Wintner's Reserve

Wintner's Reserve

A case of fiction

by Robert Wintner

Twice-Baked Books

Wintner, Robert,
Wintner's Reserve
1, Fiction. 2, Romance. Bodily function. Wit and humor.
ISBN: 979-8-9855513-7-2
Cover art by Keith Christie

Twice-Baked Books

$15.00
ISBN 979-8-9855513-7-2
51500>

9 798985 551372

Also by Robert Wintner

Fiction: Whirlaway
Lizard Blue
Touch of the Unknown Rider
Reefdog
Was Is
Solomon Kursh
A California Closing
In a Sweet Magnolia Time
Toucan Whisper, Toucan Sing
Crux
Lonely Hearts, Changing Worlds (stories)
The Modern Outlaws
Touch of the Unknown Rider
Homunculus
The Prophet Pasqual
Hagan's Trial & Other Stories

Memoir:
Brainstorm
1969 and Then Some
The Ice King

Reef Politic in narrative and photo/video:
Dragon Walk
Neptune Speaks
Reef Libre, An In-Depth Look at Cuban
   Exceptionalism & the Last, Best Reefs in the World
Every Fish Tells a Story
Some Fishes I Have Known

Author's note:

American values suffer a crisis. Whose family sets the standard?

As a two-term president with solid political chops and a great mind, Bill Clinton left a brilliant legacy, except for a lapse in judgment. On the moral imperative, Congress demanded details, as primetime writhed on a cigar and a stain.

George Bush didn't drink or smoke and waved off youthful indiscretion on cocaine, as primetime still wallowed in nitwit inanity, between drug commercials to rectify our most personal malfunctions.

Barack Obama was cool, an Ivy League intellect with a stable family, as babes on TV twerked, and the boys howled, "Woo hoo!"

Donald "I like to grab 'em by the pussy" Trump walked in on naked females, went raw dog on a porn star, lied, cheated and stole until perversion seemed normal. Trump stoked the base, made the Supreme Court Evangelical and called for insurrection, all abnormal.

Joe Biden, a wise, lovely man, struggles upstream.

We descend on stupidity, as cleavage, bodily function and rage are primetime staples. Melodrama ignites us. Power resides in the news cycle. Adrift, we stress.

Sip these pleasant fermentations to ease the journey.

And please note the count herein, borrowing from the bakers to make a vintner's dozen thirteen bottles instead of the usual, paltry twelve. As Uncle Harry often advised, "Yer gonna need it."

The Stories

The Powers that Be

Dave DeBanque didn't refer to himself in the third person by name, like a political candidate might do. Rather, he called himself an industrialist. His narrative accounts of life and adventure often assumed poignancy and lasting value, because of the industrialist dynamic in any situation.

"Put an industrialist in there," he urged, recalling the charm of the Industrial Revolution two centuries ago, when tough jobs called for the right men, who brought the world to full potential. Dave saw a light, in which his ilk glowed eternal. Industrialists would live forever, just as machines would need cogs, gears and ingenious articulation. Industry was to him the way of nature.

Some eternities die young, but Dave sensed longevity. He saw no difference, really, between modern times and the olden days, between hard drives, high speed and virtual reality on the one hand, and smokestacks, sweat shops and a sooty gray march to empire on the other. Everything still needed management and labor for optimal extraction of resources, where lesser men feared to tread. It was still the old neighborhood for Dave DeBanque.

Presenting himself in this simple caricature and then backing the bunk with vast social spending, Dave could often make contact with women. A name-dropper and a dollar dropper, Dave let them feel his grit. He was a coin with two sides, a double-edged sword, a story told coming and going; that was Dave, the yin and yang of masculine know-how, can-do and power. Could the women tell this at first blush? No, they could not. They could only sense something special, something spectacular, hidden in this man who came on tough as a mill hand. Dave could have been run hard and dried out after back-to-back swing and graveyard, a burly, shaggy fellow whose five o'clock shadow filled in by one.

Hardly shy, Dave claimed as boisterously as necessary that he'd worked the toughest job in the Arctic Circle, slinging timber yokes beside a thousand-tooth blade that was always hungry for pulp or meat. He actually said man meat for a short time, till someone mentioned the, well, er, uh, homosexual association with that phrase. Or maybe Dave figured it out for himself, maybe feeling a wrong ring in the sound of it, or maybe he sensed disappointment in an otherwise fair visage. At any rate, his brief bio kept pace: the big saw grumbled with indiscriminate appetite, needing to feed again and again. And there was Dave DeBanque, neophyte industrialist, slinging yokes. It sounded rough and tumble; slinging was so urgent, so physical, and yokes were so demanding or short order or something.

Never mind. Dave owns the mill now and a few more like it. He won't elaborate on his route to ownership but coyly suggests that our system rewards risk and nothing but. Nor will he specify gross income but hints magnitude in the two hundred million range, annually, give or take. Well, that's Canadian, converting at only seventy-six cents on the dollar, ey? So it's only around a hundred fifty million real dollars a year, give or take, which he's first to concede isn't nearly as much. Then he grins, asking how in the world he could spend it anyway.

Spending couldn't catch up to income, even hand over fisting his every whim. Take, for example, Dave's casual response when we visited him at his Florida place, where temperature and age both average eighty-two. With so many geriatrics around, a middle-ager can feel chipper on general principle. We called from two hours up the road, the wife and I. Dave knew we were on our way, but we hate to pop in. Who needs the surprise? Who wants to walk in on any manner of peculiarity so common these days?

Not to worry; it was another lovely afternoon for the likes of Dave DeBanque, who roused himself from nappy poo to acknowledge, "Mm. Yeah. Hey, whaddaya want for dinner?"

Dave and I met through mutual friends who derive their livelihoods from his timber mills. He won't call himself the Godfather, but those in the orbit of his stellar splendor do—in his presence, often eliciting the burly grin. The first time I saw Dave tell a bartender to set 'em up for the house, even the bartender did a double take. The house rambled through four different rooms, all full. Dave grinned at the bartender's disbelief, enjoying the spectacle he was about to create, of a guy who looks shabby as a stumblebum dropping two grand or four on a round of drinks. Maybe the bartender had seen it before or knew Dave—his look lasted only long enough to take the credit card dangling before him. Then he jumped to it. "That was generous, Dave," I said, as Dave's grin eased to a sanguine smile, prelude to wisdom imparted unto thee.

"They won't even notice," he said. "It's the second time I do it that gets their attention."

I'd seen him spend thousands, picking up dinner tabs for entire restaurants, ostensibly to compensate for rowdy behavior but more likely to highlight the raw power of an industrialist's back pocket.

What magnitude did we fancy for dinner down south?

"Hey, Dave. We just want to relax. We don't need a fancy pants sit-down. Okay?"

"It's okay with me. You wanna eat here?"

"Whatever suits you. You want fancy pants, that's okay, too. Or we can get some groceries and cook up."

"Okay. See you soon. My friend Stan is here. You'll like him."

We stopped for a bottle of wine but switched to tequila, because four of us drinking would get only a single round from a bottle of wine. We could have got two bottles, but we found *Sudor de las Bolas de Toro* for the first time since Mexico. It was seventy bucks, but we were going, after all, to Dave DeBanque's place.

Well, it was hail-fellows and hugs and everybody swearing that the others were looking great all around. Dave couldn't make the men's outing last year, so it had been two years since we last met. He'd shed a few pounds and eagerly affirmed the slimming process, pleased that we noticed. He didn't offer wine for twenty minutes, and then he poured lightly. We caught up on who, when and what, and in a while, he said it was a great idea to eat in, and a chef would arrive within the hour to prepare dinner.

Stan was an old friend of Dave's, the man for whom Dave DeBanque had actually worked at one point. This concept—Dave working—was allowed pause for reflection, in which Dave fed and watered our awe and wonder with the single credential, "Stan owns Northern Ontario." Northern Ontario was not followed by Inc. or LLC or LTD and also seemed conceptual, if not quaint.

We squinted for comprehension, and sure enough, Northern Ontario in simple terms was that rarely pondered swatch of the globe in blue and gray with a few longitude and latitude lines over some mountains and rivers and places where people lived and got by. Stan owned the whole swatch, Northern Ontario.

Things do have owners. Don't they? Dave nodded.

Stan discounted his role in the wealth of nations playfully, telling us, "And his assistant."

"You mean Dave was your assistant?" I asked, going along. "Or now you're his assistant?"

"No. The chef is bringing his assistant." A wry smile and rising eyebrow sparkled in playful synchronization.

Dave interceded, explaining that he bought this condo for his aging parents for only one point six and sunk another point six into the remodel, which was pushing eight by now but was still dirt cheap, if you thought about it, especially with the parents not coming down for another month. Meanwhile, the place was a godsend to him. "Oh, man, what a season," he said. He'd met a contender for the presidency of the United States of America, and they enjoyed a budding friendship, chatting now and then, including just after each primary the contender won. Sure, the competition was lackluster, but that didn't diminish grit and character in the victor. He was the people's choice and, man oh man, could have paved the way to . . . "Well, we would have done all right." Dave's candidate lost the election.

"Dave, you're Canadian. Don't they have laws about campaign financing and all that?"

"It's all corporations. I put money in one and it lends the money to another, and then a third one sells services for the money and the second one is cancelled, and before you know it, the money's where you want it to be. We could have got . . . well . . ."

Dave had also met with the Chairman of the Federal Reserve, a meeting resulting from many requests by a full-time secretary with a single assignment: to get that meeting. Dave got his meeting after he banked a hundred million dollars in an island nation in the South China Sea, the one most known for its US military installations and hardwood forests. Dave loves hardwood. I suspect he could have had a meeting with anyone for far less, but Dave is not afraid to support his intention with cash. Alas, the Fed Chair could not assist with wholesale timbering in the Philippines.

As if the presidential election loss in the US and the Philippine hardwood disaster weren't enough, another wrench fouled the works on a little beachfront development in Honduras, also known for hardwoods. Dave merely clear-cut fifty acres for three estates, one each for himself and his two partners on that project. And a few acres for a landing strip. How else can you get in there? "They have this snake wood down there. Beautiful stuff, but it grows all loop-de-loop, so you can't cut selectively. You have to take it all."

Well, the Honduran project looked simple and clean and would have stayed that way. Dave stared off. "You would not be*lieve* what my two partners built. Ten, twelve thousand square-foot haciendas with all the trimmings. Then they dug out the old mine to make a few bucks on the side. The mine was abandoned ages ago, but the gem ore is far more accessible now with modern tech. But hell, they tapped a vein or a spring, or some shit got jiggled, and released a load of arsenic into the river. You wouldn't think anything could flow upstream, and to tell you the truth it didn't. But arsenic doesn't need to flow, really. The good thing is, it killed off the piranha. Those people down there have lived in fear for generations, and now they won't need to. The bad thing was, they were getting pretty sick from the arsenic, but we fixed that. Oh, everyone was up in arms, but we solved it quick and neat. We sent in three truckloads of Evian. Hell, half a truck would have been enough." Better yet, plastic bottles of water don't go bad.

Dave let the largesse of an industrialist sink in as he glided into the kitchen to read the label on the *Sudor de las Bolas de Toro*. "I've had this." And Timothy arrived. "Whoa, Timothy! Need a hand?"

"No. I have it," Timothy insisted, burdened with packages that he set on the counter. He smiled all around on his way back to the car.

"Where's Sheila?" Dave called.

"She's not feeling well." Timothy huffed and puffed on his way out, calling over his shoulder, "She may be by later."

"Is she pregnant?" Dave called after him.

"How would I know?" Timothy's simple response pumped his glow to ruddy red and then to cranberry concentrate. Then he was out for more groceries. On reentry, he was introduced all around, though Stan had met Timothy last night at the restaurant where Timothy was head chef. This was his night off, but he loved private parties, he said, especially with a fun crowd like this one.

In spite of his apparent feeling for Sheila, Timothy seemed fay. Allison sensed it, too, and pressed him on the tender spot; he seemed so good-natured. "Is she your girlfriend?"

"I wish! Oh, she's just, well . . . perfect, if you want to know. She's beautiful and smart as they come, and her father owns this county."

"Seems to be going around," I said. "Massive ownership, I mean. I don't own all of anywhere."

Stan was easily eldest at mid-sixties and fattest at two-thirty, nonviable as a youthful sex partner. But happily buzzed, he still enjoyed the hunt in vicarious anticipation. He corrected, "She's more than beautiful. She's really something."

Timothy blushed on cue. "She's a keeper all right."

"Then why isn't she your girlfriend?"

"Oh, she knows where I stand," Timothy said, ripping the cellophane from giant packs of giant prawns, lobsters, racks of lamb, baby back ribs and steaks, piling the Styrofoam in the sink, working and talking like a well-oiled machine. "She's the kind of girl you wouldn't believe is out there. But she is. I can't really talk about my feelings with her, but I can with you, I mean, I can with others. I mean, I think she knows my opinion of her."

"And she's your assistant?"

"Yeah. Her father buys her anything she wants, as long as she works. Now, don't yell at me for this. Trust me." Timothy had shifted on the fly, meaning that we should trust the cheap cut of steak he'd brought. "London broil is tough, but we'll fix it," he said, stabbing it with fierce repetition like a serial killer with a fork, assuring us blithely that steak connoisseurs would be loathe to pierce meat like this, through the fascia to the far side, and they'd be right, except for London broil, which needs piercing so the marinade can seep in and soften the meat.

Dave twisted the tequila cap and sipped from the bottle. "Oh, that is good. I remember it now." We had a short one to get things going or keep things going. Dave said, "What the hell. Might help me sleep." Dave couldn't sleep so well lately, since he'd cut back on his blood pressure pills. Naturally, his pressure was up, with the mill hands at his first and biggest mill threatening to organize on a list of demands already presented as an ultimatum. "How do I get those nimrods to see that they leave me no choice? What do I care if they organize, if I have to meet their demands to keep them from organizing?" He stewed on the cruel paradox of human ignorance till he could will himself calmer, reducing internal pressure through repression and distraction. He explained this exercise, admitting that it sounded illogical, but it worked. Instead of adequately pissed off to kill somebody, he explained a process and only simmered.

He said his blood pressure had soared to perilous heights when the bottom dropped out of the market. It rebounded with a punch, as his biggest, most complex planer went down for a month—the most critical month of the year, with tons of raw stock on hand and mills from Ontario to Saskatchewan chewing fiber into pulp and gluing up particleboard at record levels, while he sat dead in the water. "You want to talk blood pressure?" He sighed on a short laugh and heavy head wag. "These pills are worse than the pressure, you want to know the truth. They change you. Change everything about you."

Well, the pressure was down from the worst of it, down from the bad market and broken planer depths. His blood pressure was still high enough to trouble his slumbers, and now the apnea damn near tried to kill him right there on his overstuffed sofa. Dave laughed, an industrialist who could not ditch the weight of the world, even in balmy climes, on the finest sofa money could buy.

"If it ain't one thing, it's another," I consoled.

"Yeah. Well. I'll take the other," Dave replied, knocking the sauce back to make room for another short one.

"Just a half a short one for me," Timothy said; he really was so thirsty that he hated to hit the tequila right off but would rather start with a beer and some wine.

Stan drifted to the veranda. I followed. The balmy evening, the cocktails and terrific dinner coming up had begun their soothing effect. "Timothy seems energetic."

"Yes. He's a great chef, too."

"Does he stand a chance?"

"A chance?"

"With the assistant. Sheila."

"Nah! How could he? Dave's riding first horse."

"How old is she?"

Stan shrugged. "Young. Like Timothy."

"Dave has kids older than that."

Stan shrugged again. "You wouldn't believe the effect Dave has on women. I've seen them—I'm not kidding you now—I've seen them break down and cry. I saw it last night, good-looking woman, couldn't get over what a wonderful man he is. She starts crying."

"Oy."

"I told her: wait till you get to know him. She wouldn't hear it."

"It's the money."

"Of course, it's the money. Trouble is, he'll promise them anything. Then he delivers. What a nut. Who ever heard of a hundred grand for a blow job? But very few of them will turn it down. He gets more pussy than Frank Sinatra." Stan drained his drink and on second thought laughed. "Gets as much anyway."

We talked weather, Stan and I, but the difference between Northern Ontario and Southern Florida needed little discourse. We agreed that Dave was a good guy. Stan fleshed it out, recalling the younger Dave, who paid his dues and learned the business inside out before making his first move on buying a mill. We sat blissfully, letting the marinade seep in, perhaps reflecting on Dave's dues. "Oh, he paid," Stan said. "And how."

In a while, Dave drifted out, leaving my wife Allison in the kitchen with Timothy to observe his culinary technique. We drank in thickening reverie, till Timothy filled the veranda with hardy aroma and a mountainous platter of prawn brochettes. "These are just . . . nothing," he said. "A few minutes in the marinade; stick 'em on skewers and broil them in the oven. It's so easy, I'm embarrassed." He blushed again, endearingly, as if at will. The shrimp were indescribably delicate and complex, unlike the cooked larvae that pass for modern shrimp. Timothy served extra napkins just in time for chin dribbles, and from nowhere, he served a round of cold beer that hit home like a perfect quench and balance to the tequila—and calling the flavors fabulously complimentary. Unabashed grins affirmed his case. Reduced to moans and whimpers, wrinkling our collective brow in disbelief, we sensed Timothy approaching from the rear again, monitoring our needs. We sensed his need, too, and praised the prawns as perfect. Flashing red again, he scrunched in a modern male curtsey and looked stuck as a chef caught in the headlights.

Allison asked, "*What* was *in* that marinade?"

"Oh, that. It's so dumb, I can't even tell you. You'll think I'm horrible."

"But I won't," she called, as Timothy hurried back to the kitchen.

"Ah! My lobsters!" His excitement seemed like one more ingredient of makeshift magic.

Finishing the shrimp with dispatch, we reflected on the sunset, friends and fun, those things usually surrounding Dave DeBanque. He could make things happen, and not by simply throwing scads o' dough around. Dave had imagination. I raised my glass to him.

"This kid's terrific," Dave said. "I want to fly him up for the Log Jammer. We cook gourmet for five hundred guests in a tent. It's unbelievable. It costs me a couple hundred grand, but they remember. They love it. Timothy says he can do it."

"With the assistant?" I asked.

Dave looked up.

"Timothy can't cook for five hundred all alone," I pointed out.

"No, he can't. But the Log Jammer is all men. I don't know if she'd hold up."

"You'll protect her."

"Yeah. But who'll protect me?"

"How can he get away from his job?" Allison asked.

"Oh, well, he'll be working for me by then." Dave topped us off and explained that of all the restaurants on the island, he'd picked out three and sent his accountants over to see which would be the best deal for him. How did he know they were for sale? The way anyone knows anything is for sale.

"You want to be in the restaurant business?" I asked.

"No, but I wouldn't mind, if it's a good place. I have to leave every six months now with this green card business. All I have to do is invest a million bucks and hire ten people, and I can stay year-round, no more green cards."

"That's convenient."

"Yeah. I don't need the aggravation, to tell you the truth. Like now, Stan and I want to go to Vegas tomorrow and gamble. Here it is October, and I'm up three hundred grand on the year, and my accountant has me budgeted to lose a million. So, it's time. You ever want to go to Vegas, let me know, my buddy at Versailles'll take care of you. I'm there two months ago, and I'm losing five or ten grand a hand. Let it ride. Four of a kind pays five to one, and I'm down to my last fifty grand in chips, and I get dealt three eights. The deck is down. Down. And the house limit is a hundred grand. So, I call my buddy over and tell him I want to slide this last fifty up to the betting line. I'm down about one fifty on the evening. He says sure."

Dave downs his tequila and waits for us to follow, which we do, down the hatch, and he tops us off. "I got the eight. Two hundred fifty grand, which only put me up a hundred for the night, but by this time, you know, the chef has been bringing us little snacks, and the bartender is personally serving and all that. I told 'em go pack. The whole staff. We're flying down to Cabo for a few days. Chartered a jet. Got a hotel floor. They loved it. Nothing but eating and drinking and having fun on the beach for five days. Everybody got naked."

Timothy rustled pans in the kitchen, perhaps overhearing the potential on the veranda. "Dave? You want to get a restaurant, so you can fly the guests to Cabo on a regular basis?"

"Nah! I just don't want to fly home every six months. That's all."

We sipped and nodded, and into the lull, Sheila arrived. In a flush and flurry of excuses, she prattled over so many delays, and on top of that, as if that weren't enough, and so on.

Timothy quelled her effusions with assurance. "Hey! It's okay, it's okay." She believed him, swooping to the veranda for introductions and hellos, hardly like an assistant, more like a hostess, or a deb with breeding and grooming.

Sheila was late twenties, her generic cuteness highlighted on a pixie nose, bright eyes and glistening lip-gloss over medium breasts with no bra for maximum effect on the lusts of men. Enhancing the latter: a three-button reveal on a fair bosom. Below the waist she spread a tad too far, though the optimistic observer could see lingering baby fat; she was so young. She drank heartily, catching up to our level of good cheer. Timothy had things under control, after all, and she hated to be in the way in the kitchen. Once caught up to our festive level on wine and tequila, she felt Dave and Stan, eyeballing playfully.

Allison and I observed, and Sheila preempted our assessment. "I'm getting big, but I don't care. I'll take care of it when I need to."

Stan laughed, saying she was plenty perfect so far.

Dave remained stoic or distracted. "Who'll protect me," he asked again, "when all those men start . . . pressuring you?"

"Don't you worry," she said. "I'll protect you."

"But I mean, we have to . . . We have to . . ."

Who could know what we had to do with Timothy's hot dishes filling the veranda yet again with distinct and equally compelling aroma? This one wafted from a heaping platter of lobster tails and claws, steamed to perfection, removed from their shells and served with drawn butter, garlic and lemon sauce on the side.

"What is it, Dave, that we have to do?" Allison asked, indelicately pursuing her own curiosity that nearly spilled over into the voyeuristic realm of, shall we say, questionable taste.

"We have to eat," I assured her. She took the hint, and we dove again, happier than a minute ago, enjoying the best lobster we'd ever tasted. Spared the shelling, we popped tails and claws like potato chips. We drank tequila and beer and insisted that Timothy sit and drink with us.

"I will! I will! I just have to . . ." Off to the races, he was back in a shake with the London broil, broiled to a turn and sliced thin. Timothy served deftly along with the salad course, which was three large tomatoes, sliced. He cleared, served, topped us off, watched and then sipped from the tumbler Dave poured for him. "Oh, that's good!" He primed our pump.

Engorging with gusto, we agreed.

"Sit down, Timothy. Enjoy yourself," Stan chided, embarking on a new direction, Pinot Grigio; it goes down so easily, and this one was such a pleasant surprise. Stan had picked up a case.

"No, we have to . . ." Dave began again. "I mean, you and me, if we're going up to the wilderness to stay in tents, and you're in my tent . . ." Dave set the picture, reaching for a tail and a claw in the same grab. "You know?"

"I'll be right back," Timothy said, downing his tumbler and blushing again, this time from the alcohol rush. And out he rushed, unable to sink the turd in the punchbowl. In gentler terms, he merely sought escape from the obtuse proposition before us, a crude suggestion that would have wallowed in bad taste, had it come from anyone but the tastemaker.

"No," Dave corrected. "I mean, you can share a tent with Timothy if you want to. That's okay with me."

"Oh, God!" Timothy chortled from the kitchen, jangling pans in his urgent effort to save the baby back ribs from imperfection, though we well knew the benefit of erring to excess when it comes to cooking pig meat.

"No, no. I can't. I mean, I couldn't. I mean . . . No, not me and him." This from Sheila, in a harsh, though reflective whisper. "I mean I love him and all that, but not that way. I mean, he's such a nice guy and so much better than my boyfriend. I mean my old boyfriend. I should be with a guy like Timothy. I really should. But I'm taking my time. I mean it's so hard adjusting to not having a boyfriend. Gee, I mean the sexual thing, once you get used to it, isn't that bad."

"You mean you weren't fond of sex, but now you are?" I ventured, capturing for Sheila the eyes around the table.

"No. I always loved it. It's just that when you have a boyfriend, you know. And then you don't. I mean, once a week now seems like all the time. You know?"

"Look," Dave said, leaning forward in apparently practiced body language for this stage of a negotiation. He shook his head, displaying what the years had wrought—yes, the gray stubble and wobbly jowls, but with unvanquished wisdom overall. Dave DeBanque wouldn't press for the close, because he had nothing to sell or buy. Dave wanted only his fair advantage. "I'm talking . . . What did I say?" He looked at Stan, who reminded him that the wilderness enclave for five hundred associates with gourmet cooking would run around two hundred thousand dollars. We could only presume Canadian dollars, but even at seventy-six cents per, it still shaped up as a buck-and-a-half dinner party in the woods. "Yeah, two hundred, three hundred. One number or the other; it makes no difference to me. See what I mean? Timothy cooks. You assist. You want a hundred grand?"

"To sleep with you?"

"Sure. Why not? If that's what you want."

"You'd give me a hundred thousand dollars to sleep with you?"

Dave beamed at the summit, where all roads lead to, where clarity on needs and willingness to pay most often allow a thing to proceed. We exhaled collectively, ruminant on mortality and the last gasp that could well follow the last supper. Subtle shifting indicated thickening viscosity slogging through shrinking diameters. We smiled serenely, savoring satisfaction. We smirked, playfully imagining Dave humping Sheila, or handing her a stack of bills, or seeing the bonus she might grant him, a sweet, sincere, kiss on the forehead, just like Snow White bestowed on her dwarfs, because Dave was a wonderful guy, after all. So? What's the biggie?

Yet again into the lull, though this one felt riper than the last and verily seeped with juices fit to burst, came Timothy, ebulliently balancing two platters on one arm and a third on the other. Verily giddy with excitement, he hovered extravagantly as we cleared the mess for a landing spot. And there before us, baby back ribs, steaming pungently, the scent transcending the feast already within. Like bucks in rut, we met the challenge with unreasonable, greater hunger, as if this, too, was love. "The ribs are always a hit," Timothy said. "So I make twice as much now." He didn't wait for our reaction but left us in thin air with barbecue tender, sweet and flavorful as it fell from the bone onto the tongue; the moment went to feelings. Silence reigned as we reached for ribs with fervor. He returned like a penitent to a confessional. "They're so easy, you won't believe it. I marinate them in Coke. I mean, you know, Coca Cola."

"Diet or regular," I asked.

"Regular. You want the sugar. If you just . . . nibble the little bit near the bone, you can actually taste it, but probably not if you're not looking for it."

"I've never had ribs like this," I said.

"Mm. Nnmph," Stan said.

"And here's, well, I just thought we ought to have some vegetables." The vegetables were steamed broccoli and cauliflower heads along with some mushroom caps stuffed with crab.

Dave ate two-handed at a quicker pace now, but only briefly before sliding out. "Sit down, Timothy. Eat." Timothy nodded and complied as Dave retired to the living room and came back with a bottle of port. "Five hundred bucks this stuff cost me. US." And though we all looked forward to a taste of excellent port after dinner, Dave picked up the pace no less than a marathon runner making his move. Establishing the momentum that defined his life, Dave popped the port and poured.

I honestly thought it only adequate but gave the devil his due. "Mm. Boy!" The port got swilled and poured as we found our rhythm in the ribs, until one after another, we stopped and sat back, adjusting, reaching for another smidgeon of London broil or one more mushroom cap with crab, a last little swill of Pinot Grigio and maybe a last sip or two of terribly expensive port. And what's this? A wedge of Gorgonzola? Mm, who'd a thunk? Who'd a dared? Onward, we munched, packing a bit more over what already neared bursting—but the flavor was so . . . perfect. "Pinot Grigio. Gorgonzola," I muttered, and no one said boo, as if I'd hit the nail on the head. We savored the bliss of survivors, still breathing with no taste left unturned. It was a moment of contentment, gratitude and friendship.

"I have one little story . . ." Timothy began.

"What do you think?" Dave asked Sheila directly. "Here. Drink." He topped all the glasses and mumbled about sending out for another bottle of tequila. "That stuff is good."

Sheila belched. Then she giggled. "I've never eaten this much."
Stan's eyes rolled.

She stood up to unbutton her blue jeans. "Boy." Her belly relaxed into the slack, and Dave turned to her in his seat, tapping his thigh.

"Come 'ere."

She wobbled a bit and giggled again. Holding the table she belched again, fingertips over mouth, more ladylike this time. And she eased sideways, settling daintily on Dave's thigh, asking, "Okay. Where were we?"

"I don't know," Dave said. "Where are we?"

Well, of course we were sated and drunk, leaning back in our chairs in the afterglow of a feast, watching Dave and Sheila negotiate a deal on a little you-know-what for a hundred grand. The ticklish subject led to another lull that could hardly be salvaged by Timothy with another fabulous dish, because he was among us then, drinking hard to catch up or dull the edge or ease the pain.

"Timothy. You had a little story?" I prompted, sensing that he would not speak unless beckoned.

"Oh. Well. It's just a quick little story. I . . . Well, I can't tell stories very well. This is, well, I tried Viagra . . ."

"Recently?"

"Last week. It wasn't my idea. I've never needed it, but this person I'm going out with had some and wanted me to try it, and I've never had high blood pressure, which is what you have to be careful of with Viagra. So I took it and we made love for so long—two hours, until we had to stop; it was chafing so badly I got a, you know. But I was still huuge! So we got in the shower and this person starts, you know, jacking me off, until, I'm like . . . Oh! Oh! Oh! Like for two minutes straight!"

Timothy reached for the five-hundred-dollar port and emptied it, filling his tumbler to the tippy top. Then he poured it down the hatch and turned to Dave. "It works, you know."

We all took a little drink. I asked, "Is that the end of the story?"

With his most fervent blush of the evening and a big, warm grin all around, he said, "Yeah. Well, I don't tell a story very well, but that's the one time I took Viagra."

"I think you tell a great story," Allison said. "Do you have any more?"

"Wait!" Sheila said, getting up from Dave's lap. "Wait till I get back." Sheila had to use the bathroom, the one just off the veranda, and so we waited. She only took a while and gave us another lull to enjoy. We could easily ignore the faint blending of her dainty regurgitation and the toilet flushing it all away. Truly, it was an evening to savor, with a rich, wonderful meal under our belts, a happy contentment all around, the tropical warmth, the light breeze and the crickets chirping.

The Scenic Route

Anybody with half a wit will tell you it's a bad idea to smoke dope while you're driving. Maybe on occasion some cocktail-grade legumba might be okay, like rush hour, when the steel and rubber monster crawls at two miles an hour. What's the diff? You get a jump on happy hour, and that's pure productivity, when you factor time and usage that would otherwise be wasted. You need an extra dollop of discretion, with cars scoping peripherally for a nose pick, a surreptitious phone call—or a doobie. Unless they're getting high, too, which is easy to spot if you know the motions.

Nevertheless, a little dirt weed in rush hour is a minor exception to a solid rule of practicality. Immutable to driving safety is prohibition of heavy weed, modern weed, the weed grown these days, way beyond cocktails and often leading to a separate reality. That weed deconstructs a few layers of perception and then shuffles the deck while telemetry struggles to keep it between the ditches while processing broader meaning in broken yellow juxtaposed with unbroken yellow, as such a pairing might influence human behavior behind the wheel, confined to a single lane with margins of mere inches to either side, bound as well to a single plane that may defy the time-space kaleidoscope spinning slowly but inexorably ahead, its sharp and pointy shards of sheer, garish color, as sass and innocence intercede, two more lines of reasoning in the broken-unbroken interface, hardly parallel but defying intersection, too, just ahead, speaking of yellow, that may be flashing intermittently, unless that's a steady blink in telemetry . . .

Yeah, that shit sitting in my ashtray like a reception committee after a three-hour meeting—*after hours*—starting at five. The scheduled discussion was meant to ventilate inner feelings as they may relate to workplace comfort, and/or troublesome behaviors of that most populous species, individuals of which may populate that place. That is, people irritate each other to the point of violence, but they hold back, repressing what they feel in order to preserve our way of life, our rule of law, which will be sustained and nurtured by waiting and talking. And talking and talking, spewing the obvious, down to the dry heaves, so the speaker can feel expunged and restored to the productive world, to a world that would spin ineluctably onward, should the speaker suddenly vanish, which is surely what it and she or he will do one day—and we, as a collective consciousness hoping for the best, can only anticipate such occurrence happening sooner rather than later.

Three hours! Starting at five! Five! When the rest of the world has the sense to stop, gear down, change its mind, relax and take time to enjoy life, which shall be defined here as the time occurring between the points of birth and death, with the exception of time spent in these meetings. Because we're going to be dead for a long time and these meetings only detract from our paltry few years till the big one takes us, and we have no more time to go, go, go for the more, more, more, here in the land of the free and home of the brave and the resounding NO! It's not enough!

Can we talk for a minute here about productivity as it relates to sensitivity and the needs of others?

Tuning out is good. A mind-squint lets the audio/visual plane blur to endurable fuzz, though tuning back in can be cruel and unusual. It's enough to make a sane man twitch or even question the sanity hitherto presumed, wherein the party of the first part would not shut up, no matter how many bones creaked or groans surfaced. Then came the parties of the second, third and fourth parts around the table, developing the concepts by which we work and grow together, by which we suffocate and die in a room with no windows and a sputtering air conditioner that could not possibly keep up with human metabolism and ethereal waste, including CO_2 and halitosis, along with a double order of petty thought, whim, need, hunger and craving skewered for slow roasting but without the campfire lickety-split or stars or fresh air, but . . . Time and space alter to another plane known as out-of-body.

Christ on a crutch; it could have been camel shit and heroin in my car ashtray and I'd have reached for it to blot whatever short circuitry still sparked stray electrons in my cramped brain.

Call me addictive. Call me addled and insensitive. Call me indifferent. Call me callous. Call me willfully ignorant of the needs of others.

Call me adaptive: I, survivor.

Just so, the deconstruction began, resuscitating the ingrained knowledge of a fair and practical world, in which it's okay to get high, and better still to use good judgment. Motivation combines with practicality to recall what is known in the heart and mind, namely: that you don't keep smoking this shit till you're stoned. As I pulled on the little roach with a vengeance, I also recalled the little cartoon angel of my youth, who sang out, "You'll be sorrryyy . . ." Rules for practicality allow a single hit—okay, two hits—and then you set the implement of altered consciousness back down in the ashtray and wait. If you smoke it till you're stoned, you will not get the few orbits of adjustment and settling prior to blasting through the stratosphere. No, you burn rocket fuel unnecessarily to seer the edges of gravity-free space—fuck time. What time? And onward you blast, free of coordinates or concern for higher, deeper or farther sideways and moreover blazing inward, shattering the ionosphere and blogosphere, where I saw only yesterday, or maybe it was last week, that the THC in today's cannabis is astronomically greater than a decade or two ago, which may result from hybridization techniques many growers now incorporate to achieve stellar heights on minimal encumbrance. Did they say incorporate? Like in big bidness? Well, the growth companies do represent jobs for the people and strive to bottom-line efficiency, so it makes sense. Or would that be the growing companies? Grow companies?

But the encumbrance issue may be open to challenge; not that the ditches are likely to pull me in, but damn! This stuff keeps on coming on, feeling like a spaceship in the rough between Mach IX and hyper speed, where a few rumbles convert to mild twitches in a human, and surely reflect residual sludge from the arid, lifeless planet shrinking in the rearview—and up ahead—look out!

Thirst incoming!

Yes, well, dehydration is a great thing to avoid, like the ditches but more subtle, sinister in its way, not threatening with obvious consequence, like driving into a ditch, but with a microscopic grain of diabolical debris, uric or calcium, that will accrue even tinier bits over time, with no fluids to wash them away, till the agglomeration spells k-i-d-n-e-y s-t-o-n-e. Fie on that, with numbnuts, the kidney stone guy, blathering tedious and obvious taunts in obtrusive proximity to my face about the problems of "allowing ourselves" to get kidney stones. Well, fuck, duh, what was your first clue?

No, the kidney stone was no fun, so, in the spirit of healthful living and stone prevention, which is not at all like stoned prevention, which was already avoided by the ultimate antidote, making me feel circumlocutive at least *and* slightly encumbered, I called for my little cooler. "Where's my fucking cooler full of beer when I need it?" I pondered, feisty as a roundtable ventilator after hours.

"It's right behind your seat," the more prepared, more service-oriented self replied. I didn't reach for it, because that could have strained my rotator, still ginger from an old badminton injury.

I am a seasoned, careful driver who planned salvation in detail, for the evening at least. If I did not plan adequately to spare myself the reach, then synchronous events covered my needs as they will do more often than we'd like to admit. Obstacles in life can disappear with a little help from a friend, in this case sparing me another dislocation, on the advent of another reality. What was I thinking? I thought with reasonable certainty that I should have paused on one hit, or two, to avoid euphoric overload, but regret is another ditch to avoid, so we move on.

From the door panel pocket comes the little bottle opener shaped like a shark's head, and keeping in character with what we know of these apex predators at feeding time, it frenzies on the bottle top. The seasoned driver knows to scan, front and rear and side to side for MADD mothers and cops, and so I did, front and rear and left side anyway, when the beer, likely affected by gravity-free conditions in deep space, floated up, hovered briefly and then docked expertly at the glug glug glug portal for in-flight refueling, giving rise to further observation on the age-consumption continuum.

That is, a boy begins his trek across the tundra to manhood when on first realizing that hops, malt, grain and water do not taste bitter but combine to deliver the taste of life, or, more accurately the taste of good life, which absolves the rest of life.

That is, the recognition of soda pop as a repulsive, sugary taste comes with new insight to tastes and new meaning, new frontiers and value in life. Then come the decades, where two beers are twice as good as one beer, and three hold up with economy of scale, and on occasion four and five seem more perfect still, making a man wonder if six or eight will one day be the summit, before the far side and diminishing return.

Along with greater return on consumption comes a more startling absorption rate, allowing beer to virtually pour down the gullet for a deep quench, making the absorber feel like one of those paper-thin sponges that go fat and fluffy and full of life. And joy. Just add water. Or beer, recalling Benjamin Franklin's best insight, that beer is proof of God's love. Well, if not Ben's best insight it was certainly near the top.

Just so, the first went down the hatch in mere seconds, not so much as a trivial task to get out of the way but as a giant step for man. In terms of value, that first beer changed things for the better. Hardly incidental, it helped as a soothing balm on a wound. Sliding the dead soldier under my seat, I reached for another as part of a theme, as it were, seeking a better world. I laughed: did I cause this carnage? No, I did not.

But! Did I adequately respond?

Yes, I did.

I felt good and better and better yet, yet woeful interruption intervened: emergency response. That is, a cop had backed off the road behind a bush the way they do, to remain unseen until you're just out front with your dick in the pickle slicer, so to speak. In this case the patrol car sat perpendicular to the road as the perp passed within the speed limit, not swerving or otherwise appearing to threaten society, except for the cold brewskie descending from the glug portal with a few inches of brew remaining, along with the perp practically confessing in the visible fear spasm up his spine and the faint skunk smell wafting skyward out the inch of his barely open window. The beer snugged between his legs and the joint in the ashtray completed the tableau. Did time enough ever exist in the space-time continuum to explain, Your Honor, the arid tundra recently left behind, a vacuum so lifeless as to separate any man from decorum, productivity, appropriateness and the rest?

Emergency response in deep space is tricky. With sheer, raw existence broken down to analysis, with pros and cons drifting weightless about the cockpit, most frontline synapses are deactivated, virtually eliminating the secondary phases covering, in a word, downside potential. Okay, that was two words. And two frames: 1) the cop car hiding behind the bush with the ominous caption, *Did he see me?* He must have—at any rate, an astronaut must trust his gauges, even as he senses malfunction in support modifiers. What else can he do? Then came 2) a tree that would allow the briefest but possibly adequate cover in which to ditch the evidence.

So I hurled the bottle by the neck with extra oomph to make the ditch beyond the passenger window, underscoring the original premise here, that you simply should not smoke dope while you're driving.

The window was closed.

I knew that, kind of, but then events and glass so rudely converged in the space/time interface that I nearly did put the bottle in the ditch, packaged in a car.

Pressing the rewind button for a minute or two will allow a second track to lay down, to supplement and enhance those elusive laws of physics so presumptuously discarded only moments prior.

Humanity's most heinous pursuit is more apparent in the United States of America than anywhere in the history of the world. That would be the struggle for more. Liberation from material pursuit brings a twitchy aftermath and blessed relief— call it freedom, which isn't free. These colors don't run. Support our troops. For purple mountain majesty and amber waves of grain, never mind the gridlock, the nag and worry and constant bills. A hard-pressed commuter seeking to open a door of differing perception is willing to set aside the laws of practicality and the laws of the land simply to stabilize. Yes, I had anticipated as early as sunrise the onset—onslaught—of post-meeting compression, along with the mortal challenge to reason and sensibility, pressing any sentient being to the precipice, delaminating senses with the deliberate sadism of a dictator who hates freedom, who turns on his own people, who *has* weapons of mass . . .

Don't get me started. The point is, I had planned accordingly for proper response to nuclear levels of discomfort, with a cooler, a few beers on ice and a doobie in the ashtray hardly an inch long and leftover from who-knows-when, kept for emergency use only, and this was it.

Left to instincts and primitive devices I tried to get the nub lit, which must occur before pressing the roach to the lips. Trying to light a roach so short already in the lips will scorch a nose, nearly always resulting in a far different consciousness than the one desired, leading as well to tomorrow and the incessant question: What happened to your nose?

I wasn't exactly steering with my knees. Yes, they played a key role, with the joint in one hand and the lighter in the other, knees in critical assist mode, ready to take over, as seasoned knees should be. But my hands were still inches from the steering wheel, so we were covered on sudden swerves, which really rarely happen. Besides all that, it was way after dark in unusually thick traffic moving slowly. For all I knew, these drivers had also survived the rigors of materialism outpacing its headlights, and they, too, struggled with doobie ignition.

Just then I looked up to see a young female between sixteen and twenty-eight—I can't tell anymore, because, frankly, they look the same. This one seemed unique, with her classic pretty face, notably thin arms and silver serpents coiled from her elbow to her deltoid on the right side, the side she dismissively offered with her hooked thumb outstretched. A light rain had begun, begging the question of grace. That is, every man fantasizes the perfect hitchhiker: young, thin, pretty, of legal age, discreet and hygienic, smart, good manners, pithy, engaging and so on—a perfect female who knows how to apply the lip gloss, who understands wisdom and gratitude. But she's never there.

And there she was.

Are you crazy? This is the avoidable pothole, so deep and wide that anybody could see it, but nobody would run right over it, except for a politician. Who needs to belabor liability, risk, health hazard and real danger, much less the crime of soliciting a minor for sex and offering her narcotics? Not that I would do either one, but that's how it would come out in the wash. Wouldn't it? Of course, it would.

Yet knowing these things, I pulled over. What? A guy gets so old and paranoid, so afraid of media morality, so removed from life itself that he can't give a lift to a woman in the rain? The joint became a minor prop in a one-act play. "Where you going?" I asked.

"Your direction," she said, getting in, then turning to the smelly roach as the lighter finally flamed.

"Seven dollars for a lighter, and it won't even work right. Hold the wheel for a minute, please. Will you?"

"Geez," she said, taking the wheel in one hand. "You're a hippie."

I laughed. "No, I'm not. I just came from my job. And I bathed this morning."

"Yeah, yeah. So did all the hippies. That's what happened to you guys."

"I don't know. Maybe. At least I don't drink whiskey. And I still stick to my guns on the important stuff. You know, world peace, eating vegetables. That stuff."

"Yeah. Whiskey is rough. You're not supposed to use clichés like sticking to your guns. Guns are violent. You're a flower child."

I got the joint going and took a hit or two and didn't think twice about not offering it, not these days with social diseases everywhere and lip residue and DNA and the whole general malaise of what used to be a fairly fun world. But then not offering seemed so rude. "How old are you?"

She reached over and took the roach. "How old do you think?"

"Nineteen."

"Hey. You guessed it right on the button."

"No I didn't."

"So what. How old are you?"

"Take a guess."

"Nah. It doesn't matter. You're cool."

"You mean it comes down to cool or not cool?"

"No. Cool or uncool."

"How do you know I'm cool?"

"Maybe you're not cool. I mean uncool. But you were steering with your knees trying to light a joint. That's better than threatening to slap the shit out of a bunch of screaming brats in the back seat and listening to elevator music."

"Yeah. I'm cool."

"Hey, you want to come over?"

That was fast. I couldn't get a decent look at her—not that physical appearance would have changed anything—and turning on the dome light seemed nearly as rude as not offering any reefer. "Come over where?"

"To my place."

"Your place. What for?" I hadn't felt so dumb for asking such a dumb question since I was her age, which was decades ago, no matter how old she was—we passed under a streetlight, illuminating the inventory between us, wrinkles and hinted jowls but not yet wattles on my side, fair skin, an emerging figure and damn good teeth on her side. Dental hygiene is important; a girl who takes care of her teeth will likely take care of the rest.

"You know. Hang out. I think I like you."

"Just that quick?"

She shrugged.

"I'm way older than you."

She shrugged.

I reminded her, maybe encouraging her, "You know old guys are different. People of ages so different as you and me are different."

"Duh."

"We have no peer subjects or common experience."

"I didn't ask if you want to come over and get married."

"You mean come over and . . . watch TV?"

"I mean come over. You didn't ask so many questions in the hippie days, did you? You guys redefined anarchy. You didn't need to nail down the coordinates then, did you? You probably sold out and got a job with a big corporation, didn't you?"

Yes, and I stayed on for years, to the point where I wanted to hang myself instead of attend another meeting where I learned all about the sensitivities of others. I let her cruel insight sink in.

I tried further discouragement; or maybe it was only a disclaimer. "You know old guys get tired real quick."

"Yeah. That would be a relief."

I looked at her again, perhaps rethinking the health hazards. She caught me looking at my watch and scoffed.

"You need to hurry and get home to the little lady? That's cool. Besides, I'm feeling too frisky for a tired guy."

Suddenly removing herself from availability put a new light on things. "I don't, like, fall asleep or anything," I said.

"Okay, we can try it."

That's when I most regretted three hits, or was it five, instead of one. Coordinates had melted, overlapping the vertical interstice with the horizontal, calling for a beer to separate the dimensions, so we could proceed in this dynamic change of scenery from only minutes ago, on to new horizons only minutes hence, away from my lost dreams to fantasy fulfilled.

I still felt rude about not offering a beer, but beer had a practical override. All the kids smoke reefer, Your Honor. She was stoned when she got in the car. Sex? Pshaw. She asked for a ride home. It was a dark and stormy night, so that's where we were headed, so I could drop her off at home.

Besides, I only had two beers on hand, because driving after drinking three beers is foolish. But I really needed two in the true spirit of medicinal purposes only. Don't forget: I had major internal twitching to remedy. So, I didn't offer her a beer. I did break down and ask, however, "Do you drink beer?"

"Nah. That's cool. I know guys like beer. I'm not old enough anyway."

Great. I wondered just how rude I would sound, asking to see her driver's license. I wondered if she was an undercover cop. That's when I saw the cop on the side of the road. She saw the cop first and with practiced efficiency unhooked her seatbelt and leaned my way, putting her face in my lap, as it were, as she fished under my seat for the empty—adding the last stroke to the tableau, so drinking and doping and driving were compounded by sexual advance from a minor, or so the appearance/reality matrix had us intertwined.

I wasn't so loaded that I forgot she was there; that level of inebriation behind the wheel would be irresponsible, not to mention inappropriate. I did suffer momentary memory lapse, however, on the window being closed; what the fuck; you smoke Redstone rocket fuel and guzzle two brewskies; you're going to lose a few details.

The big picture blossomed like a bud in time-lapse. It couldn't have looked worse, like a blow job from a minor who could be a cop. Can they nail you for that?

Then I smashed glass all over the inside of my car.

The flashing blue light came next.

Okay, back when I stopped to pick up Heather—which could have been her name, unless it was Ashley or Tiffany—reality was already in a jumble, moving in slow traffic, yes, which should have been a good thing but posed greater risk, since slow speed allowed for shorter distance between cars, allowing my car to be more easily remembered and recalled: make, model, color and license number. Not that a crime had been committed, but the world we live in puts crime potential on the same road as great adventure. A young, svelte, female hitchhiker at night represented a chance on the bright side as well. Didn't she?

The chink in the cosmosphere got quirkier when the car behind us tailgated on into the shoulder and stopped in front of the cop car. The driver got out at the same time as the cop, making me wonder if she was the undercover cop and had called in a perv 513 in progress, with aiding and abetting, alcohol to a minor, narcotics possession and distribution to a minor—called in the bunco squad and DEA, the FBI, ATF and the PTA. Unless the chickie riding shotgun was also undercover and dove on the first bottle to snag that juicy piece o' prima facie for the closer, Exhibit A, Your Honor. Or B, since the roach remnant was still in the ashtray.

Except that the tailgater was Allison, my wife, who should have been home on the couch watching another two-star movie but had come out to the grocery to take advantage of my absence. Not that my presence was ever a problem for her, but she did love my long hours, she often said, because they let her get things done. Anyway, if anyone had recorded my license plate—or recognized it—when I pulled over to pick up Heather, it was Allison, who now approached from the rear on a dicey step, what with her six-inch heels and the shoulder gravel.

Six-inch heels? For the grocery?

Approaching cautiously, one hand on her hip, like she might need to draw her piece and blow me away in self-defense, she leaned in. She didn't say anything stupid, like, "What's going on here?" She said, "What are you doing?"

The cop saved me from answering by asking for my license and registration, the former of which I was groping in my back pocket to find, the latter of which Heather had already retrieved from the glove box—and apparently read in the dim glow of the map light I'd hesitated to order at $220, which never ceased to piss me off, the way they take advantage on a five-dollar flashlight just because it's built-in, till then.

"Hi, Mrs. Fetteroff," Heather called. "It's me, Heather. You remember? I'm Alan's kid."

Talk about seizing the moment—or the day, week, month, year. This kid had it coming and going. Allison gave us her superior smirk to assure that she was neither inclined nor able to sort my associates, colleagues and acquaintances and surely not my friends, especially those with unctuous strumpet daughters— silver snakes up her arms? Pulleeze.

The cop eyeballed the two cards then stooped to peek in. "What's going on here?"

"My fault, Officer," Heather called. "My dad is in rehab, and I get so mad at him for leaving empty bottles around that I just wanted to throw them out the window."

"That's illegal."

"Yeah. Good thing the window was closed."

Yes, I know, it seemed contrived, with the silver snakes, old Dad and rehab. It would have played like the old Statue of Liberty, but the cop and Allison standing in the rain and thickening bullshit and lingering skunk smell didn't make for progress down this field.

"Is this your dad?" Boy. What a cop.

"No. This is my dad's friend. He stopped to give me a ride. You know, nighttime and rain and all."

She was good, so far, till the cop asked how the bottles got in the car in the first place unless someone was drinking and driving—asked me, pointedly and up close.

Not to worry, Heather leaned over. "They're Bud's. He's such an inconsiderate asshole. You know? Mr. Fetteroff goes out of his way to help our dad, and Bud drinks beer in his car. Mr. Fetteroff's car. You know?"

She leaned hard on complexity, but the parts slid into place like a Chinese puzzle, difficult till it's solved. I would look back on her delivery, sincerity and conscientious teen aplomb with admiration. In the moment, I could only look down with humility, as she rubbed my thigh.

The cop showed his hand by exhaling just prior to the next question, indicating his willingness to be fooled into the end zone. "What were you doing out at night alone?"

"Oh, that. I had a practice for the school play, you know, a rehearsal. We're doing *Inherit the Wind*, you know, about the Scopes trial and evolution and all. Then I missed my ride because of the cramps. I thought it was diarrhea, so I thought I'd be out in a minute, because I hadn't eaten much all day, you know, but then it turned out to be my period. I'm one of those women who get it really hard at the beginning. You know?"

With everyone safely back in their cars and either headed home or proceeding with a good-guy errand or hiding by the roadside to catch irresponsible drivers, the evening felt productive. Sure, I would spend a few hundred bucks on a new window and would have been better off all around, skipping the meeting with an excuse nobody could challenge, like diarrhea that turned into the heavy part of my period. "Did you just make that up?"

"Well, I can't really take credit for the diarrhea part. Let's face it; that shit's old. Ha! Get it?"

"Yes. I get it."

"Same for the period stuff, but I did figure out that putting the two together can be compelling. I'm so young, and men can't stand to hear about diarrhea and my period, so it usually works."

"You'd call that little routine part of your repertoire?"

"Yeah . . . Hey. I like that. My repertoire. Hey. Turn left at the next street. Hey. You want to come in? We don't need to do anything. You know?"

"I don't think so. That wore me out."

"Oh, you mean like old-guy tired?"

"Yeah. Like that."

But she was cute, and said she had some buds that would put this stuff to shame and cold beer in the fridge. That sounded good, especially in light of the novel concept she'd put forth, that we wouldn't have to do anything. I liked that. We seemed like kindred spirits, so why not have a friendship?

But then she said, "Oh, shit. They're home." Meaning the parents, who weren't due till tomorrow, or at least till later tonight. "Hey, maybe another time. Okay? You were a gas back there, the way you just went with the flow. Not many guys could do that. You know? Young or old, they just don't get it. They all have to run their big, stupid gobs so *they* can save the day, because they're so big and strong and smart. Not you. You're something."

"Thanks."

"Thank you." She leaned over and kissed my cheek.

"What were you doing out alone at night?"

"I told you: rehearsal. The monkey trial play. I guess you're senile, too. That'll be fun, when I have to remind you what we did."

"The little routine was real?"

"No. I was supposed to get a ride with my boyfriend—make that my ex-boyfriend. He's so rude. So self-centered. So single-minded. Is it any wonder I'm ready for an older guy? I don't mean older. I mean more seasoned. Like you."

She got out and went in, waving back from the door.

Man, these kids today. But she did put a new sheen on the Universe, didn't she? And it's good to feel young again, yet in a few short blocks, back on my regular route home I wondered: did that just happen? Any of it? Or does the aging process bear risks equal to those of doping while driving?

What? Did I just think something?

I've cruised at times, suddenly seeking a few frames from the last ten minutes, or thirty. Beamed forward from point A to point B, I arrive in warped time, holey as Swiss cheese. Yes, it's the dope, sometimes. Yes, the miles lost were easily displaced by distraction and daydream, but this was different. She happened all right, yet I saw no clue or the least iota of her presence. Oh, yeah, broken glass everywhere.

The rare evening warranted another beer, or maybe another round of two beers. I didn't want to get out of the car and back in with broken glass everywhere. So I pulled over to sift the ashtray for the last little butt. It was too small to pinch but adequate for laying right onto the hot part of the car lighter and presto, ignition for a nose hit or two—mm, yeah . . .

Call me addictive. Or is that addicted? I'm not; I just don't like to run out.

Better yet, call me romantic. I wiped my sooty fingers on my pants like a camper in a forest. Who cared? Which was not to ask who gave a flat flying fuck, because "attitude" is most often bad, most often reflecting urban constraint with an absence of leadership, cooperation and sensitivity. Hey, I had ignition yet again, ready and willing as a dreamer who could scrounge the ashes for one more flight, another redemption among the stars, another reach for the adventure I was born to live—call me free, free at last, till tomorrow anyway.

Then liftoff, and we soared homeward on the wings of doves, me and my doves. Or were they ravens, for their matching black and perfect stealth? Oo! No. Nighthawks, for their raptor fierceness. Or owls! Yes. I like owls, with their big pie faces and wise eyes.

No! Phoenix wings! Yes. Out of the ashes and into the night we soared, stopping first at a *24/7 Stuff-U-Want* for a whiskbroom and a six-pack and maybe just a small bag of ice to better prepare for the moonlit clouds ahead.

We'll Always Have Chicago

Late in nesting season, around Thanksgiving, we were all surprised when Dr. Leisure discovered Orion's last clutch at Little Beach, and the nest yielded three babies on a Friday night. Dr. Leisure got his name on his commitment to beachcombing. And practicality prevails in the rural tropics.

He called Carol, playing his part in hawksbill turtle survival for that year. Sea turtles motivate some humans to step up against terrible odds, to help delay another extinction. Media can motivate those people, in whom humility is best seasoned with a dash of recognition. They're deemed heroic for helping nature in trying times, for caring and making a difference. What cause touches wild hearts more than turtle salvation? We loved the turtles, and the Maui Snooze was on hand.

It's actually the *Maui News* but is commonly called the Snooze in a kinder, gentler rendition of prevailing assessment. Calling it the Snooze was more polite than calling it the Corporate Missionary Propaganda Rag.

Turtle love transcended differences in our dedicated group; a reptile species that had won our hearts. On that occasion, another group mixed with ours, challenging our adaptive skills, as turtles never would. That is, Little Beach access requires climbing the cinder cone hill called *Pu'u Olai* at the north end of Big Beach. This two-handed challenge made Little Beach tastefully suitable as the nude beach. Decades ago, Little Beach attracted people who wanted to be naked, merely naked, in the flesh, to soak sunbeams and feel the ocean slosh more freely, or to compensate constraint elsewhere. The next wave took nudity from objective freedom to sexual fantasy. One nude segment openly expressed its appetite at Little Beach with arousal and foreplay; eyebrows also rose over disgruntled murmurs.

The New Age crowd came next, accepting the alternate sexual preference crowd. Then came the lookers and families who wanted to see or experiment, and then the construction workers from other cultures, who stared, who had taken off their tool belts but left their boots on.

The crowds blended more or less in the future upon us. More esoteric and psychically reaching, the cosmic crowd bared body, mind, spirit and then some, their comprehensive nakedness revealing needs to the point of troubling extreme. Down to bare metal, they challenged the politically correct label of special. Demonstrating that everything is everything, it is what it is and whatever happens happens, they looked nutty. They reached for an audience, abrasive as sand on shells and glass fragments rolling in the surf.

Little Beach got seedy, marginally creepy and at times egregious, needs and shore break tumbling, bare flesh and raw nerves sparking voltage, arcing synapses. People in a zone talked to themselves or to Nature, herself, with a time and season to every purpose. It wasn't for the fainthearted.

One purpose to that time and season was a nesting female of the hawksbill species. A mature female might lay only one season in three or four, laying several nests in that season. Orion was a favorite on Maui, returning on schedule to deposit four nests good for hundreds of viable hatchlings over that summer. We loved her and all she stood for, which, in our way, we hoped to stand for, too. We followed her as fans follow celebrities, though her path was simpler with far fewer flings, DUI arrests, divorces, tawdry revelations and remorse. With the patience and virtue of a true conservationist, as if by choice, she held still for installation of a satellite signal unit, staying high and dry for hours, after depositing a clutch of eggs, so the bonding epoxy could harden with minimal catalyst, generating minimal heat that could, if excessive, burn her shell. Once secured, the sending unit tracked her search around the islands for tasty little sponges and turtle love, giving way to currents, crossing channels or hanging close to a particular beach for the nibbles available there.

That Orion would lay a fifth nest at Little Beach was icing on our cake, proof of her magnanimity and shared sense of urgency. With hawksbills listed as critically endangered, and Orion as the only nesting female known by humans to visit Maui that year, we also shared a sense of history in the making. In more difficult terms that remained unspoken: last call.

The Dawn Patrol walked known nesting beaches looking for tracks, so nests could be spotted and watched for incubation, eight weeks, more or less. The nests remained unmarked and never fenced off; with turtles near extinction and humanity pressing eight billion, too many humans still want to eat the eggs, accounting for our group's misanthropy, also unspoken. Carol monitored every other nest known that year, along with volunteers who slept on the beach in the last days of incubation, because hatching occurs at night nearly every time—cooler sand triggers the hatch for greater survival prospects in the dark.

As hatch time approached, monitoring went round the clock. Once hatchlings emerged, three days were allowed for stragglers, and then came excavation, to retrieve egg casings, unhatched eggs and, most important, viable hatchlings that failed to surface, either from lack of energy or impedance by invasive roots, rocks or debris. An excavation could liberate three more baby hawksbills or twenty-five more, so the event drew observers— including kids torn from their TVs, who whined and stomped, whose parents wanted them to feel something that would soon be gone. Some of them watched the hatchlings hit the foam.

Hawksbill babies are exposed to ghost crabs and feral cats, but darkness helps avoid dogs, scissortail frigate birds, mongooses and, most dangerous of all, reef predators. Hawksbill babies are not countershaded on the bottom and present an easy target if backlit by daylight. Excavations occur at dusk, so liberated hatchlings can scramble to the sea to swim through the surf and beyond as night falls.

The nest was below the crotch formed by limbs of a fallen tree. This location also served as the drummer's seat for Sunday raves, when many people gathered naked to bare their spirits and rejuvenate in nature with cosmic, mystical forces. They felt chosen to be here, now, as conduits of magic on Earth, as power brokers, translators, channels, spirit guides, wizards, witches, nymphs, gnomes, and generally elevated beings, some bearing spectacular racks and bulbous tallywhackers.

Among the latter was a gaunt fellow about six feet tall, painfully thin but sporting a straw boater, big, dark sunglasses, a dazzling gold chain around his neck and a huge kielbasa sausage bouncing off his knee caps. A freak of nature in any other venue, he assumed the summit at Little Beach. Unctuous aplomb underscored his reality. Hands on hips, he swaggered left, right, left with pendulous rhythm, the big tuber swinging to and fro but going wide when he turned to a greeting, as he smiled and called back, oblivious to consequence in his playful way.

Was it not natural?

Eye-poppingly huge and a certain focal point for some in need of a closer look, this bratwurst swung casually, as if all pork links were equal.

Some women winced. His girlfriend or wife or mother didn't look at it but shared his natural view, in disregard of the clothed on the beach and their implements. Her crotch, unlike that of the tree, was not adequately concise to form a seat for a conga drummer. It hung open, ghastly, from time and usage, reminiscent of the Japanese monster porn classic, *The Vagina that Devoured Chicago.* Parental discretion advised.

As events unfolded, these two played key roles, beginning with Chicago climbing the lesser branches up to the main trunk above the crotch. The tree had fallen seaward on a slope, putting her seat above the crowd and the excavation, putting her at eye level, unfortunately, for adults and impressionable juveniles brought along for seasoning. Scanning to both sides, she engaged with her mate in pelvic dialogue, their discourse seeming practiced, their genitalia aligned. Displaying her most personal self, she challenged anyone to answer or question her naturalness. Two preteen boys, admirably brave and honest, called, "Eeyieeww!" An adult female nearby admonished them to stop that right now. They did but sneaked peeks and giggled, which served everyone as a tension release.

Meanwhile, from her superior vantage point, Chicago yelled at the nest excavators:

"Stop! I don't like this. You're too rough!"

Her man paced the perimeter, akimbo, head and member wagging to and fro in apparent agreement.

Her awkward spectacle and aggressive demeanor rendered her apart and goofy—especially among the clothed and concerned.

Her man called, "That's right."

We agreed but remained silent.

The chief nest excavator was Bumpy Lowe, a career employee of the Division of Aquatic Resources, with the "authority" to excavate turtle nests "legally," an oxymoron combining the State of Hawaii with management of nature, especially regarding species near extinction. The bureaucratic approach to vanishing habitat and species was wrong, deferential to commercial interests and hazardous to our health and the health of what we love. Could any government manage what it failed to protect?

Some of us cringed and nodded agreement with Chicago and her man.

Bumpy Lowe had no more sense of balance in nature than a bag boy has of brain surgery. His tool of choice in a critically endangered hawksbill nest was a garden shovel. Nobody said boo, but if they had, Bumpy would have explained that he was the only person authorized by the department to excavate turtle nests, and he had to do the green turtle nests, too, and that's a whole bunch of sand to push by hand.

This painful scenario had been bandied and resisted for years—among us. Nobody had openly complained until then, and that's the way it was—until Chicago bleated the plain, naked truth, in revelation of what we'd known all along! Like many removals from common sense in Paradise, Bumpy's stupidity and behavior had continued in deference to "authority."

And Bumpy had staying power. He was born here and could speak in complete sentences, demonstrating public school viability and the potential awaiting future generations, if they could get off the dope and out of the surf to hit the books. Bumpy's chronic grin and severe overbite imbued him with a look of continual good cheer. People in the tropics value good cheer and humility, so Bumpy was regarded as a good guy in a good mood.

His bad habit of using a garden shovel on turtle nests, risking the fragile last chance, was overlooked, like a foul smell on an elevator; it would be over soon, so let's just stay civil. He'd heard the complaints, but "authority" ruled—until this dig.

This crowd was a different mix than usual, taking in the naked, the passionately naked, the nakedly passionate, the nakedly naked and—never mind; a shudder and murmur rounded the area as Bumpy Lowe, oblivious or putting an overbite on a tough situation, angled the blade and stepped on it.

"Oh . . ."

Chicago called out. "Stop that! What are you doing? That's a . . . a shovel! What do you want to hurt them? We're their mother! No! Wait . . . They're our mother! Yes! No. Wait . . . Yes! They're our mother, and we have to . . . We have to be more careful!"

Awkward verbally as well, she was poignantly accurate on her cut and slash to the harsh truth we'd failed to resolve. Her nakedness seemed incidental to the bare facts on baby turtles and a garden shovel. Gross mismanagement on the humanity/nature interface got more dramatic when an elderly man ambled up beside the fallen tree and climbed on to sit behind Chicago. His chins, stomachs, flabby folds, moles and freckles rested in enough hair to stuff a sofa. Like a man of the street, gone to the beach, he wore his body like rags, in need of washing but comfortable enough for now. More noticeable than nudity was the guitar strapped at an angle over his back. Once nestled higher on the trunk, he swung the guitar around and strummed a single chord. Shifting to another chord, he accompanied himself with a didgeridoo impression, tweaking his vocal cords to sound like the outback instrument. He would have put an oddly benign mood on the twilight activity, but things shaped up otherwise, darkening, seeming confused and overpopulated, and more hazardous on each thrust of the shovel blade.

Among the soft chatter surrounding Bumpy's sweaty grunts was the topic of the nest location, directly below the drum for eight weeks, causing compaction in the sand and many little turtle headaches as well. Nobody belabored the strange taste for raw drumming, hours on end, like it was musical or harmonious or anything but incessant and overbearing. What could we say to those who craved the *boom boom, boom boom, boom ba ba boom boom* among us, ass to elbow, so to speak?

When turtles hatch, they move out of their egg casings on their way to the surface, loosening the sand around them. Given that a few hatchlings had already emerged, Bumpy dug for looser sand that would indicate the main part of the nest. He didn't find it. The sand got tighter, apparently recompressed on further tamping in conga frenzies. The sand became dense enough to resist the shovel, taking probability for survivors precipitously close to zero. Whether from belated sensitivity or fear of mob reaction, Bumpy set his garden shovel aside and went to hands and knees. He used a garden trowel but did not protest when a few bystanders joined with their hands to loosen and remove the sand gently, as if to show him how.

Daylight and hope waned, yet turtle love and circumstance motivated those hands to seek what life might wait in the sand, until a dark spot, a baby turtle's head, got gently cleared with one finger. Then came the body, dead—no, wait. It's alive, but barely. Into the bucket it went, onto the wet sand at the bottom, with a stop on the way for weighing and measuring, as if a flop and a stretch for the scale and tape measure would be no more ignominious to this noble infant than weeks of conga drumming on the head.

More hatchlings came out in minutes, till the bucket bottom crawled with baby turtles. Bumpy's associate Lynette moved quickly with her scale, tape measure and clip board, recording stats for science, so the sum total of hundreds of baby turtles would let us know they were of average size and weight, or that they comprised an average or were below average or that they assured another pay period for state-employed scientists, whose stats would be unassailable in any environment, including the one with more extinct species than any other place in the world . . .

I digress. The stats are crucial, in case the sand itself is determined to be toxic, or in case of many potentials that may tell why this species went extinct and who would be to blame, which might help to slow the next extinction.

Carol also moved quickly, carrying the bucket to the top of the runway that had been cleared, a path about ten yards wide beginning about twenty yards above the waterline. The idea was to set the hatchlings down in view of the sea rather than setting them into the sea. Scientific data indicate that hatchling turtles seek open space and light—starlight or moonlight—in the sky and reflected on the water. That's why coastal lights, either residential or urban, have killed so many turtles, leading them inland, where they die.

The babies are also thought to be hardwired with a "frenzy" phase that lasts around three days from emergence, in which their tiny flippers go like hell. Theories abound. The frenzy period may vary geographically to coincide with each location's distance to offshore feeding grounds, which aren't grounds at all but currents carrying tidbits suitable to sustain turtle life.

Who the hell knows? The fact is: the turtle runway at Little Beach was lined with well-intentioned humans ready to assist the babies, the first of whom struggled weakly seaward. One crawled into a footprint and needed rescue. Another crawled into a wispy coconut husk and needed untangling. Most just sat, too weak to move. They looked dead, but if picked up, they moved. The technical term applied to hatchlings weakened as a result of human behavior is "compromised."

The reporter from the Snooze further discouraged and frustrated those of us struggling in the natural/scientific/tragedy matrix. A mean-faced, twitchy fellow with a fixed sourpuss, seemingly stuck in place from facial palsy or karmic resolution, he got little sympathy. His approach to anything was barbed, remedial and superior. His tedious ingratiation to the powers that were felt toxic and worse than no news. As a newcomer to conservation heroism, he mingled, asking around, "Is this your first turtle release?" He wanted to know what people thought, and wasn't it grand, and what about these kids, having this terrific chance to experience this wonderful miracle and rejoice in this wonderfully miraculous place we're so lucky to live in.

His story in the Snooze would say just that, with no mention of major mortality or the tree crotch or Chicago or anything but a happy-face rendition of another outing the Chamber of Commerce could appropriately support. He was a nuisance and distraction to those of us who saw sixty compromised babies of a critically endangered species being sent to certain death.

The first hatchlings at the top of the runway who couldn't move were picked up and moved a foot forward, such as children will move their toy soldiers. In a minute or two they were moved again, along with the second bucket bunch, making spurious progress toward the surf.

Stars twinkled.

The waves came in sets, till the first babies were far enough along to be taken by the biggest waves of the sets. But a wave can only take those babies who take the wave, who propel into it. Otherwise, the babies lay flat on the sand as the wave pounds them. The second or third wave might roll them over. A few got rolled back up and then back down for a while. Some were plucked off the sand and tossed into the next wave, where they began the process of drowning.

In the damn near dark, I went to Bumpy Lowe, knowing the severe pressure of the state's guidelines for handling endangered species, and the severe pressure at hand. I shared an experience from Mexico, where the government sponsors seaside hotels to actually care for hatchlings for ninety days before releasing them, thereby changing hatchling mortality from ninety-eight percent to ten percent, saving several species that had also been critically close to extinction. The hotels invite guests to participate in the nursery process, feeding the hatchlings small pieces of fish, gratifying the guests with lasting impressions of a thoughtful country and a species worth saving.

Bumpy winced at this suggestion that he break a state law, saying that it was wrong—that it would be tampering with nature, that you must not, cannot, will not tamper with nature, because you'll get it wrong, and nature will be hurt forever.

I reminded him that resort development hosting seven million tourists annually in twenty thousand rooms may be a tampering of a different magnitude. And that many of his "local" friends shed great wads of monofilament and braided nylon fishing line wantonly onto reefs, with big barbed hooks soon entangling and hooking many turtles.

He sweated visibly in the dark and seemed more upset. "Yeah. You teach a turtle to eat little pieces of fish; next thing you know, you get one hook buried in that little piece of fish. Then what you going say?" He hadn't heard me—had ignored me like a perfect employee of the state.

He left me speechless. I could have yelled at him, but that couldn't change sixty certain deaths. When forty-five of the hatchlings had been committed to the deep to drown, the circle of humans, naked and otherwise bared, gathered around the listless few hatchlings remaining.

Bumpy Lowe, in darkness and ignorance as certain as the death before us, and as willfully oblivious to nature, had no more to say. Bumpy was never a bad guy; nobody wished him this situation, without the balls or brains to do something, anything but be a bureaucrat.

We simmered, until Bumpy spoke of rationale for something or other, stating the fact before us, that sixty babies got retrieved but were compromised because of severe compaction because of drumming and . . . and . . . "Carol. You want to take these home?"

The moment was monumental, with authority going to a white gal from the mainland with a graduate degree. Carol watched a few more waves wash, perhaps assessing scientific method and consequence, finally making the call on one hatchling and then, after a few more waves, making the call on another. The listless babies selected were placed back in the bucket. Agreed was that they would spend the night at Carol's, in the bucket on the wet sand, thereby generating the strength to scramble into the surf tomorrow. That is, they would recover by internal fortitude. They would not be fed—Bumpy's ruling.

I did not ask if anybody wanted to skip dinner, drink no water, hold the late snacks and then go for a swim at sunrise out past the reef. No, because you reach a point in personal development where non-dissension can best facilitate practicality. A few glances my way may have served to question my polite deferral, but that, too, was conjectural in the dark, and nothing remained of nuance or eye contact, except where starlight glinted. No, it was time to come together, to love each other and the world we live in, to move on, join hands and rejoice that here is our place, and now is our time, and the circle of life goes round and round, yadda, yadda, blah blah blah.

The bad news was brief. Twelve of the fourteen turtles carried home in the bucket with the wet sand at the bottom didn't die until morning. The other two weren't tossed into the surf, because free of peer pressure, humans are capable of correct behavior, to a point. The remaining two were not fed and hung on till the following afternoon. Then they died, too.

Two or three days later came the Snooze account, glowing with turtle enthusiasm and what the release team was up against—darkness, intricacy, delicacy, little bitty babies, so cute, and of course commitment, beauty, et al ad nauseam. Then came dates of milestones in the turtle epic, like when the state finally stopped its sustainability program on Hawaiian green turtles. That program had safeguarded the species by limiting the catch to twenty-five percent of the population per year, so the numbers would always be protected, because three quarters of the green turtles would always remain. This argument and these numbers actually prevailed at the state capitol. The story ended by noting some core individuals (humans) for tenure in the turtle crusade and the legislature.

We laughed. Not really, though she did appear to smile. I swiped her easy enough there in the dark, playing my little cooperative shell game, slipping this one into my vest pocket along with my sunglasses. I call her Chicago, for the nostalgia.

The other bad news is that turtle babies don't want to be force-fed anymore than any babies—don't like it and will resist it. The secret is shmushing the fish to a pulp and getting the mouth to open to push the fish in and then down the gullet with a cotton swab. This challenge resolves to proper perspective once love is tempered by fatigue and gets tougher. The good news is that any baby not properly weaned—or in the case of a sea turtle, not properly frenzied to the tidbit currents—will accept mushy food in a few days. And don't forget the greens.

Chicago grew from one point five to six inches across in ninety days, following scientific consensus that turtle size is more a function of diet than age. I'd never seen a fat turtle, so she got all she wanted. A six-inch shell seemed so much bigger than an inch and a half; we went for a swim. She followed me. But turtles are not pups; they're solitary by nature, like some humans, except for social activities, like feeding, sex or basking. When she drifted away, I followed her—couldn't help it. That is, like any worried dad, I didn't feel my baby was ready for deep water. So, we came back home. Then her time with me became a year, to eighteen inches across.

She most often faced the ocean, and her pool was too small, and changing the saltwater was a heavy task requiring many trips from the beach and heavy lifting and constant vigilance to keep her wet and out of trouble—and to keep her hidden, to keep me out of trouble.

We scheduled another swim, not so deep but out and around the north end of the reef at the south end of the Prince Hotel beach, where green turtles gather by the dozen to feed on limu growing on the rocks there, and an occasional hawksbill drifts through. Hawksbills eat sponges, harder to find, but she should, and some turtle socialization couldn't hurt. I thought hanging out with green turtles might give her some shark sense, too. The greens know when to lay low.

I do, too. Do not try this at home; it's a federal offense punishable by fines and/or imprisonment. And it's never good to tamper with nature, unless of course you feel the runaway madness reaching full gallop, and you need to correct what's gone wrong. I remember green-eared turtles for sale at the dime store (The dime store? Who remembers that?) with a little flower painted on the shell. I remember chameleons for sale, 29¢ each with a little chain around its neck and a safety pin at the other end to pin to a shirt. A wet mint would stick it to the shirt near the chameleon, who could lick it all day, and it was okay, even at school. A kid could race home to catch flies and maim them, so Larry or Igor could catch them easily. The world was big and endless, and nature was an amusement.

I got some red-orange nail polish and daubed her trailing edge dry and printed:

I brake for reefs. Go Cubbies!

I saw her again a few weeks ago, feeding near the limu ledge, casually, unafraid and adapted. A few huge green turtles in the three-hundred-pound range rode the gentle surge, grazing limu along the ledge. Chicago made me proud, working the bottom just below, tipping rocks in search of little sponges. Did she figure that out? Did she observe it?

Did she see me? I think she did but wouldn't let me too near, perhaps fearing a return to the plastic pool. That's good, a little fear of humans among those you love in nature. Hawksbills were hunted to near extinction for their red shells, used for mirror handles or eyeglass frames. Chicago's bumper sticker was holding up, so maybe she'd stand a better chance.

I still look for her, but I think she's off somewhere deep or far away, refitting the puzzle parts, sorting instincts, approaching a suitable male, I hope. Maybe I harbor some regret that we can't cruise together, though I hope to see her again in twenty years or thirty, when she comes home to nest and remember those difficult, early days.

Bigger than Mike Quinlan

I wrestled my first match at fourteen, five one, a hundred-three, second boy out after Nicky G at ninety-five. Nicky stayed there three years but had to fight his natural weight gain in our senior year, when he took the district championship but lost in the first round of the state tournament, weak from dehydration. He'd been slurping ExLax and chewing rubber bands to spit over the side while sitting on the pot. He shaved his arms and legs and clipped fingernails to ditch another half gram.

I grew up a few classes but got nowhere near one eighty-five, where Mike Quinlan wrestled—not for forty years anyway. From one oh-three, looking up to one eighty-five is gigantic, a reality of magnitude, a beanstalk to the sky, unlimited growth, a force of nature.

Mike Quinlan was a junior and a gridiron all-star, so he couldn't get too excited about rolling around on a mat in tights. He went along good-naturedly, not so much indifferent to the drama but more resigned to wrestling's status as a filler between football seasons. Football was the meaning of life for Mike. Wrestling was a diversion, a pastime, an amusement.

Mike seemed eager to win his matches. Why not? But still, they were wrestling matches, win some, lose some, and not football, with winners and losers. He said lying on his back, being pinned, was like nappy poo compared to a pileup on the two-yard line, where life could pass before your eyes—a short, painful life with all too little of the you-know-what as yet in the bag.

Mike had been there, on the two-yard line and rounding the bases with his girlfriend, so he knew. He could nearly doze off, flat on his back in the wrestling room, which was hardly the case on the gridiron, where a hundred eighty-five pounds made him one of the smaller guys out there. Thundering momentum in a defensive line could stack mortally against him, coming on like a ram-charged steamroller. KABLAMMO! That was the sentiment of football contact, no cushy rubber mat about it. Mike got respect and awe for his muscle mass and athletic prowess—and because he was a great guy among the wrestlers.

On the gridiron, he was somebody else, all tooth and nail, hard-driving furor up the middle, do-or-die on every carry.

Football guys had to stay fit for next year, even the heroes. So Mike went along, into wrestling, laughing like a good sport, as he donned the skimpy togs with the caveman shoulder straps. He'd be our heavyweight, and he joked about one thing and another as we looked up to him with hope, because now, at last, with all-star running back Mike Quinlan as our cleanup wrestler instead of that fat ass Sandy Snyder, we might have a chance to win for a change. The heavyweights are last out, which is tough, with eleven matches to sit through while your stomach churns. Worse yet, a tie in team scores could bring the ultimate team decision to the heavyweight. The last match often told the tale and made an indelible imprint on the teachers, the other kids, the coaches and cheerleaders.

Mike was cool, like he didn't care. He did care, because good guys care, but then it wouldn't matter, really, this wrestling thing, because it was indoors and not at all the same. He could hardly consider it a real sport like football. Besides, he'd be an all-star running back next year no matter what, even if he got rolled on his back and pinned like a cream puff. He might even have a smile on his face, which he'd never have at the bottom of a pileup. A grimace maybe, but never a smile.

Wrestling wasn't exactly a goof, but it was a long way from football and filled the post season much easier than basketball, which Mike said was for pussies. We loved him for that, knowing that wrestling couldn't compare to next fall, when Mike Quinlan would take the handoff and show his moves to any other heavyweight on the field who thought they could take him down. Then we'd see who smacked snot out of who. I mean whom.

Mike was cavalier at first but dropped the constant joking once we'd had a little chat, he and I. It happened at practice, reviewing the basics, like proper ride height for the waist/ankle ride, effective leverage for the breakdown, efficient moves to perpendicular for the half nelson turn, the far-leg turn and, of course, the neck-and-knee cradle, which was the only move in amateur wrestling that allowed a wrestler's hands to clasp. Mike had been tying his shoes; untying them and tying them again, then untying again and trying an ankle wrap before re-retying. He wasn't paying attention, which was no big deal for those of us who'd heard this stuff and practiced to second nature and then tried it out in a match because it had become accessible to us. But Mike was green, so I told him, "This is important."

"I'm trying to get it right. I just can't tell if I want them to dangle, or if I should take a wrap on my ankles."

"Not that. I had my shoes tied in the locker room. This. You got to know how to ride."

He looked up to see who was talking to him. He looked over at Coach Dale's demonstration and smiled. "I know how to ride."

"How do you know?"

He laughed short at something so obvious, as if to ask back: How does an all-star running back know how to walk, or eat or sleep or anything? Or everything. "Don't worry," he said. "Nobody you know is going to ride me like that."

"Why not?"

He'd returned to his shoelaces. "Because. I won't let them."

I knew what he meant; that his brute force made certain things certain. But I also knew that not being ridden wasn't a certainty to count on. "It doesn't work that way," I said.

He looked back up. "How does it work?"

"It's not a huff and puff and blow your little house down. We got twelve different weight classes so you get an even playing field. It's a system of mechanical advantage, with action, response and counter response that favor the guy with the best moves. That's why we practice the moves. Without the moves, you got nothing."

"Yeah? You got moves, and I got nothing?"

In essence, no, that was not the case; nor was my explanation nearly so concise. But that's what I meant. What I said at the time was, "Look." I got him to take the defensive stance on his hands and knees. I took a knee beside him, with my near arm around his waist, and grasped his elbow with my other hand.

Coach Dale saw us and scowled. It was rude to practice while Coach was talking and strictly forbidden to practice two levels outside your weight class, much less eight levels, but Coach Dale hadn't wanted to tell Mike Quinlan to quit lollygagging with his shoelaces and pay attention, and then he had an inkling that a nagging, chronic problem might be solved here without anybody yelling at anybody else. So he called out, "Ready . . . Wrestle!"

Of course, Mike Quinlan was casual, he was so big and didn't want to look like a bully against a hundred-three-pounder. I moved sideways over Mike's back, and he laughed, like a mosquito might need to be slapped. I switched to my other arm around his waist and picked up his far ankle. He laughed again, like I was Tinkerbell sprinkling pixie dust on his ankle. I nudged him forward and slightly to the side and broke him down from what was then a top-heavy stance—both hands and one knee. He tried to stand up, but I had his ankle raised by then so his heel was pressing his ass. I hooked the top of his foot with my thigh and held it in place there with all I had to give as he lifted his torso off the mat. I broke him down again by catching him off guard with a sideways swat to his elbow. It all went quick but covered two breakdowns and continued control. I stayed with him through his rigorous shake off, and then rode him across the mat as he tried to shimmy out from under with a rapid hand and knee walk. My part was simple, rudimentary application of basic mechanical advantage. But he was Mike Quinlan, heavyweight, who soon huffed and puffed, erupting free of pitiful constraint—up and turning, flushed red, crouched low and charging like a linebacker into some slam tango . . .

Coach Dale blew his whistle on that head of steam.

Mike Quinlan stood there one easy motion from pounding me into the foam, till he nodded and smiled, realizing what I'd shown him, besides showing him up, that the wrestling mat doesn't work like the gridiron; no, it's as much gamesmanship as sportsmanship. But it's not a game like football. It's more like chess, but then you have the oomph and drive on top of the mentality, so it's really not like chess. But it's not like football, and that was tough to sort. The point was that Mike started paying attention, and I guess that's when we started to be friends, and he became more aware that his teammates wrestled to win and shouldn't be let down, because looking up to him as Mike Quinlan, all-star running back, was only a context, and it was *our* heavyweight on the mat that counted most.

If he approached things casually and lost, well, that would be like someone else getting to second base with Patty Larew, and Mike thinking, *Ah, well, that's life for you.* Patty Larew was

Mike Quinlan's girlfriend and captain of the cheerleaders with a few moves of her own. She seemed natural and profoundly affirmed by her full-fledged shape and the molten warmth rolling down her slopes with seemingly unstoppable power. Mike gained clarity on the importance of winning at such an inconsequential thing as wrestling, when hearing it compared to keeping his girlfriend true. It seemed a time of growth for him, seeing the motley scrubs who were his teammates as viable as the sellout crowd at homecoming.

Most of the team were more like me than Mike, with no girlfriend or gridiron glory to fall back on, and not much else either. I for one had sparse identity other than the profile every kid hates, of an uncertain, shy and formative boy. I kept to myself in tight pants and hand-me-down sweaters, outdated and non-preppy, generating sympathy for the exigencies of poverty but hardly magnetic to the girls. I wrestled with personal status, grappling with self-esteem: I'd show them. The mat would stage my valor. Or defeat. I'd show them, or maybe prove what they already suspected.

You could pluck phrases from the hallway hubbub; the news was that Mike Quinlan would be wrestling junior varsity. What a laugh. He laughed, too. He didn't care, because the varsity heavy was Harvey Binder, second in state last year. Most people thought Harvey should have been state champ. He only lost by a point on a squirrelly call in the last seconds. And he was the epitome of classic wrestling: no body fat, short legs, long arms, a low center of gravity and team spirit that balanced fairness with can-do perseverance. Harvey Binder tipped the scales at a cool two-ten with muscles on his muscles and gave up nothing by way of notoriety or popularity to Mike Quinlan on JV. They were teammates and friends, in the limelight together, because Mike was an all-star running back, after all, and went the distance with Harvey Binder, giving up thirty pounds and hanging in there unpinned, a tribute to Whippets everywhere.

We practiced a month before our first match of the season. After that it would be a match each week for eight weeks, but the rest of the season shrank to miniscule proportion behind the first show, where we would see whose perfection would remain intact, and who would fail. The fear crept in a few days prior like a phantom pain in a brave boy who thought he'd ditched his anxiety. Like seasickness on an ocean crossing, the fear made its rude presence unavoidable. Most boys hid it, what with everyone else on board having such a frolicking good time. I thought it was stomach flu at first, compounded by a neurological disorder, just when I was ready to make a good impression on the other students, the teachers and cheerleaders. I would transform from ill-fitting hand-me-downs to warrior wrestler and show my stuff with grace, rough and tumble.

I didn't sleep the night before, couldn't eat the day of, and the hour before was down to cold sweats, no warm-up required. But I went through the motions, because nobody wants to be seen sweating while sitting still, and the little warm-up shuffle Coach Dale showed us was a good place to put the nervous energy.

Looking back on the components in play, marginal skills and monumental fear stand out. I think fear won the day, making it a first day in the process every boy should go through, of feeling fear conquer all and then losing and then seeing that fear may not be avoidable but losing is. That is: fear should not influence an outcome, because win or lose, things roll inexorably onward.

I lost. The fear vanished in the first few seconds, after first contact, fake, duck under and take down, which put me two points up and confirmed what I'd known all along, that eternal greatness was mine to claim, until the other boy pulled a reversal with such amazing strength and alacrity that I felt in my heart he was far more experienced, perhaps more deserving and most assuredly meant to win this thing. I pulled back, mentally speaking, and the body went along. I should have won but let things degenerate to grab ass; arms and legs flailed, weeks of practice went out the window, no moves, only reaction, no deliberation or conviction.

This perspective sorted out in a few days, but the immediate aftermath was shocking realization that the student body's assessment of me was accurate. I walked back to our side in amazement that it was over so fast, though I'd gone the full three rounds and lost by two points. I'd stayed ahead on points, just like Harvey Binder in the state finals, when I got turned over, but not pinned—never pinned. But you lose five points in a reversal and near pin. I got three of them back, but it wasn't enough.

The team sat on the floor, scrunched up along a wall that was too short for twelve boys. Mike Quinlan gave me the half nod and said to sit in front of him. He ruffled my hair and said, "Nice hustle." I gave him a look that said, yeah, yeah, but he said, "No. No kidding. That was a great scramble. I thought you were gonna pull it off."

"Pull it off? I had it pulled, till I choked." My smile was crooked and pained.

Mike's girlfriend, Patty Larew, was about my size but seemed much bigger; she was so mature and nice, so stacked and beautiful. That was her second year in a row as captain of the cheerleaders—she'd been captain as a junior; she was so good. That she was a senior and going steady with Mike Quinlan, a junior, seemed about as exotic as if she'd been Little Miss Sunbeam, and he was Mojimbo.

It proved how cool he was, if he needed proof, which he didn't. He was everything to everyone, the greatest guy ever, and everyone knew it, including the popular kids, the hoods, the scrubs, nerds, spooks, pizza faces, eggheads, do-gooders, brown noses and flunkies. Everyone liked Mike, because he liked everyone, and called them all by their first names, because that's how he was.

Patty led a cheer with two jumps and a split in appreciation of my effort, and all the guys leaned forward and called my way in agreement; I'd hustled nicely. That helped, after visualizing my match as two scrawny boys on a foam mat for six minutes looking like kids at a jammy party in a pillow fight without the pillows. With everyone calling my hustle nice, things found a better perspective. Then Patty Larew came over and stood there until I could look her in the eye. She leaned over smiling and caressed my shoulder and said, "You're really something. You're gonna be great."

I felt greater already, like I'd won instead of lost, sitting in front of Mike Quinlan, getting strokes from his girlfriend. Mike watched over us, Patty and me, like a benevolent giant safeguarding two very important little people.

Mike still didn't know much about wrestling, but he won that day with a default to what he did know. It was easy, once he figured out that the other guy was scoring points on reversals and escapes. He laughed when the ref yelled, "Two!" That was two points for the other guy. Mike laughed every time, until Coach Dale yelled for Mike to stop horsing around and get serious. Then Mike got so serious you could see it on his face, all the mirth displaced by intense determination, just like homecoming with seven seconds left, down by five inside the twenty. He went slack for an instant then slid in kind of sideways for a manhandle move we never practiced. With a short step shuffle, he grabbed the bull by the horns in a stalemate of brute strength, till their four hundred pounds tilted too far and plummeted to the mat, piled up in our favor. Mike cinched up on impact, stealing the other guy's wind and getting the pin. The ref was down and peeking and counting one, two, three and slapping the mat for a Whippet win. Mike Quinlan came up flushed, brushing off a pesky but necessary task, helping the other guy up for a hug before ascending yet again to the top of his own private Olympus. Patty Larew ran across the mat full speed, leaving terra firma five feet out and flying into his arms, where she lit like a little bird and something else, never mind the sweat and mat goobers; Mike Quinlan was every girl's dream.

Mike never learned the wrestling moves, because his heart was on the gridiron, and learning both seemed like too much, what with all the plays already stacked up in his brain box. He could tie up though, ear to ear with the other guy, holding the neck and one arm. Most wrestlers like to fake a lunge up and dive under for a two-leg takedown, or duck around for a waist grab and throw down. Nobody faked Mike Quinlan. He wouldn't budge up or down; he was just that strong. He might laugh at a failed fake. Nobody took Mike Quinlan down. He took them down, every one, with a move up they all thought was a fake, till it kept going up, advantage to the most muscular, Mike Quinlan.

Sure it was only junior varsity, but they were all heavies. He bulldogged Harvey Binder once, too, before Harvey figured out the perfect counter, a drop away fake that hooked a biceps on the way down into a rolling sit out.

Mike laughed and said, "Hey. Do that again, wouldja?"

Next time Harvey tried, he may as well have tried it on a statue, a laughing one. Immovable Mike stepped in, replanted and grasped Harvey by the triceps. Harvey shook his head just as Mike sat down and flipped him to the mat—Harvey Binder on his back! Second in state! It was the greatest move Mike ever made, and Coach Dale blew the whistle for a gather round. Coach told everyone to listen up, and he waited for silence. "That's not a wrestling move. That's grab ass."

Mike looked down.

"And that's what it comes down to sometimes. One move. It comes from right here." Coach Dale patted his heart. "It can take the day. Harvey? Am I right?"

Harvey Binder paid attention as Coach Dale walked through Mike's move, explaining the overwhelming effect of brute strength properly blended with balance and timing.

Mike's eyes stayed down for unexpected praise, as Coach Dale demonstrated several variations requiring less brute force for those of the, shall we say, more mechanical inclination.

Coach had Mike come up, then curled his arm under Mike's armpit, from where he could twist, sit, flip and come down in a pinning position instead of two points, because if you don't look for the pin, you can end up a few points shy. He demonstrated variations on a pancake, with more oomph and finesse than a grab ass boy might imagine.

The other gem glimpsed for the first time that day was equally brief but just as brilliant: a shared insight to Coach Dale's Olympic past. Coach Dale hadn't been a shoo-in any more than any boy or young man, but the center podium and gold medal appeared to be his by rights at one time, until he lost. He couldn't understand loss any better than Mike Quinlan could grasp the importance of wrestling, and any reference to Olympic greatness or what might have been was met with a quick discount, a brief laugh, a change of subject, a wise word on the importance of developing both the body and the mind. If pressed specifically, Coach Dale offered the sheepish grin and mumbled that he'd lost on points, perhaps taking marginal solace in going the distance, or maybe seeking only to move through the subject quickly and on to something else. Yet that day his loss seemed to be airing out. We all knew it was a pancake out of nowhere that got him down, and here he was, flipping pancakes of every stripe, as it were, sorting out the myriad nuance, twists and turns a pancake can take, with humble innuendo that now he would know what to do, if another came at him out of the blue.

Coach Dale was a heavyweight, too, much older, married with a house and kids of his own, thirty-four already. He died eight years later over a two-month period from an inoperable brain tumor, resigned at the end to the inevitable chicanery of the phantom pancake waiting out there to take you down. He faded as humbly as he'd lived, perplexed in the end that nobody had figured that one out.

But eight years is two lifetimes for a high school sophomore. I ended that second year with a junior varsity record just over five hundred, right in there with the rest of the win some, lose some, so-so scrubs. Coach Dale advised me that spring to get a set of weights, nothing fancy, just a barbell and a couple of dumbbells and a hundred pounds or so. I was so skinny that I had to depend on the leverage moves, which I fairly slicked, but I needed range, to keep them guessing. Coach said the leverage moves were good and would put me a cut above the rest, who never took the time to learn them because they all thought wrestling was for grab asses, like Mike Quinlan. "Never mind the weight gain. Let's see what you got in there."

So every night between the dresser mirror and the foot of the bed, with the radio playing "Louie, Louie," or "Bend Over, Let Me See You Shake a Tail Feather," "Your Love is Lifting Me Higher," or "Midnight Hour," or the whole host of rhythm and blues inspirationals as yet to be discovered by most white kids, I curled, cleaned and pressed, until slight swelling appeared above the elbows; faint deltoids defined the shoulders, and the radius and ulna were no longer perceivable above the wrists because of the thickening that got in the way. I didn't exactly bulk up but did put some muscle on the bones, gaining poundage through two weight classes to one-twenty, which seemed powerfully big from one-oh-three, until power and weight became two more relative concepts, and the world turned like it always had, with no discernible difference. I still sprawled on the couch, watched TV, walked down the hallway at school, fiddled in my locker, watched girls and thought they didn't see me staring—and wondered when and how and what if. Those were the years of natural growth and wonder and seeing things as they might well be, someday, somehow.

Never a good student, I got by, neatly balancing my steady D in history, which was no fault of my own but rather a result of the most thorough disconnect between student and teacher in the history of education. To whom did he imagine speaking? Then again, some kids got A's. I still wonder what they heard, and how they responded when Nick Adzick (the Great Greek) talked in tongues, spewing phrases, names, dates, concepts, ideologies, vast intellectual movements rolling across the Purchase just like the Expedition up the Trail but without the undercurrent undermining the substrata of the underbelly, or as Frederick Jackson Turner would have it, the underpinning of the Great Conestoga . . . the Great Conestoga . . . the Great Conestoga . . . Movement! If you will. A clock never took more time to cover forty-five minutes.

Where was I? Where am I? Oh, yes, balance. It occurred in exposition, or expository writing, as profiled in the curricula. I had flow. Youthfully obtrusive, obstreperously vigorous and verbose, my sophomoric prose nonetheless blended some sprightly spices while spinning a few good yarns and chewing some generous fat. All the writing counselors had to do was pare down the vigor and verbosity, then unmix the metaphors, *et voilà*! I would be a facile communicator, or at least a cut above your average high school student, a true Whippet expositor.

Did I say writing counselors? Yes, I did, because the Whippets were not your average high school students but in general hailed from old money, seasoned neurosis and delusional flare. A privileged background presumed but did not guarantee the flow. I worked menial, degrading jobs from age fourteen, and the flow came naturally to me. I had it. The writing counselors recognized it and helped me bring it along, beginning with Mrs. Hussong, a staunch stalwart of starched syntax, usage and grammar, who met with me one-on-one, expressing no less than gratitude for what I brought to the table. Yes. A historian might grimace at this accounting—let him—but a writer I could surely be. Mrs. Hussong, the rectitudinal matriarch of the constant vigil for awkward construction, run-on sentences, transposed points and unclarity, nay, the Virgin Queen of Verb Predicate Confusion, gave me A's in a steady flow of her own, right up to the end of the term and a culmination of effort on the final exam for a glowing, history-be-damned A+.

A writer could live quite well, given adequate fame. No sweat. I'd be there. And I wouldn't give a snit about history—or algebra, chemistry, French or the rest. I would some years hence actually spend time in France and pick up the language at will in a few short months, making me wonder yet again what was going on among the Whippets. Anyway, into year three of high school, with prospects for a varsity letter in wrestling and some of the girls I watched beginning to watch back and blink and smile and some of the girls I hadn't watched beginning to grow more watchable, I strode boldly into a new season of exposition, emboldened by my singular victory with the Hussong. You what? You got an A+ from Mrs. Hussong? Did you kiss her?

Mrs. Hussong was very old. I did not kiss her, but I would have, in gratitude for what she taught me.

Janet Swope, on the other hand, was twenty-seven, which seems old and experienced, too, and seasoned and all-around-the-block if you're only sixteen or even seventeen. To capitalize on her single feminine attribute, she stood, walked, leaned, sat and, we can safely presume, lay prone, with a most acute swagger in her hips. From her hips, a dramatic curvature sucked way to the inside under her ribs, only to sweep in a dazzling hairpin back the other way in a most suggestive parabola, perhaps identical to the path of Cupid's original arrow. She had no breasts to speak of, a gaunt face with dark, sunken sockets around olive eyes deep in the recess. Most unfortunate was the nose, long and twice humped, once just under the bridge and again halfway between there and the cruelly pointed tip. A sparrow of a woman with a notable ass, Mrs. Swope seemed keen on showing us something.

These days she would have the nose reduced and the breasts enlarged, or, as they say, enhanced. Back then, a girl could only call on her own devices, primarily those of compensation by wit and charm, which is not my recollection of Janet Swope's compensatory skills, but rather what she deemed them to be.

She introduced herself as Janet Swope, generating a mild titter in the classroom. In those more formal days, we sometimes never learned a teacher's first name. "Should we call you Janet?" Davy Wood asked.

Davy was big, not as big as Mike Quinlan, and far from all-star, but he was a running back and often a joker. He was considered most popular by the other kids, especially the boys, who looked up to him when he told several times weekly of what he had to go through to get that week's blow job from his girlfriend, Meredith Wilkes-Bashford Bush, no relation to the Washington via Texas/Maine Bushes but nonetheless wealthy in extremis and just as appropriately proper. Meredith had notably buoyant and spherical breasts, not huge like muskmelons but big as honeydews and certainly heftier than Mrs. Swope's. She had a bad overbite, but Davy said she must have practiced in the mirror or something, because it never got in the way. Meredith Wilkes-

Bashford Bush did not utter one syllable to me in hundreds of hallway passings or chance encounters outside school in the four years we were classmates. So, naturally, I, too, listened eagerly to Davy's accounts of having to first chat with Meredith's mother and then make some lame excuse for wanting to check something out in the basement and then having to make out with Meredith for about an hour and then finally getting her to unhook her bra and feeling her melons, till she put her foot down and flat refused to go farther, because nice girls didn't, and then relenting to the blow job just to, you know, help Davy out. Getting her to swallow was easy, once he assured her that her mother would know instantly if she drooled, and they could only rest easy by disposing of the evidence, all of it.

"No," Janet Swope tittered, blushing and batting her lashes over her dark eyes. "Call me Mrs. Swope."

"Mrs?" Davy asked, holding the boys enrapt, because we knew what Davy had in mind, and here he was, making his first move in the first minute of the first day of school in front of the whole class.

"Yeh heh hes!" Mrs. Swope tittered, blushing and batting again in this unexpected flurry of engagement.

"Is he in the navy?" Davy asked. "Like, you know, on a submarine or something?"

"No ho ho," she insisted. "He's . . . He's a . . . He has a job. You're bad, aren't you?"

"No." Davy sat back. "I'm good."

Some of the other kids laughed. Mrs. Swope gave him a look much as a B-girl might scan a soldier to buy her a drink. And so the term began. "I don't know what it is," Davy said after class. "But I want to fuck her. I really want to fuck her."

"You want to fuck 'um all, Davy."

"I don't want to fuck Hussong."

Ha! All the boys laughed in the clubhouse privacy of shop class. Anything deemed cool gains momentum in a student body, so several other boys began to flirt with flat-chested, bird-beaked, broad-bottomed Mrs. Swope.

I was annoyed, first with the boys fluffing plumage on her behalf. What was that? Then with her, for playing along with the endless titter, blush and batting. It was embarrassing for one thing, to see my friend Joel Schuman arrive at school soon after the beginning of the notorious interplay in Mrs. Swope's English class, wearing jams, then known as boondockers—strange pants that stopped just below the knees—cowboy boots and a bandana around his neck. She said he looked dashing, like a buccaneer. He swaggered, puffing his chest and holding his arms out wide, as if his latissimus dorsi muscles were so big they pushed his arms aloft. We sometimes lifted weights together, but come on.

Joel wrestled one-thirty-three and knew nothing but was really ready to rumble. He ended up winning the district finals but got pinned in the first ten seconds of the state competition. I didn't see him after that but heard he'd failed at suicide in Chicago after succeeding at romance for the first time ever with a woman, who, for some reason, could not reconcile the differences between them, or between their parents. She was black. He was Jewish—and perhaps fatalistically depressed. I heard some years later—not too long ago—that he finally succeeded at suicide. I still wonder why so many of them died, but that wonder was also displaced for the best.

On the day of the cowboy boots, bandanna and jams that made him look like a French homosexual (we didn't have gays in '64), he handed in his first assignment in expository writing to Mrs. Swope. *What is the allegorical connection between Holden Caulfield and society? What is meant by "allegorical connection?"* We had begun the reading season with *Catcher in the Rye*; no small accident to my mind, that our first selection would pivot on the f-word.

The papers were returned the next day. Joel got an A. I got a C-. Ah, well, I thought. Good for him, I thought. But then Davy Wood got an A, too, and though he could give a spellbinding blow-by-blow on the rules of romance with Meredith Wilkes-Bashford Bush, Davy was a dunce. Huh. Uh huh. Uh huh huh huh huh. Huh. Davy Wood didn't know an allegory from a participle. The elusive A went as well to several other boys in that class who ranged between Davy Wood and me in their level of flow, all of whom did their best to leave no doubt with Janet Swope that they, too would like to you-know-what if she ever, you know, wanted to, you know, or anything like that.

This tedious sexual innuendo touched the proverbial nerve. Mrs. Swope was not a sexual being, for starters, nor could she claim the least intimacy to literature. Next came Hemingway,

Across the River and Into the Trees. "Say, Mrs. Janet—I mean Mrs. Swope . . ."

Titter titter blush blush bat bat.

"Did you ever cross a river and head into the trees?" Titter titter, et al, ad nauseam. Okay, on to the meat of the situation: What does crossing a river symbolize? What is transcendence? How does it apply in this story? Does friendship prevail? Endure? Subsume?

To make a tedious tale short, each boy in the front row got an A, with rises in their Levi's, wearing ridiculous hats and sashes and carrying on like male whores for the last bitch in town. I got a C-, after displaying thorough grasp of symbolism, rivers, transcendence, friendship and endurance, though in the end I was subsumed.

Next came James Fenimore Cooper and the romantic side of the American frontier relative to Natty Bumpo's hyperbolic accuracy with a shooting iron in a context of brutally hard times. This was dangerously close to history but in fact was the other extreme, highlighting the good stuff, the colorful, daring feats of heroism. I knew this stuff. But it was A to the rest. C- to me.

And so the autumn phase proceeded in a steady stream: A to others, C- to me, through Mark Twain, Nathaniel Hawthorn, Herman Melville, Thomas Hardy and Edgar Poe.

Macbeth would change things. As it happened, Sissy was a junior at the private university in town that same year I was a junior at Whippet High. The private U was known for its literary wing; that's why Sissy went there. The flow ran in the family.

Sissy read *Macbeth* the same week I did, and got an assignment quite similar to my own. She got an A. So I copied her essay verbatim and handed it in and got a C-.

Gotcha.

Well, the next private session between Mrs. Swope and me was difficult and embarrassing for her. I loved it, giving her the news point-blank, along with advising her of moral failure in giving me a nonstop C- because I didn't flirt with her. She should be ashamed, first for flirting and foremost for penalizing me. I needed a new writing counselor posthaste, and the Hussong would do nicely, if she was available.

Mrs. Swope cast her huge sockets downward and muttered, "We can work this out. I want to work this out. I need to work this out, if you'll let me. I'm asking you to let me work this out."

"There's nothing to work out. I'm an A writer, but you have denied me for foul reasons. You're sick. But that's not my business and hardly why I'm here. You need to work this out with a licensed professional. I'm a kid. You may not be an adult, but you have adult problems. I won't suffer them anymore."

"No. I know. You're right. You'll get the grades you deserve. I promise. Please."

"Your call," I said, standing and ending the session after two minutes, taking my copy of Sissy's A paper that looked bludgeoned by Janet Swope's red pen, tucking it under Sissy's original, pure as the driven snow except for the big A at the top and the brief praise, *This is really very good.* "Psh . . . You're pathetic."

The next week the Hussong gave me an A on my own *Macbeth* composition and two more A's on the last two compositions of the term, giving me an overall grade for the term of A. The Hussong went along with Mrs. Swope's fix, tactfully avoiding the topic directly, but nodding sanguinely when I assured her that I didn't mean to appear so bellicose, but I felt that the proper accolade should accrue adroitly to me, and it wasn't; so I felt *very* dyspeptic but hoped, in time, to curb my acrimonious inclination.

Mrs. Hussong's wry smile perhaps reflected her feelings of well-being and job security. I'd used five vocabulary words in two sentences, justifying many more hours of advanced counseling.

Davy Wood was a waiter in LA for a couple decades, waiting on his break in the movies, I think. His parents had a deli in St. Louis, and when his father finally died, Davy took over and is chipping beef to this day at Solly's Finest, keeping Solly's spirit among us.

Meredith Wilkes-Bashford Bush married a very well-to-do fellow and lives as she always lived, in the next block over from where she grew up.

My mother overheard her mother in the beauty salon, bragging, as it were, that Meredith had never been without a boyfriend since age twelve, yet she remained a virgin till her wedding day, with her virtue intact, as it were, her popularity still surging.

Sissy married as well, perhaps less virtuously. She had three children, two of whom had children of their own.

I called Mrs. Hussong about twenty years after the fact. She remembered me, or at least said she did. I told her I wanted to thank her. She assured me I was very welcome. She died a few years after that.

Mrs. Swope went away after that year, never to be seen or heard from again. She was rumored to have been unmarried and not twenty-seven but thirty-nine, so maybe it's no wonder she behaved so poorly, lonely and desperate as she was.

I wasn't nearly as resentful then as I came to feel in later years, which underscores the importance of every child, especially adolescents, viewing adults as mortal people, with mental and emotional infirmities just like other children might have. Otherwise, these adults, these so-called paragons of behavior and right thinking, get away with murder, most often resulting in damages that linger for years.

But at the time it seemed a good turn of events, an adequate airing out and call to justice, and wrestling season was underway directly. I felt good. I made the varsity team by defeating Mark Thurman in a match most memorable for the whole team, watching to see if I would wrestle as usual when beginning from the top position. That is, with my chin nestled into Mark Thurman's back. Mark Thurman had terrible acne, not as bad as some—Johnny Walker was known as Pizza Face. Some kids didn't know his name was Johnny Walker, which could have been a perfect name for a popular athlete in a V-neck sweater, creamy beige with cable stitching, over a button-down collar, khaki pants and Weejuns. But it wasn't. It was the given name of Pizza Face, a hump-shouldered, clinically depressed and introversive boy who couldn't look you in the eye because of the tomato sauce and cheese oozing out his pores.

Mark Thurman's acne was mostly dormant on his face, reducing ridicule and the tired joke that his after-school job was playing goalie for a dart team. Mark was nearly over the pus and bleeding that left craters that would fill in over the next thirty years. But his back still erupted. Mark, pleasant otherwise, was prone to loss on the wrestling mat, usually after a few near pins that would stretch and open the gooey vesicles, till they oozed like a failing drain field. What a mess.

The boys mumbled. Some continued practicing on the periphery, glancing obliquely at our elimination match.

Mark, ever friendly, advised me not to worry about his skin because he would wear an extra T-shirt under his sweatshirt.

"I'm not worried," I lied.

"You'll win anyway," he said.

"How do you know?" I asked.

"Because. You're a better wrestler," he said.

Mark was an egghead, a class of student that preceded the computer age and nerds. Mark was an A student in chemistry and physics. I was supposed to say something to the effect that nobody knew who would win, or that a good hustle can surprise you, or that giving up isn't part of this. But Mark wouldn't win because he didn't want to, didn't want to be varsity but rather yearned for junior varsity. Given the chance to beat me, he'd pull back. So I said, "You'll get better grades than me."

He laughed, "Yeah."

In a few short years Mark Thurman got a job in a great new industry, nuclear energy. He walked into the power plant one day and was never seen or heard from again. Perhaps the ambient radiation cleared up his skin.

At the moment, we squared off to begin round one. Mark smiled. I took him down, and he laughed briefly. I controlled him easily by the waist and one ankle, and finally decided to get this over; he reeked of Clearasil, half a tube spread over his back. It had no more effect than a bag of sawdust sprinkled over an oil spill. I surged ahead in the spirit of expedience, swinging to the perpendicular, pivoting with my chest on his lower back. I turned him with a half nelson and went for the pin. Too late; the bell rang. He laughed again, rising and straightening his many layers as groans rose from out of bounds.

Mark's back had stretched and festered, sprouting red and yellow wet spots across his back.

He won the toss for round two and chose bottom, innocently enough, putting me on top. I settled to one knee, grasped his left elbow and put my arm around his waist slowly, gaining time to find a safe place to nestle my chin. I reckoned three inches to the left of the spine, just below the shoulder blade, unless of course a soft pustule waited just under the cotton for some slight chin pressure. But what could I do? I settled gently to a dry spot on his T-shirt, touching my chin to it with a half-gram of pressure.

Coach Dale knelt in front of us with one hand raised, ready to blow his whistle and begin the action. He hesitated, puzzled at my unorthodox chin spot, but then he shrugged and chirped. What followed was neither nice nor memorable. Motivated at that point to minimize the agony for both Mark Thurman and me, I drove for the pin straight away, far more ruggedly, aggressively and brutally than Mark Thurman warranted.

Afterward Coach Dale took me aside and asked why I hadn't done that last year in every single match that I lost, which, by the way, I should have won. I began my excuse, as a boy will do, seeing quickly that it was a trick question with no correct answer. The question of loss went nowhere, allowing a silent interlude in which to glimpse another side of knowing.

Maybe Coach Dale's little insight spurred me on, that first year of varsity wrestling. Consensus among my teammates was that my nine and oh record was attributable to lifting weights off-season. I didn't argue, though I knew the weights were only partly responsible. The big difference was the transition from the vigor a boy might muster, to the power that, for better or worse, makes him a man. I couldn't very well extemporize on manhood, though it was plain to see: I'd gained a gear since last year, and shifting up as necessary got the job done like it hadn't been done before.

Mike Quinlan also made varsity that year.

Harvey Binder had graduated after a miserable loss in the district finals when he had the flu and could hardly breathe. He'd enrolled in a trade school where he was learning to be a pipe fitter, where he'd earn fourteen dollars an hour to start, with time and a half for overtime, and he'd be working alongside his father, making both of them happy. Harvey came to all our matches but looked different in his work clothes, less strident, more content, carrying his winning attitude into life itself. Harvey had continuing confidence that he could finish any job he started, and he owed that fortitude to wrestling.

Tom Reardon was also a bit of a joker. Some of the boys liked him and some didn't. He smoked outside before a match, said it loosened him up and relaxed him. Harvey Binder didn't like him, and nearly made a move on him when Tom asked what the hell it was that Harvey could finish, besides another day at his knuckle-buster job and the cold lunch in his pail. Tom drank a fair share, too, and would die just after his forty-eighth birthday, when his liver would quit and he'd follow, way down on the transplant waiting list with no celebrity status. He was haggard and yellow by then, but during a smoke break after a match many years prior, just after insulting Harvey Binder, Tom laughed out loud at Harvey or any fool who thought a job was a good thing. Tom tended bar for thirty years before he croaked.

Mike Quinlan hadn't done nearly as well on the varsity squad, going against varsity heavies keenly intent on winning with moves, strength and speed. He could beat the big fat guys who went sixty or a hundred pounds heavier, except for Frank Mantrell, who looked like Haystack Calhoun but was fast and agile as a state champ, which he proved to be. He pinned Mike, the first and only guy to do so, which was okay.

Mantrell was great, and it was an away match, so the cheerleaders weren't there.

Mike was four and five going into our last match at Soldan High School. I avoided talk of district finals or the state competition, because it made me sick with anxiety. I didn't mind losing so much as contemplating loss or worse, disgrace; what if I turned out to be the biggest pussy who ever stepped onto a wrestling mat? What if I got pinned in the first round? Well, it could happen, and the thought was frightful.

At the summit of my nauseating prospects stood Jonnie Ray Green, the hundred-twenty-pounder for Soldan. All black and much different in their movements, the Soldan cheerleaders didn't pom-pom or rah-rah, or jump with twists or splays. They got down, got funky, got loose. "Come on, Sugar! Whoop up on him! He *know* you can! I got something for you."

I thought their unusual dialect and rhythm a ploy, a psychological diversion on their part. How could they know that I knew he could? Yet I did know. Jonnie Ray Green took second in state last year—because he had the flu like Harvey Binder, because it was going around. Jonnie Ray ran a fever of a hundred three but defended the title because he took first in state two years ago. As a freshman, first in state! He came off his sickbed last year with a shrug: "Hell, it only six minute." Technically, he lost, yet morally, he was still the undefeated champ, going three rounds with a raging flu and losing by one point on a questionable call.

Jonnie Ray Green had no neck. While we warmed up on neck bridging, arching our backs with the tops of our heads pressed to the mat, Jonnie Ray only watched and smiled. He couldn't do neck bridges because his head was mounted on towering trapezium perched on spherical deltoids that rose from biceps the size and shape of grapefruit. He looked twenty-seven or thirty-two with a few hard laps around the block.

I told Coach Dale he was a ringer, recruited from the mean streets for a sure win against a kid like me. I was seventeen and still crawling out of adolescence.

Jonnie Ray was all man and looked familiar with the worst conditions.

I wanted to puke.

Coach Dale looked and nodded and finally said, "Well."

Oh, great. I shrugged and shook, like a boxer, kind of.

Coach Dale patted me on the back and consoled: "Just get in there and mix it up. Like, you know, you got nothing to lose."

"How can you do this to me?"

"What am I doing to you?"

"You're scaring the shit out of me." This exchange would make the rounds with me saying shit to Coach D and he responding like we were just two guys dialoguing on a point. "You're supposed to tell me what to do, Coach, not that I got nothing to lose."

"It's not me who's scaring you. It's you. That's how it works. And nothing to lose is exactly what you got. What do you think, you got it in the bag already? Sheesh."

Jonnie Ray had ripples on the lumps on his muscles and veins popping everywhere. He'd warmed to a sheen and stared at me, sweat rolling off his shaved head. His grin was playfully dominant with too many teeth too perfect to be real. I didn't sense his scorn but rather his bemused approach to this trick of fate; after all he'd been through, now he would face a so-called "undefeated" child of opportunity and advantage. When I stared back, he made a move, not a wrestling move but a dance move, like the cheerleaders. He'd gone through a few beats when the cheerleaders caught the action and picked up the step and howled a few bars of the funky banshee. What a festive occasion this was shaping up to be, like a pig roast with a blazing fire under a full moon in a druid rite of passage. Oink.

Coach Dale pulled me away, shielding his mouth and speaking directly into my ear to keep Jonnie Ray from lip reading our secret strategy. "Don't tie up. Don't let him get under you to your legs. Don't go in low. He'll catch you in the armpits for a pancake." Coach Dale thought it through and nodded.

I waited and finally asked, "What *can* I do?"

Coach Dale smiled. "I don't know. Stay away from him for now. Let's see how it goes."

Mickey Schisler wrestled one-twenty-seven that year, right after me. Mickey had carrot red hair and massive freckles and came to our school from the same military "academy" as Tom Reardon, so he, too, smoked and drank heavily. He went on to spend twenty years behind the wheel of a tour bus in Santa Fe, really getting the feel of the place while growing his flashy locks to shoulder length and delivering a compelling narrative on the history and insights to Santa Fe, his natural humor in no way compromising his rebellious disposition. Just then he said, "Fuck it, man. Like Coach says, you got nothing to lose. This guy's gonna kill you. What the fuck? Tear it up some. Have some fun." This analysis would also make the rounds, in the end trumping my shit story.

I looked at Coach Dale, who shrugged, unable to argue.

Sitting through the first three matches at ninety-five, a-hundred-three and one-twelve took forever. I had to use the bathroom twice, both times sitting idly, focused on this same time tomorrow, when I'd have nothing to do but rest in peace. Prognostication on the long term held equal sway, say twenty years ahead, when I'd be a successful something or other and could look back in mild amusement at my grab-ass wrestling days, and the silly way I got nauseated over nothing, or what would become nothing, given time.

Of course by then I wouldn't be straining to take a dump in the Soldan High School boys locker room in a tiny booth heavily rusted with carved initials, phone numbers and illustrations. No, I'd have some elbowroom by then, with a decently elongated bowl, and tile on the floor with a little foot rug and a window with a view and some ventilation. I might smoke a pipe. Or maybe I'd only smoke my pipe at my desk. Either way, I'd have a well-stocked magazine rack alongside, and the toilet paper dispenser would be just askance of my knees or an easy reach out front, so I could pluck freely without spinal contortions required to twist around behind. Why do they do that? Oh, and two-ply, and a reading light. Best of all, I'd be sitting there for a reason, to take a dump, unlike that agonizing moment of delusion before my match with Jonnie Ray Green, when no dump was anywhere near ready; it was my guts doing takedowns and pancakes.

Mike Quinlan came in during my second try and took the booth next to mine. Cutting loose on a massive load at will, he sighed heavily and said, "Hey. You got to relax. Give it your best—no! Give it your very best. Go the limit and then go farther. You know?"

"Yeah, yeah."

"Losing is all part of it. I mean, I lost plenty this year."

"I haven't."

"I know."

And that was that, save the rudimentary motions of personal hygiene and anxiety repression. Back out front, it was round three of the one-twelve class, both camps screaming for victory. I couldn't tell who was ahead and didn't care. I started the little shuffle dance. Coach said don't look him in the eye, but I sneaked a peek and saw him grinning back like an old friend who just pulled the perfect practical joke on rosy-cheek, lily-white, soft-touch me.

I wouldn't say Jonnie Ray and I ever got to be close friends, but I did see him from time to time over the years, especially after he got out of the used-car business and opened his restaurant specializing in pig snoot, so the brothers wouldn't have to haul ass all the way over the bridge to the eastside every time they got a taste for snoot. He kept the snoot on the menu but shifted his promotional focus to ribs 'n chicken over the next two or three decades, hoping to expand his market as any businessman will, knowing that Mom, Dad, Bud and Sis might want to come down to Jonnie Ray's for a half slab, a quarter chicken or a mutton sandwich, so snoot went to the back burner, so it wouldn't intimidate them into staying home in the burbs.

We went down to J.R.'s for the snoot, maybe hanging on to old times as aging people will, gradually letting go of the leather-tough, disgusting pig noses in time, especially when they got so popular at your better chain pet shops. Jonnie Ray knew ribs and, more importantly, understood sauce, which, after all, is the main reason anybody eats ribs in the first place, as a vehicle for the sauce, and they'll keep coming back to the right balance of vinegar and sugar. You can't eat that stuff too often, but every now and then, I'd head down with the guys. J.R.'s had an unbelievable secret sauce and a great reputation, so why not?

He grinned at everybody by then, sometimes working the fire but that was just for show. He was the host, glad-hander and showman, and when he grinned at me, I thought that was just part of it; he didn't recognize me. People change over the years; it had been a few, and who would ever have guessed that one day I'd be bigger than Mike Quinlan?

But he did squint through the changes as he stepped up and leaned in with a coarse laugh and gruff whisper, "Come on, brotherman. Three quick ones." Then he cupped my neck with a grip like a bull python and knuckle-rubbed my head, which wasn't as aggressive as met the eye but more of a private joke between two survivors. Then he laughed out loud. We hugged, both tensing, in case somebody had a pancake in mind, and we laughed at our success.

Some years prior, however, things got dead serious when we circled the center of the mat and the whole world fell away. I think Jonnie Ray Green was always playful and never mean spirited. So when he dropped in a blink and swooped casual as a raptor gathering a rodent, sweeping my knees in one arm and putting my butt on the mat, I thought: Damn.

"Two!"

This guy makes it look easy. I rolled over quick to avoid the pin and thought him presumptuous for jumping high onto my back and leaning all his weight on a forearm squarely between my shoulder blades. That made him top heavy and I could throw him off, theoretically. Pondering the throw off, with my chest and chin pressed to the mat, I glanced up to see the Soldan cheerleaders screaming bloody murder. I heard nothing but my heart pounding in formidable currents of blood and sweat.

Shrieking in transcendent silence, the Soldan cheerleaders went to gyroscopic choreography, loving Jonnie Ray's antics. He knuckle-rubbed my head, which didn't feel too good but was, I had to admit, intimidating and humorous. It also led to the next surprises, the whistle stopping the action and a penalty point awarded to me.

"Da fuck, man!" Jonnie Ray whined.

It was my second best move so far, putting a point in my column and narrowing the score. This expletive was not penalized; Jonnie Ray said fuck whenever he wanted.

We began again with him in the top position, where he rode for a while, unable to turn me or break me down, till I squirmed free on the brief opening between his shift from left to right, giving me another point on the escape as round one ended with the score tied. That is, Jonnie Ray Green and I scored the same number of points in two minutes!

I won the toss and took the down position. Unlike Mark Thurman, I didn't know I would lose. I also didn't think I could ride Jonnie for two minutes any more than I could catch a giant catfish with my bare hands. Moreover, I'd just proven that I could fend him off. Sho nuff, he got a point for riding time but couldn't turn me over, but he was up by a point at the bell, going into round three.

Jonnie Ray hunkered down, fingertips on the mat. I knelt beside him with my right arm around his waist, my left hand on his left elbow. He felt solid as a fire hydrant.

Coach Dale squatted by our bench and yelled, "Watch for the sit out! Watch for the sit out!" The sit out indeed seemed likely, in which the bottom wrestler swings his left leg under his right leg, arching and bringing all his weight down on the other guy's arm, especially if the arm is still trying to control the waist. Successfully executed, the sit out will make the top guy's arm collapse, and so will his body, allowing the bottom guy to roll over and become the top guy, two points. The catch is that the guy attempting the sit out must have adequate muscular strength to make the move work. Oy vay.

In an instant two choices appeared. The first was to jump back, let him up, sacrifice a point on the escape and go from there. That seemed crazy, giving up the match on points, since he'd surely take me down. I went for the second choice, driving all my weight forward and into him at the whistle in a perfect anticipation of the sit out. Anticipation is dangerous in any endeavor, if the perfect counter awaits, instead of the move anticipated.

In this case, Jonnie Ray could have lunged forward and up, neutralizing my move and escaping. But Jonnie Ray went for the sit out; he was so strong. My move worked, and with more than four minutes behind us and both of us huffing and puffing, he went to his chest, broke down on the mat.

My heart fluttered at the mere glimpse of victory over Jonnie Ray Green. Then it compressed under Jonnie Ray's weight; who ever heard of a rolling sit out? You can't sit out unless you're on your hands and knees. You can't sit out if you're lying down. Yet there I was, on the bottom, chin and chest digging into the mat with Jonnie Ray's forearm between my shoulder blades again.

"Two!" the ref yelled, triggering another bloody murder chorus from the Soldan Fly Girls, who went gaga ballistic on a mixed bag of walking the dog, soul strut and funky chicken. So? I'd lose by two, unless I got careless and let him turn me. I was way too vulnerable in the prone position, but he couldn't turn me with his forearm pressed into my back.

I took a rest. When he swung around to perpendicular, I made my move, up to hands and knees just as his hand grasped my neck. The world constricted in horror, flashing images of the quick flip that would put him on top and me on my back.

Later, Coach D would assure me that it wasn't a vision or gifted insight but the luckiest grab-ass move he'd ever seen, in which the bottom guy locks onto the top guy's half nelson and not only volunteers the flip but kicks into it with all he's got, building a momentum that might just roll on over, especially if the top guy is so muscular and strong, he rides too high, too confident. I locked, huffed and lunged on around, pushing with both feet while arching into a backbreaking neck bridge.

And what do you know?

"Two!" the ref yelled. I checked my bearings, on top, so the two points had to be for me. It would stay tied if I could ride him for the minute remaining. Fat chance.

Jonnie Ray said, "Sheeyit" and stood up casual as a debutante leaving a tea party, till he turned and took me down again easy as lemon chiffon.

"One! And two!" the ref yelled, putting Jonnie ahead by three. And there it would have ended, had not Yolanda Washington pleaded that Jonnie Ray bring it on home, Sugar; I got something for you.

Jonnie Ray and I looked up at her generous offer and remarkable demonstration of team spirit. Jonnie Ray grinned; I lunged into it—into his momentary lapse, I hooked his arm from the back and spun, shoulder to shoulder, verily leaping off the mat, levitating my legs and letting it fall—Jonnie Ray, me, the works, down and over for "Two!"

And onto Jonnie Ray's back, where his shoulders touched the mat for a split second before his recoil sprung him back over, but it was enough for the near-pin and . . .

"Two!"

Except that Jonnie could grab ass, too, continuing his roll again like I was too dumb to learn from the first one—back on top and, "Two!"

The reversal was his, but who knew the tally by then? I thought we were tied, maybe, just as happy to cruise on into a well fought match that I'd lose by only one point—till Coach D yelled, "You're down by one. Escape! Escape!"

Oh, sure, you fat fuck. Easy for you to say, I thought, more or less chewing the nasty foam beneath us, glancing up as far as my eyeballs could roll in their sockets, glimpsing Mike Quinlan, who'd taken a knee next to Coach D with a soft, amused look on his face, a haunting half-smile and a murmur: "Hey. Get up."

It wasn't so easy, but Jonnie Ray was chewing as much carbon dioxide as I was chewing foam. Struggling first to my knees, I pushed up with my hands, crabbing sideways when he lunged for the breakdown. Grunting into that next phase out of boyhood, I lunged, hardly escaping the brutal situation but escaping in the technical sense for a "One!"

Jonnie Ray stared as if at a shooting star, knowing what his wish would be. Grounded in the next moment, he closed like a predator, demanding that I, the prey, should submit and roll over.

Jonnie Ray had a strange little hand jive meant to distract, his fingers stretching odd ways, down and up and in your eye before he dropped and shot in. But I went low with him and met him arm to shoulder and vice versa till he pushed me out of bounds again and again at each attempt to take me down.

The bell rang on a tie, an acceptable end to my undefeated season. A tie with Jonnie Ray Green indicated equal skill levels. I could have won on a fluke but didn't, and that was okay, because I didn't lose and didn't get pinned or even turned over. *Eeeyihaa!* I thought.

The ref had us shake hands and held our hands aloft as Jonnie Ray said, so everyone could hear, "Man, da buhshit!"

I felt ten feet tall and taller still when Jonnie Ray, a head shorter, stepped near for a back slap and a gruff whisper, "You awright, brotherman. You awright."

Greatness is a function of consistency and is not proven by a single win. But don't try to tell a high school junior about greatness, once he's tied a three-time state champion, which Jonnie Ray went on to be, with a three-season record of 46-1-1.

I won the District Finals but lost in the first round of the state finals to a guy from the southeast corner, lankier than me and with a way of turning me (over) that I hadn't yet seen or imagined till too late, but woeful lapses fade quickly in recollection of glory.

I would inventory the images of the night I tied Jonnie Ray, one of which came years later when I second-glanced at a girlishly cute woman in her mid-thirties who'd done a double take on me, too, in the next moment gaining mutual recognition. Patty Larew was still a looker, even in a plush overcoat. She let it fall open to show she could still lead a cheer in any ballpark. We were both in a hurry, both on our way home and eager to laugh out loud at the bigger hurry the years seemed to take.

But we dropped everything and bellied up to the bar for a round of recollection. What a sweet little while we spent catching up, filling each other's eyes and feeling what was in the air. She praised Mike Quinlan, who'd gone off to engineering school even after she'd stayed home so they could date, but that was best; he'd become such a terrific engineer. He'd married a great little gal he hadn't known that well when she got preggers, leaving a game but honorable guy like Mike no choice, and that was also for the best because of the three great kids they had and the house in the suburbs with a reasonable payment. Mike worked for General Electric or Motors or Foods and . . . and . . .

I wanted to ask her back to my place for some pizza or fried chicken or something. But it seemed like a violation of nature, like we were siblings, or at least half-siblings with the same Spirit Father, the same guiding hand and role model. We went our separate ways, exchanging phone numbers but never calling, maybe sensing an aftermath or a strain. All grown up, more or less, we shared loving memories. I was willing to consummate that love, but I get ahead of myself with distraction and fantasy. Are you kidding; Patty Larew and me? That would be a sit out to ponder. But the call never went or came, maybe as a fluke of nature or nature's way.

A more lasting if less loving image came at the end of the Soldan meet, when we filed back to the locker room with our heads held high, having lost the team score by less than half of what had been predicted. There in the crowd beside Coach Dale's wife was Mrs. Swope, staring at me. I turned sideways and saw that Mike Quinlan was right behind me, and I sensed she wanted to strut her stuff in front of the all-star running back, maybe to recruit him to her list of hopefuls. Moving as best we could through the well-wishers, family and friends who'd made the journey to support the Whippets at Soldan, we neared until close enough to speak.

I nodded hello but she reached to touch and say, "You were fantastic!" Practically pulling me over, she came in close. What the hell was she doing there? "I'm so proud of you!"

Oh, come on. I didn't say that but looked puzzled.

"Really!"

"Fantastic? Proud? It was a tie! A tie!" I didn't expect everyone to stop, but they did.

Mike Quinlan smiled beatifically as he had a few minutes prior, coaching me to stand up to manhood.

"That's like kissing your sister!"

Mike knuckle-rubbed my head as Jonnie Ray had done.

Mrs. Swope glanced up at him, then wrapped her arms around me. Of all the stories spinning off this stellar event, the one most told was of Mrs. Swope, shall we say, finding me. The crowd pressed us into an embrace with a writhe.

And it was over. All eyes turned back to the mat and Yolanda Washington—or Queen Zambuga, as she came to be known a few years later—breaking into an early rendition of the *Ngube Night Sky Dance*.

In the din spoke Swope, something heartfelt, something sincere, something contrite or hopeful. The ebb and flood pulled us apart, pulled me through the swinging doors into the locker room, leaving her outside, where she didn't want to be. But alas.

The next day at school we approached in the hall, Mrs. Swope and I. We hesitated, wondering what next. I waited, a Varsity grappler riding high but stuck in perplexity. She wore a plunging V-neck suggesting a phantom rack or hinting her own rebellion against social demands or compensating with spirit what she might lack in flesh. She trembled, doubtful, till something broke—the iceberg calved, revealing blue clarity.

I was not a great wrestler but could scrap with the very best. I was a top tier writer and had been all along. She saw it but couldn't say it, much less give me my rightful grade, because her strange isolation had bound her in longing. She was woman— twenty-seven or thirty-nine, Mrs. or Miss, skinny or thin; they mattered no more than hope and glory. Hey, that's what I saw, face-to-face and toe-to-toe with my expository nemesis cum grappler groupie. Knowing then what I know now, I would have embraced her, would have whispered that love must rule our time on Earth.

Which I did, kinda sorta. Come on: I was seventeen. She was twice that. Putting one foot forward I brushed past, advising *en passant*, "Stand up straight, bitch."

She beamed—my A at last, signaling round two, all tied up.

A Flea-Bit Painted Monkey

Jimmy Levin was dead when they found him, not exactly smiling serenely but then not exactly not. Those of us who knew Jimmy sensed his serenity at the end, his surly aplomb sustained into the next phase, his expression practically asking, *Yeah? So?*

Jimmy overdosed on downers, Tuinals, yellow pills that weren't called yellows, not like Seconals were called reds. Both were trademark names, for what that was worth, which was millions to Big Pharma. Slang drug names had spurious value for us, too, as a cultural component, as Mick Jagger narrated:

> *And though she's not really ill,*
> *There's a little yellow pill.*
> *She goes running for the shelter of a mother's little helper,*
> *And it helps her on her way, gets her through her busy day.*

Chief among memories of Jimmy Levin was his Mick Jagger routine. This was back in '69 with his hip-hugger bell bottoms, green-and-pink-striped with paisley ribbons down the sides or, near the end, the pants he wouldn't take off, leather and sixty bucks, "the last pants you'll ever need." And so they were.

Jimmy had zero body fat, like Mick, though Jimmy stayed skinny shooting speed, likely far more than Mick ever did, if Mick ever did. Like Mick, Jimmy's Elizabethan blouse hung open to show his ribs and concave stomach. He'd hunker down, sink his head into his shoulders, raise one knee as if to counterbalance emotions within, point a crooked finger at the future, and with the other hand grasp a broomstick for a microphone. He sang along in perfect synch:

I'm a flea-bit painted monkey . . .
All my friends are junkies . . .

And so on through the groove, syllable for syllable, twitch for twitch, short-circuited but young enough to override the system internal, to the polite disclaimer:

I hope I'm not too messianic
Or a trifle too satanic . . .

To the finale, squealed in a plaintiff pitch between falsetto and a rodent's death throes:

I'm a mon-keeeeeeeey . . .

I'm a mon-keeeeeeeey . . .

Percussion and guitar fairly worked Jimmy like puppet strings in spastic hands, with agony and ecstasy in the pitch and sentiment of the moment.

Then he slumped, exhausted, for quick repose between tracks, following on a ballad, a personal fave, since Mick Jagger obviously had Jimmy Levin in mind for the sad tale:

I was standing in line with Mr. Jimmy . . .

It wasn't all Stones, though "The Devil's Banquet" best connected the dots between Jimmy Levin and the way things were. The Stones didn't replace the Velvet Underground. They couldn't. They went to a new phase, unanticipated. Besides that, Jimmy needed to move on from his Velvet Underground routine, in which he and Greg Buckstein would heat their junk spoons, tie off, find a vein, draw some red stuff back into the syringe, and hold it right there while somebody—maybe one of them—would reach over to set the other needle onto the first groove. Jimmy and Greg would get about three seconds of vinyl hiss to push the plunger and get the drug coursing brainward. Ideally, Lou Reed came in on cue just as the drug reached the top floor:

I . . .
Don't . . .
Know . . .
Just where I'm going.

But I'm gonna try for the kingdom if I can
'Cause it makes me feel like I'm a man . . .

And so on to the money lines. Jimmy would come in and fade out, keeping the beat and waiting, anticipating, rejuvenating to the heady downbeat where he'd get visibly lit and giddy:

Heh . . .
Roh . . .
Win . . .
Be the death of me
Heroin, it's my wife and it's my life, ha ha
Because a mainer to my vein
Leads to a center in my head
And then I'm better off than dead

Because when the smack begins to flow
I really don't care anymore . . .

Rhythm and rhyme flowed forth on precise timing and soft touch, and just like Houston Control, we had liftoff. Greg and Jimmy looked sincere before they looked dumb, without synapse, without hope—or with hope that they'd got it right, which they did, just then. Survival felt like splashdown, back on terra firma, heroic to the inner circle who watched in awe, perhaps wondering if someday they would also launch or think not. Meanwhile,

Jimmy and Greg took a while to reenter, so to speak, easing into giddy giggles and the fuzzy glow of success.

Jimmy and Greg were out there by choice, further out than anybody else, also by choice, or by compulsion. Yet with grounded practicality, they reserved their hard-drug rock 'n roll anarchy and the Underground's ultimate cut for special occasions, lest they tire of the music or hit too much junk. Speed was no easier but seemed less threatening, and though the boys would have wilted in their boots at any hint of conservatism, they deferred to survival with honor. They agreed that hitting speed for the synchronous merge with "Heroin" would keep the Reaper amused and at bay, too. Ole Reap was such a rascal, insisting on the tease, from where he would leap from lethargy for snacks on the run.

It made sense. They moved on, lead ponies on the wild frontier, until Greg laughed out loud in certain scoff if not scorn. Shooting LSD would be crazy, like stepping off a curb in front of a bus. For fun? Are you shitting me? Greg was no pussy, no way, and he wasn't crazy, too. Well, you could shoot LSD. Nobody said you couldn't. You could shoot anything. We talked about peanut butter. Didn't we talk about that? What a goof. But LSD? That would be like, you know, using a Mack truck for a golf cart or a nuclear warhead instead of a cherry bomb.

Man, golf. What a goof.

Mainlining LSD was Jimmy's modest proposal: "Hey. Would it be a fuckin' goof, man, if we like spiked some Owsley or some microdots? Or some fuckin', some fuckin' sunshine, man? Uh huh! It'd be the ultimate gas!" Jimmy saw LSD injection as a brave scout might, like seeing an easy way to cross the canyon out front. The canyon was metaphorical but present, changing form with time and, uh, progress.

*Ev*eryone was eating LSD, and that was cool, but that was all it was, college kids getting off to get their shit together. Jimmy needed more, something way out front. Jimmy wanted to hang ten over the cutting edge. Never mind the toes; he'd grow new ones—like a lizard! Uh huh.

Always happy, playful and daring, Jimmy's radical view was meant to be sporting and brave, such as courage could describe a bold innovator, if not a role model. "Fuck it," Jimmy often said with a grin. He'd wake the Reaper and slap snot out of that silly fucker. On a serious note, Jimmy had responsibilities, like, you know, thinking this shit up and checking it out, you know, for the kids. He'd looked around for something new to shoot up, till it hit like lightning—the idea—twisting his face on a sort of grin.

He called the idea original; he invented it. Nobody yet had spiked acid. Now there was the space shot to reckon. Besides, what could it do, take you out six dimensions on a bumpy ride? So? What's wrong with that?

Jimmy hit some acid by himself, like a test pilot, because Greg wasn't a pussy, but given the experimental nature of the thing, would be best engaged working the record player, because once you hit acid, setting the needle—the other needle—into the groove and volume control get tricky, hard to manage or monitor, and missing in heavy Gs, an acidnaut could spend a day and night staring at the grooves in search of the lost one. Greg at the controls was best. Jimmy loved all his music as a parent loves all his kids, each for its unique character. He picked Led Zeppelin to shoot acid to, "You Need Love," perfect, and Greg got it right. Jimmy sat on the floor, pressed the plunger and leaned back against the wall, staring and twitching.

Greg tweaked treble and bass then untied Jimmy and laughed, "What's it like, man?"

Jimmy's mouth went all floppy, and he laughed, too, kind of, and made some noises but couldn't talk too well, which everyone agreed was like Houston Control losing contact with Major Tom. Then Jimmy nodded. Then he stared at the record player and said, "It's off."

Greg said, "It sounds off. That's all. You're accelerating, man. You're breaking out of suborbital. It's not off. Get all the way, man. It's on. It's right on . . . man."

We hung out for a while, watching Jimmy get all the way, but then we started getting off, too, maybe forty-five minutes later, because we'd only swallowed our acid. We drifted apart to roam the universe. Some of us may still be out there.

A few days later, he had Greg convinced that it was a stoned gas, and maybe somebody who didn't try it would never know, wouldn't *experience*, which would not do, which is what happened to our parents, and look how they ended up.

They bantered further, working together to get Greg pumped up to try it. Greg was game, already feeling a little bit second fiddle, with Jimmy telling everyone how it was, and he, Greg, grinning and nodding like a bump on a log while Jimmy debriefed on his journey to where no human had ever been and returned from, the outer galaxy. "It's like, man, you're just sitting there one second, and the next second, you're like . . . tripping your fucking brains out, man."

What a nut. But what a character, true to form and tragically so and colorfully, too. Many called him a waste of everything. He wasn't. He wasted his human potential in material productivity, as intended. Jimmy achieved bliss and died, which is different than suicide. Performance art was incidental, part of the fun until the day he died and, for all we know, beyond that. As a warm, fun-loving guy, he seemed no more depressed than anyone and set himself apart on a commitment—not to drugs; they were his vehicle. He wanted to be the tungsten in the bulb. He wasted no time resenting his parents and their seemingly silly lives, their suburban needs and fears, their addiction to creature comfort and so-called security, their tastes and fads that looked ridiculous a few years later, like huge cars, plastic-covered furniture, zoysia grass, split-level ranch style and on and on.

Jimmy's mother had high hair. Father drank highballs. The country club proved success, and life in America had big fins and chrome as evidence of the future upon us, superior and real, along with the prescription drugs Mom and Dad popped like M & fucking M's, man.

Jimmy openly loved his parents, which was as radical then as ear staples, eyebrow spikes, nose rings, tongue bearings and lip brackets might be today. Oddly enough, I met him in unfriendly circumstances—not met, really, but saw him.

Jimmy wrestled in high school for Ladue, our archrival. Small, wiry and punked out, his arrogance matched two severe cowlicks clipped short. A spike-headed kid with an aggressive smirk, he was undefeated at ninety-five pounds near the end of the season. He was easy to dislike, stepping out of his team circle, walking halfway to ours and staring, till he picked out Nick Geiss, his opponent. Laughing, he sneered with ridicule, aping Mick Jagger a few years before Mick did it.

Nick Geiss was my good friend, also undefeated, so this match would preview the district finals, with the winner going on to the state tournament. Jimmy was a villain. He pinned my good friend and made it look easy. Then he did a little strut with the smirk that would stay with him to the State University, where he wouldn't wrestle. The sneer would stay with him.

Yeah? So?

I got to like him one summer in the heart of it, when we both wound up in Boulder, Colorado at Stevie Getman's apartment, where Stevie went to summer school to catch up. Stevie and I were friends in high school, and he was friends with Greg Buckstein, whose parents played golf at the same country club. What a goof: golf, country clubs and parents, cocktails, Cadillacs and pills. Greg and Jimmy were on the road together, and there we were in Boulder, a couple years into the revolution with everything on its head, or rather in its head, man. Jimmy came on like an old friend, with excited banter over several drugs, some new and untried, perhaps refining experience as we'd known it. He didn't remember me from Adam or the peanut gallery when he pinned my friend, as his cheerleaders had chanted: *Jimmy Levin! Get the pin!*

I never asked why he was such an asshole back then but mentioned that I'd wrestled for my high school and saw him wrestle Nick Geiss. He didn't mention the win or the pin or his progress to the state finals but lit up. "Oh, man! Nick Geiss! How's he doing, man?" With impressive humility, Jimmy set the stage for higher times, ditching social values that proved harmful. Competition and victory had become culprits, grist for the jungle war. It raged and threatened.

Anybody who didn't know how good Nick Geiss was and how easily Jimmy pinned him could miss Jimmy's selflessness in passing. With formidable presence, however, Jimmy didn't take drugs but sought what the drugs could teach him, at least in the beginning. He learned, good and bad, but stayed with it. Then he learned about overdose, maybe.

Sure, it was part of the times, setting aside conventional concepts, like winners and losers. And Jimmy was a fun time guy, one o' the troops in that summer of survival. I stopped in Boulder by chance on my way to San Francisco, our Mecca of Freedom. Hitchhiking was faster and easier than a car then and waiting for a ride rarely took more than a few minutes. Vietnam draft age kids were all sisters and brothers. I stayed in Boulder a few weeks to goof with the guys. Why not?

That was the year Greg Buckstein got nicknamed after a Magnavox TV, the Quasar, merchandized for discreet and easy access to controls. Quasar, the TV with its *Works in a Drawer*. Greg was Captain Quasar, with his works in his drawers. He and Jimmy were hitting junk that summer, in Boulder's first infusion of heroin and the associated crime wave. My bicycle got stolen three days in and still makes me laugh. Theft was a bummer, but hitchhiking with a bicycle underscored the times. "Yeah. That's cool, man. We'll strap it to the roof." One ride after another tied it to the roof or put it in the microbus. Then we'd get stoned, heading west.

Junk wasn't cool. It segregated the brothers and sisters from the junkies, in most cases. Greg and Jimmy were exceptions, remaining cool. Their parents gave them cash and credit cards to keep them off the street, with no need to steal. Greg and Jimmy were discreet as well, hitting up in the bathroom, because heroin was still very, very heavy, man, a certain taboo, even among major hell-raisers, and good breeding and upbringing didn't count for nothing, not yet anyway.

Everything was a goof, and Stevie Getman and I giggled like hyenas when I reminded him of the shit-fit Sylvia and the Wolf man would have, if they knew who was running smack in Stevie's bathroom. Sylvia was Stevie's mother, the Wolf man her second husband; they did a great imitation of Ike and Mamie Eisenhower and held the pose longer than Ike and Mamie.

We got some mescaline and went to see Leon Russell, who looked like the old man on the mountain in a top hat and long gray hair that hung down into his long gray beard. He was a rhythm 'n blues god, and Mary McCreary, his eventual wife, had a body for everyboy's dream. She sang and danced, her Amazon-African physique a certain jaw dropper for the boys gaping up from the front row at her perfect melons bouncing to the pulse of life while Leon rolled away the stone. All the joy and light, the insight of Truth and Being, filled us with warmth and camaraderie like never before, till the show was over, and we were spent but still tripping or maybe all tripped out with nowhere to go.

That's when Greg, with his distinct downward inclination, asked, "God, man. I wonder what it's like to be dead. Man. It must be the trippiest fuckin' trip in the world. It must be like . . ."

Dead? The fuck was he talking dead for? Well, maybe dead was cool. Nobody said anything, because we were tripping and not nearly as seasoned as Greg or Jimmy. Stevie and I scanned the files for dead and trippy, since anything could be cool. We had the Grateful Dead, with the skulls and everything. They were cool, and tripping was not your usual life-form, and it was cool, but then Jimmy summarized the situation:

"It's not like anything, man. You're fuckin' dead." The guy was full of surprises.

I saw him the day before he died, at his parents' house. He said it was cool for a while, to get his head together and figure out some shit and maybe get his shit together and then maybe get his trip together, you know. I was in town and heard he was there and stopped by for a goof, to smoke a joint and say hey. His mother tried not to look, sound and behave like June Cleaver but failed. She chirped cheerfully that Jimmy was "in his place," the garage, converted with a bed, a small fridge, a table and a chair to make Jimmy feel comfortable at home, not confined.

I went on back. He slouched over a bowl of cereal to slurp it out of the spoon, head askew to make room for the cat, who sipped more daintily alongside without a spoon.

"Hey, Jimmy."

"Hey, man. Want some cereal?"

"Nah."

"I'm into cereal. Do you realize? Cereal, man. It's too much."

"I used to eat cereal."

"Yeah?"

"What are you doing?"

"Nothing. What are you doing?"

"Nothing. I might go back to Columbia tonight. Nothing going on here. You got anything going on?"

"No, man. But I got an idea, man." He sat up to check my take on this breaking news, that Mr. Jimmy had a new idea. He seemed pleased, coming up with something dynamic, forward-thinking and a few inches out front of the cutting edge. "I'm gonna hit some Tuinals."

He didn't ask if I wanted to join him. I wasn't on his level. He knew that and didn't want to put me on the spot. It was cool; we understood that hitting Tuinals wasn't in the cards for me, because I never hit anything, because needles wigged me, stuck in me or anyone. But it was cool. We all fairly knew each other's level and stayed cool on freedom from judgment. Everything was everything, and that was cool, too. Jimmy's level with drugs was ultimate, not only comfortable with any drug in any mode but hungry for something to test, something that might break out, break in, *break on through to the other side* (cf. Jim Morrison). I didn't do needles, didn't want to and couldn't watch without the dizzies.

Besides that, I couldn't handle downers. I tried a red Mike Dunn gave me. He stole them from his mother, who bought them by the bottle and didn't miss them. He popped two and advised two, because one Seconal wouldn't get it. I told him I'd try one and take another in a while, as necessary. The one turned my legs to jelly, then my hips, torso, arms, eyes, brain and so on. I eased back in the grass and got up six hours later, sunburned with a hammering headache. Mike asked, "Cool, huh? You want another?"

"No."

"You sure?"

"Yeah. I'm sure."

"Suit yourself."

"Okay."

Jimmy waited for my reaction, my approval, amazement and admiration, but all I could conjure was my go with a red. I nodded and finally said, "That'll be like . . . jumping off a cliff."

"Yeah, man. That's good, because it's downers. I mean it's all like a big cliff with anything you hit, but like, with downers, you jump off and keep on, you know, going down."

"Yeah," I said, but I didn't know. This was years before bungee jumping, so I couldn't imagine springing back, only a nosedive at terminal velocity.

"You like downers?"

I shrugged. "I couldn't get into downers."

"Yeah," he said, turning back to the last of the cereal.

"Well, I gotta go. See you, Jimmy."

He nodded, slurping, calling out when I was at the door. "Hey, man. I'll let you know how it went."

"Yeah."

Dead by the weekend, Jimmy let everyone know how it went. Everybody was shocked but not surprised. Sadness prevailed, until Jeanette's lament, stock audio from the aggrieved parents file: "Such a waste!" Jeanette and Harold had been oblivious that Jimmy was wasted long ago. Denial was also sad, as she cried over Jimmy nearly deciding to join ranks with the doctahs of the world or the lawyahs, or an *accountant* wouldn't be too bad.

What did we know? Jimmy wasn't stupid. He made bad calls. Maybe Jeanette should have hoped for a pharmacist. But maybe not. Blind to Jimmy's emaciated appearance after six years as a speed-freak junkie dabbling in downers, Jeanette had effervesced. Maybe she put a nice face on a tough situation or believed that Jimmy would snap out of it and go to his room for a nice club tie and a Brooks Brothers shirt. Then he'd marry a nice Jewish girl and begin a family. And why not, Mr. Smarty Pants?

I sometimes ask myself, WWJD? What Would Jimmy Do? Or say?

Harold and Jeanette Levin died within a month of each other some years later from old age and broken hearts—what Jimmy would have called their usual routine. Harold was quiet, not so much unthinking but tuned out like Jimmy but with nothing else to tune into. Jeanette babbled to the end, her blue bouffant and big costume jewelry sticking her in time like an old joke.

I imagined Jimmy's comment on their demise to go something like, *Yeah. It's cool. They never were really, you know, into much.*

The Musical Fruit

Like some women do, Ramona Marano acquired quirky habits in self-defense, masking her beauty to accommodate normal life, ducking under breaking waves of need and sexual innuendo. Big surf had felt incessant, as if an eyeball scan or pelvic suggestion might win her heart. She dressed down and went plain. Yet alas, her efforts failed; beauty shone through, radiant as a country sunrise.

She let her armpits and legs grow hairy. She belched like a sailor, like one of the guys. She bathed less and scratched her hindside in public, into the fulsome crevasse, moaning relief. Yet in mere moments she emoted again, pretty as a portrait.

Her efforts came to naught but to make her mental, I thought, till life's wily ways put me in a defensive mode of my own.

I'd moved to a neighborhood near Market and Castro in '81, just prior to the dreaded disease going public. It wasn't called AIDS for a year but presented early with baffling symptoms on homosexual men, as they were known. The purple splotches were soon identified as Kaposi's sarcoma, historically affecting African or Eastern European men. Notable Kaposi characteristics are malignancy and contagion. How did it spread? Rapacious fluid exchange and heavy friction, with blood and/or jism and/or dukey in the mix. Pardon my vernacular. Socially agreeable phrasing would be gay, ejaculate and feces, but semantics evolve, and this was early, still in the discovery phase of those swashbuckling, speed-bumping, stairway-to-heaven days. Eye contact meant yes, we're on, anything goes, except fist-fucking on a first date, but then who knew?

Slim and trim at a hundred-forty then, I could hardly grasp a turnip at the produce counter without a game flirtation from a willing shopper in rutabagas. I discouraged the randy boys, as I'd seen Ramona do. I belched, picked my nose and scratched my ass. But a svelte, sinewy fellow with robust muscle tone, good skin and no apparent boyfriend can't fend off the kings of testosterone quite so simply. Methodical repulsion didn't always work. The boys came on and on. I called Ramona to say hello, to seek consolation and guidance in a troublesome world.

Catching up and sparking the old voltage, I said I missed her and didn't know why it had been so long. I knew. I'd written her off. She was too beautiful, too perfect to go for me, just another pogo stick, and she fended off all males. Call it attitudinal or a failure of confidence, I thought Ramona flawless, except for rough intervals by design.

I was flawed. I thought she filled her personal needs with discreet spontaneity, rarely seeing a lucky fellow twice but rather disclosing at the outset she was using him. Would he mind?

She'd missed me, too, she said, also puzzled by our lapse. I was such a decent man to spend time with, she said. I didn't linger on decency, though it sounded painfully similar to nice, safe, harmless or hardly in the running. I let it pass, recalling her luscious self, her curvature, her scent, her inaccessibility. Voluptuous, warm and soft, she felt present, even on the phone. I said her defense against men must have worked on me, too.

"I didn't mean to turn *you* off," she said.

Or turn me on. "I'm not sure you could turn me off," I said. "But you discouraged me." There I went again, putting her on the spot, invading her space with puppy dog infatuation.

Had she made the transition from the pole to the hole, as they said in the neighborhood? No. "I got to tell you, it's tough" she said. "I got so good at it, and now I might meet someone I like and try to turn it off, but it won't go off. I think I'm getting old. And fat. I don't have a boyfriend but not because I don't want one. I don't mean just anyone, but some guys I like and things don't work out. Geez, Louise, I gotta get laid—that's not what I meant. That sounded wrong. How are you?"

Was I a candidate? I commiserated with my own social woes in general and specifically with fending off homosexuals.

"You mean gays?"

"Yes. I mean gays."

Well, yes, she could give me a few pointers, because sexual harassment can go both ways. I should come over anyway, what the hell, and she'd show me a technique or two but not on the phone. "It's visual. Not really visual but sensual, but not sexy sensual. You know?" City people often entangle in mental webs, wrapping themselves in complexity where simple meaning would do. A drive across town was a challenge in any circumstance, but greater drives prevailed. Ramona on the eyes was like cream on strawberries. Oh, boy, I thought, as if discovering an old shirt with a C-note in the pocket: Ramona.

Oh, boy, but what a mixed message. What if our playful affection plays out? Will she shut up for some real nitty-gritty? My excitement got curbed on visions of hairy legs and armpits, skin gone sallow and blemished, but she wouldn't go that far. Would she? She could be hefty—she'd called her comfort level incredible. Had she gone to seed in the spirit of liberation?

Well, I played defense, too, thinking the worst-case scenario: she was still a beauty who'd love me but not in that way.

The curtain rose, as it were, the stage set for resolution. Grip my chest with heart-wrenching desire, she knew that I knew— had to know. Sheer rayon pants clung to her hips. Profiling her ass seems profane but, alas, it was perfect. What man could see this shape and not be inspired? Could she present this show without a dress rehearsal in the mirror? No. The frikkin' Pope would sit up and take note of this wondrous work that God hath wrought. Draped loosely from her shoulders, the blouse hung pointedly out front, defying gravity while generating its own gravitational field, keeping my eyeballs in orbit like lesser moons. The midsection screamed perfection where the blouse stopped not quite below the breasts.

Men have asked through the ages, "Why do they do that?"

The answer is also old: for the power.

Ramona unleashed primitive instinct. No wonder romance was problematic. With a body like that sizzling his brain pan, what man could ponder meaning? My response was simple, as unworthy of detail as a description of her hind side. I wanted to drop a pencil under my desk and look up for the beaver shot. But I had no pencil or desk, and we weren't in junior high. What could I do, not stare? I could not not stare and knew that I should not, so I put my eyes on hers and stepped into her open arms.

"You get the picture," she said in my ear, her warm breath and throaty voice sensual as a siren's song. "I got used to the staring. What the hell? It's the . . . advances I hate."

Oh, great. There I was, getting something straight between us, unwittingly primed for a move and filled with doubt. "You know, Ramona, the way you dress encourages sexual advances. You invite them."

"I don't."

"Don't you? You look great. You feel great. You are great."

What friendship survives lust? But look at her. I was no monk, and I felt our friendship sound, even as she rendered me knock, knock, knocking on heaven's door. So? Was I the man for the job? Or was this a sad and poignant example of mankind gone to seed? Would we soon experience alienation of the subcultures relative to and socially misaligned by gender? I didn't think so, yet I dared not imagine the pot of gold at the end of the rainbow. It glowed in my mind—what she'd call my fantasy—but she was merely human, like me, engaging in what we both thought was open and honest. She'd admitted on the phone hardly an hour ago that she was open to romance, and there we were, on the verge of having our cake and eating it, too. What a dish.

What a spirit. Ramona's liberal thinking, her sense of humor and fun-loving disposition were no fantasy but a palpable reality I could feel. I wanted to lift the veil to feel it better, to show her that the fine line between friendship and romance was not a boundary but a line of communion.

But no! Feeling her breasts would be obtrusive. Better to lay hands on gluteus maximus, in friendship. She didn't seem to mind, even when things meandered. Perseverant as Lewis and Clark in my own private wilderness, I wandered onward in the spirit of discovery, over the hills and into the valley.

She blinked. Was that a smile? And she farted, briefly, like a trumpet finding A. I ignored it, just as she ignored me, in mutual tolerance. Or rather I thought I ignored it, even as my hands veered laterally, up and out from the crevasse. She squeezed me tighter, eased back a bit and held our intimate proximity as if oblivious. She glowed, her skin smooth and pink. Her moist, full lips and perfect teeth lured me in. I would kiss her but feared that she'd turn a cheek and end the dream, but a life of doubt and regret loomed more fearfully. And a friendly peck on those succulent lips might easily lead to a juicy thereafter and fantasy running free. I wallowed in visions—till her soft, serene whisper: "Look at this." She hiked her blouse, revealing the all of all that rendered me utterly, speechlessly, gawking.

This reverie, too, was shattered by obtrusive tones from below. My eyes couldn't bug any bigger; it seemed so odd, maybe not so brash and brazen as "Seventy Six Trombones," but she did approximate "Melancholy Baby" at four beats to the measure. Was her little recital intentional, a conscientious score to our warm and fuzzy lyric? Smiling sweetly, she put her lips to my ear. "I eat beans. Don't you see?"

I hadn't seen but quickly realized I could sooner throw stones at heaven's door than knock on it.

Ramona had found refuge in beans. Inured to social consequence, she ate many beans. Beans and rice. Chili with beans. Navy bean soup. Lima beans. Butter beans. Bean burritos. Beans Florentine. She whispered, "The beans will set you free."

Ramona could rip last night's beans without missing a beat, blowing raspberries as casual as waving hello, effectively decoding the sociopolitical matrix of sexual dominance seekers in an urban context. Her little polemic would have seemed oddly mental under any circumstance, but her free-range flatulence made me feel somehow licensed to take further liberties, whatever they might be, until the ammoniac fume singed my septum, snapping my head like Mike Tyson's near the end.

The gender game was over. She'd won.

I was down in the red zone, gang tackled, limp and lifeless with the ampoule under my nose and no chance of scoring.

She scrunched her nose, cute as a pixie. "Brazilian black beans are amazing. I'm used to it. But I get careless. Sorry . . ."

Careless? How about hazardous? I thought she'd need to change her skivvies, or at least tidy up in the bathroom after that last aftershock. I put it at about 5.5 on the Richter scale.

San Franciscans love to show earthquake aplomb, but this was a push. Then again, she meant to address a global social crisis. Leading me by the hand to the bathroom down the hall, she ducked in for a private moment, releasing me in the doorway, or rather one step inside. Stepping to the commode, she smiled sweetly and dropped her pantaloons to reveal what would have been Act II of my fantasy. Sitting down for a casual blast off, she maintained her stride and stridency, untwisting the sociopolitical matrix of urban love or romance or something or other as it relates to black beans. Like a Redstone rocket, she nearly lifted off before settling back to allow passage of post-ignition debris. She shrugged. "Okay. Tell me what's wrong with you. What's your . . . dilemma?" She smiled again, waiting for my response, airing out, as it were, spewing exhaust and stragglers as if at will.

I turned around, plugging my ears. When she cut loose on another broadside, I sang.

She faintly called, "What?"

I dug in deeper till I couldn't hear her. I glanced at the movement in the mirror as she prepped a few squares of tissue. I walked back up the hall, still plugged and singing lowly.

Soon she stepped in front, as I wiggled fingers in ears and sang, "This old man. He played three. He played knickknack on my knee. With a knickknack paddy whack, give a dog a . . ."

"What are you doing?" she asked, effusing the brightest of womanly lights, her eyes big and dark, her rich black hair tussled, full lips, supple hands and a lusty posture to stop a song.

"I'm singing."

"Why do you have your fingers in your ears?"

"It helps me get the tone right."

"Right for what?"

"Right for you?"

"I got my own tone. Don't you get it?"

"I get it. You eat beans and blow your bugle."

"Yes, but I love beans. They work so well. Who'd a thought about beans?"

"*You* thought about beans. But you said on the phone you didn't want it to work anymore."

"Yeah. That's mostly true. I guess you run into jerks forever, no matter what. Anyway, I wanted to show you this. It really works better than anything."

"Yeah. Well . . . Ramona, do you think . . ." I turned to open a window, to slough the awkward presence between us and regain my composure. "Do you think . . . uh . . ."

She smiled coyly. "Yes?"

"Do you want to have dinner with me?"

"Sure. Why wouldn't I?"

"No, I mean, like a date. I mean, not beans—not even Mexican. I mean, because, I . . ." It felt like now or never, a classic case of reward or regret—or rejection. How quickly the downside flashed: Y*ou . . . prick! I don't ever want to see you* *again! I thought you were different!* Yet there she stood, angelic, the dazzling rack daring me to displace a lifetime of failure. I inched forward till my toes dangled over the edge. I looked down at the heaving bosom. I hooked her half shirt with a finger and raised it again.

"Because why?"

"Because . . . Because . . ."

"Are you going to fondle my breasts?"

"Okay." It was like an exam. She took it briefly, tolerant as a friend, maybe working up another head of steam to prove her hypothesis. A deluge began outside, wind whipping the torrents through the open window, and she pulled away.

"Hey! You let in the rain!"

"Sorry. I meant to show my feelings."

"Don't be silly. What about my feelings?"

"What's silly?"

"We're friends."

"So? We're heterosexual. You're still hetero, aren't you?

"I think so. It's just that . . . I like you."

"I like you, too."

"I get it; this is supposed to be natural." Did she accuse me? I shrugged.

She turned away, pouting. "It's not natural. We're friends. Friends don't do that."

"Don't do what?"

"Have sex."

"Are you kidding? Do you think a successful marriage precludes friendship?"

"Most of the time it does."

"I said successful."

"Is this a proposal?"

"Ramona, I hardly . . ."

"You hardly know me?" I shrugged again; she'd made my case. "Okay. Let's try it." She stepped up, hiked her blouse again and coaxed. "Come on. Tongue." It felt off but rare, like a scene I might soon savor with little else to recall. I complied, briefly till she blew reveille, which the little trooper mistook for taps and fell asleep.

"Ramona."

"What?"

"Must you?"

"I think so. If we're friends, you won't mind."

"It's embarrassing. Friends can get embarrassed for each other."

"You think sex isn't embarrassing?"

"It doesn't have to be."

"Fine. I think farting doesn't have to be embarrassing. Especially among friends. I know what you guys do, fart out loud and laugh your asses off. Right?"

"Sometimes. We're friends, so why not. It doesn't interfere with romance, which we pursue with women."

"Ha, ha. I get it."

"I don't think you do."

"But I do. And I'd fuck a man to death if he could get it, too." She harrumphed, point proven, dropping the curtain abruptly and folding her arms to barricade the set. She huffed.

"You want to . . . uh . . . you want to have sex while you're blowing air out your ass."

"*I* would have put it more delicately. But . . . yes."

"How would you have put it?"

"I think romance should transcend bodily function."

"Have you considered that you might have an anal fetish?"

"I do not have an anal fetish. I want to cut the crap."

"We could, I suppose . . . um . . . try it. But . . ."

"What?"

"Nothing."

"That's not cutting the crap. Come on. Come clean."

"What makes you think you can maintain pressure?"

She played two refrains of "Row, Row, Row Your Boat." "What makes you think I can't?"

What a nut. What a woman. I would not complain that a fantasy cannot be fulfilled with stringent burdens in place. I remained honest with my friend. "Maybe I could get used to it." I stepped aside to reopen the window, this time from the top, for marginal air but no rain. "Can we keep the window open?"

"Why do we need the window open?"

"Ramona. We don't need the window open. I love you. I've always loved you. You know this. Don't say you didn't know it, because we both know you knew it, just as we know your farts stink. Yes, I love you and don't care if you leave the bathroom door open or fart all night. I'll get used to anything, because I love you. And if you love me, you'll grant me a little tolerance in the short-term while I adapt to higher standards than I've practiced in the past."

She looked thoughtful, a profile in sociopolitical rectitude, like a woman toyed with once too often, dispensing justice to the next defendant. But then, playful as a new toy, she eased into the warmth we'd often shared. She smiled. Pulling her blouse clean off, she came in with a hug. "You're such a fool," she said. "Of course you've always loved me, and we both knew it. So why have you been so blind to my feelings for you?"

I leaned back. "You? For me?"

"Who else? I've asked myself nearly every day why you never called. Now you have."

"Why I never called? Why didn't you call me?"

She shrugged. "A girl can't very well invite a man over for a serenade on the sousaphone, can she? How would that work? You took the initiative. It's the hormone thing. That's the only way it could have worked."

"The hormone thing? I thought that was your nemesis."

Coy again, she wiggled free of her pantaloons and eased my buttons. "Not with the right guy," she said, as heaven's doorknocker echoed down those hallowed halls, as, from the top, with feeling, she blew "Stars and Stripes Forever."

That we'll live happily ever after remains to be seen. But we've given love a start, working through our issues with sacrifice, understanding and a keen eye for the needs of the other.

We cut way back on our beans, because we don't need them anymore. Ramona knows I love her. With her on my arm, the wild boys out rooting for truffles can plainly see I'm hooked on hetero.

Every now and then, we do like to simmer a vat o' meatless chili, eat to our hearts' content, sit back, relax, let good feelings flow and then head on down to the village for the show, our show—our own little marching band. I usually play tuba and double on trumpet. She's dabbling in blues trombone—and she sings. The neighborhood likes a jazzy touch and seems receptive to two-part harmony.

Reunion

I went to high school in a Midwest suburb, a paved patch on the map, a place with chronology but no history, a street culture of commerce, no lore or legend. As a moneyed welt on a massive sprawl, it festered affluence. Shopping centers served subdivisions flush with luxury cars and self-absorption. New money was gauche but not us, twenty years in and tasteful.

Mentality characterized one segment of the student body, while most strove to be cool, presuming that posing avant suburban would keep up with modern times. The little burb reinvented itself as necessary, slowly and to small purpose.

Highschool kids watched TV, *Hogan's Heroes*, Gilligan and the Beaver moderately influential, while *Shindig* and Ed Sullivan rocked our world. The Billies came and went with few kids aware of a classic. Most saw hillbillies who didn't comprehend value— material, that is: split level, country clubs.

One cool kid's family wasn't wealthy but sustained hope. He advised acquiring nice things in youth. Otherwise, forty years old comes on with no nice things. Who wants to start then, with everyone else so far ahead? He preferred a genuine tortoiseshell hairbrush instead of a wooden one, an ivory shoehorn instead of plastic, doeskin shoes instead of (ugh) cow leather. Anybody will need new shoes before forty, and tasteful habits help. Doeskin sets a pattern early, on quality, identity and need.

I shitchu not. This was spiritual development where I went to high school.

Things changed rarely, adaptation more awkward than natural. Sporting prowess, good grades or wealth indicated comfort in the future, with a home in the enviable burb and spending power. On graduation, those kids went Ivy League, for best contacts. Other kids went somewhere else.

We loosely formed three groups. The biggest was the vast middle who did their homework to get good grades. After college, life on 2.7 children and 1.7 cars, as due. Next was a fringe amalgam of hoods, tight pants, pompadours, beer drinkers and school skippers. This second group ruled the pool tables at the community center and cruised into a future of no limits, except for their wits and luck. The third group, core elite, was cool, their fathers in suits and European sedans. They would rule the future by inheritance.

I was not core elite or a hood. I did wear tight pants and skip school often. I thought about college but doubted Andover or Yale. Who would pay my way? I worked forty hours a week at fourteen, more fringe than middle, destined for a future of rubbing two nickels to get twelve cents.

One evening, I had occasion to stop by a popular boy's house to drop something off and pick something up. One of the cheerleaders, a heavyset girl generally liked for her chronic smile and cheerful demeanor, had managed to steal a copy of Mr. Barthel's history final. I made the loop on that one, having acquired Mrs. Swope's English literature final; I was willing to trade. Trading would generate many A grades in history and English, but I didn't care, and I'd be on the top tier.

With only weeks to go until graduation, we felt worldly. A half dozen boys from the popular crowd were at the house where the trade would be made, and I was invited in. I was offered a drink, a highball, like our parents drank. The other boys wore dress slacks, creased, some of them high-end Sansabelts with the patented elastic waistband for the sleek suburbanite look, and oxford shirts in sky blue with button-down collars, light starch. They all wore Weejuns, soft, pliable and heavily shined. A few wore cardigan sweaters, partly buttoned like Ward Cleaver's or Frank Sinatra's.

Again, I shitchu not. Lounging on the sofa or plush chairs with their drinks, legs crossed, they smoked cigarettes and nodded to Lou Rawls on the hi-fi. They shared a moan of pleasure, "Oh, man . . ." when Sinatra came on. This was 1966, dawn of the Revolution, and these guys wanted to swing, to be cool, Daddy, like Dino and Lawford. And Sammy; what a groove, what a crazy cat, what a kick. Some went on to Princeton or Harvard or Yale. I got into the State U on a loan/charity combo and majored in coed leg, LSD and reefer.

I digress, but what better path goes back so many decades, than one stepping-stone to the next? Every piece counts in the great puzzle.

Forty years later, they found me. The roster and email addresses told what some of them were up to. Some could be traced to a mug, though most of the website shots were old, taken at forty-something. Not all the roster had email. Some were not yet found. I recognized about a fourth of the names, and half as many faces. *Deceased* followed some.

Tom Reardon was deceased, his exit making the circuit far and wide, first to remind us that growing up includes college, marriage, children, divorce, remarriage or grandchildren, divorce and death. It waited for us, too. Tom Reardon was a shocker but no surprise, dead at forty-nine from too much liquor. Tom had dressed like core elite but remained hardcore fringe. He said he hated military school but did learn to drink, fight and fuck. He also skipped school, to shoot pool and cruised. Tom's acerbic wit and compulsory insults put some people off, but we were friends. He'd call me a fool and point out a foible of his own, laughs on us. Tom was cool but a hood, but not a greaser, but he smoked cigarettes and drank heavily and let the cheerleaders know what he could do for them. And he gave shit to the cool guys at random, sometimes squaring off. He didn't care.

Street smart but a sorry student, Tom gave advice on the world and pussy in exchange for doing his geometry homework. He'd discovered liquor at age seven and had some every day till he died of liver failure, failing to move up the transplant list as well. He discovered pussy four long years after his first drink and knew instantly that the two went well together. He specialized in other guys' girlfriends, believing that they all wanted what their lame ass boyfriends couldn't give them, but he could—and he didn't even have to buy them dinner.

People didn't like his cocky way, but I sensed the truth on one or two girlfriends. He told me at graduation that the senior poll had a category for most naïve, and I'd won it hands down, but they scratched it so I wouldn't feel bad.

"What's wrong with being naïve?"

He shook his head, like I'd never get it and never get laid, too. Then he told a few leg stories while we crammed for the geometry final.

I stayed at his house one summer after high school, along with his mother and Uncle Harry. The three of them would drink a case or two of beer and some bourbon and scotch daily but only got drunk on weekends, in the spirit of moderation. Weekends were hell. Uncle Harry would get drunk and want coffee and stiffen it with scotch and tell of his first date with Elizabeth von Durfelhauser III, who discovered no spoon to stir her coffee. She fell in love with Harry, who stirred it with his pecker. He told the story often, as if remembering something fresh.

Harry would add more scotch to his coffee and stir it with his pecker. It was funny once. I lasted a month at Tom's but counted him as a friend in need.

Each reunion update ended on a request for $25 "so we can firm up our plans, and please help us find anyone we haven't found yet." The plan was a get-together Friday night, softball on Saturday, and dinner Saturday night to include "spouses or significant others! And *please* let us know if you have any ideas to make our reunion *even better!*" Fifty-eight years old and still living the pep rally.

The former girl heading up the search team summarized the last forty years for herself, with children grown and grandchildren in Seattle. Besides children and grandchildren, the last four decades had included thirty-seven years in a small appliance repair shop that was finally sold ("for a nifty profit, I might add"), which bought a medium RV for roaming the country six months of the year—including *Seattle!*

The former girl heading up the scheduling team urged anyone to join the team by letting her know. She'd been Roseanne Markowitz but had become Brigitte Montray. Did she marry and/or divorce or choose a new handle? She was not listed as Markowitz-Montray, but simply Montray. The change from Roseanne to Brigitte remained a mystery, and so did highlights and low points of her own four decades since.

Among the unfound, a toady boy widely seen as unfortunate who strove to be cool, to integrate with the core elite. He wore only khaki pants, sky blue button-downs and, in winter, bulky V-neck sweaters with cable stitching and a daring stripe. Slovenly fat, flabby with jowls, chins and liver lips, he demonstrated fortitude in *black* Weejuns, shined to a dazzle (by the maid) to match his thick black glasses and black wavy hair, Brylcreemed to a tall wave. Grout-like skin was backdrop to flared zits, moderate by count but resplendent in fiery bases and molten cores. Enough braces on his uppers and lowers to build a stainless-steel chicken coop were to be seen as affluence.

Kevin Hojax was rich. Or rather his parents were rich. They bought him anything a kid could want and taught him how to toad. Where else would he learn it? He would let you ride his moped, if you would be his friend and could be cool. He wanted cool friends, not uncool friends. He walked with a shuffle to be cool, but he couldn't be cool, yet, but maybe, if . . .

He pondered, assessing coolness potential, if only . . .

Like Piggy in *Lord of the Flies*, Hojax was dependent and superior. Hojax was also ugly inside and out.

Insisting that I ride his moped once, he introduced me to motorized happiness on two wheels. But I proved uncool. I didn't mix well with the core elite, who could have ridden the moped but opted for Weejuns and a cool shuffle.

Davy Wood was cool. He drove Hojax's car more than Hojax did—sometimes cramming it full of cool kids until there was no room left. Hojax whined on the curb, "Come on, Davy. It's *my car*!" Davy would laugh and assure Hojax, "Next time. Next time, Kev, for sure." Davy Wood was big and bigger in a wool sweater with cable knit and a crew neck. He looked twenty-three at sixteen, except for the occasional volcano zit on his big schnoz. Everybody liked him; he was friendly, got bad grades, played varsity fullback, didn't fumble too much and shared sex adventures in shop class. Back then, boys took shop and girls took home economics: cooking, sewing and girl stuff, though it's not girl stuff anymore.

Anyway, Davy Wood took time to hear Kevin Hojax's plan for the great things they would do together. Sometimes Hojax got to ride in the back seat when Davy cruised with Meredith Wilkes-Bashford Bush. Hojax had a Hillman Minx, an odd little upside-down bathtub car that Mr. and Mrs. Hojax loved for the x in it, or maybe because Kevin and the car were both so cute.

Davy drove. Meredith rode shotgun, holding her hair in place with one hand. Kevin rode in back. The top stayed down. Meredith's overbite wouldn't have been so noticeable if not for a puffy upper lip, her a chronic pout way before collagen. She spoke only to the worthy, but few minded; so snooty and aloof, in the jargon of the day, conceited. On her behalf, I now suspect she was simpleminded and shy, sensitive to her deficiency. Her huge rack at fifteen was foremost of prominent sets in our class. Davy Wood got access to see, feel, suckle, whatever, whenever, from fifteen through seventeen. Davy's fondness for Meredith was evident in their easy, relaxed company, sharing confidences in the hallway, holding hands and cruising in Hojax's convertible. It seemed a match of physical attributes, minimal intellect and affable simplicity.

Known for breeding and Lip Gloss, Meredith shone with good posture and attitude. Mrs. Wilkes-Bashford Bush called her daughter's virtue secure till her wedding day by way of personal pledge, and that day could include Davy Wood; such a nice-looking boy from a lovely family, a bit poverty struck, perhaps, but hey; he was a fullback, too, which seemed more appropriate for Meredith than a halfback.

These details got dispensed Mondays, Wednesdays and Fridays to those of us with shop projects requiring a vice or a lathe—dispensed by Davy Wood, who worked on a candy dish for his mother. Casually, one day, turning his maple dish on the lathe, Davy announced the problem solved in the W-B Bush basement. That was the problem of damn near bursting after working over Meredith's rack. Davy unbuckled and unzipped his pants for a little breathing room and to show Meredith the monster she'd created. She stared at it, as she often stared.

But then, glory, glory hallelujah, Davy suggested that she might, you know, put it in her mouth. She didn't whimper, whine or hesitate but engorged it, nodding till Davy made like Old Faithful, a messy go at first but a great relief for her, too, keeping virtue and Christian morality intact.

Davy's replays on when, where, how long, how much and strange peripherals on Meredith's blow jobs got old. In time, they broke up. All Davy wanted was to hang out in the basement.

At that juncture, Davy got a huge growler on his nose. He blamed Meredith.

Meredith rebounded with renewed popularity, never wanting for a date from the backfield, the frontline, the infield, the guards, forwards and the center. She may have set a record for the Fighting Whippets, the first homecoming queen in school history uttering fewer than fifty words in public, ever.

Fighting Whippets? No wonder we were known as mental.

Davy Wood scored more snatch than most guys early on, big, cheerful, an athlete. He regaled me with a story once of a lucky stroke the night before with Dianna Rosen, who showed up out of nowhere and "fucked my brains loose. Man!"

I'd had a crush on Dianna Rosen for years and, not too long after Davy's tale of a wild night, ended up hanging out with her and living with her and being married to her for a few years. Davy apologized for being such a jerk soon after. I shrugged it off. Dianna was horny, and of all the guys who got in her pants in the years I knew her, he was the least difficult. I saw him on a trip home a few years ago but didn't recognize him till ten paces out. Shorter, shoulders stooped, vulture neck, he looked about sixty-five. We were fifty-two. We turned around at the same time, turned back and kept walking. I thought he'd shrunk. My height hadn't changed, though I'd gained forty pounds, so maybe everyone from back then would look smaller. I'd heard he went to LA to cash in on his good looks and got on as production assistant at a sports radio station, where the dots might connect. They didn't. He didn't get a part.

The End.

Years earlier, I was so uncool that one day Kevin Hojax hung out in the hall near some cool guys and thought to score some points. When I passed, he called, "Hey, come here."

I stopped to see what he wanted.

He stepped up and stepped on my shoe, grinding his shoe into mine, in his best Peter Lorre voice saying, "You're nothing.

Now you can go." It was a presentation to the cool guys, like letting them ride his moped, kind of.

I slammed him into a locker and dulled his shoeshine. The cool guys laughed, but the scene lingered.

I hit Reply All on the original email and said:

Odd as it might seem, Kevin Hojax & I became close friends only a few years after WHS. Asshole buddies? Well, yes, I suppose so, in our strange way. You would have been amazed at the changes he went through. He'd already lost 4 lbs., got his braces thinned and had his face sandblasted.

We took a trip to Costa Rica. In the jungle, eco-adventuring among flora & fauna, the tour guide cried out that we should take to the trees, because the wild pigs were coming!

Alas, Kevin was too slow & got tugged out of his tree by a khaki pants cuff and hit his head on a rock. Of some consolation is that he was thought to be already dead, I mean deceased, when the pigs ate him.

This seemed brilliant to me. It withstood the test of time. I added: *The reunion sounds terrific. How about after softball we have a swim party at the park pool with clothing optional for spouses or significant others under fifty?*

It was a goof. I would never have sent a group message like that forty years ago. For one thing, our high school culture was inhibited. For another, we had no email then. Life had become easier on both counts. I also knew that resolution in all things had become easier: I would not attend. Of the many places I'd lived, only one had no lingering contact. Well, I fixed that easy enough by touching a fingertip to a little mouse's nose with the cursor on Send. It would be my first and last return to that group of people in forty years, and in the moments following, I could imagine a few old classmates laughing.

The End.

A few email addresses ended with company domains, what destiny had held in store. I checked out Richard Levitt, who called himself Richie, a self-endearment to match his massive grin that wasn't the Cheshire variety but more like a dog beaten so bad he bares fang, tail tucked. Richard Levitt at six feet even then was a string bean seeking coolness. He couldn't quite get it; awkward at basketball, frail at football, his big nose a standout on a gaunt physique. He also toaded but only made second string there, too, behind Kev Hojax. He greeted me with a toothy, *I'm okay/you're okay* grin when I was new, till I proved uncool in tight pants and pointy, Marvin Gaye shoes. Then he taunted. That imagery also lingered. I googled him and got zero, so I went to his domain website, a restaurant supply store. No shame there, yet restaurant supply did seem satisfyingly tedious and dull for a lightweight climber.

Nobody could be completely cool. Petro Hazloff's family was rich, but Petro was not an athlete. It was his house where I got my first glimpse of the cool guys' idea of life after high school, in slacks with cocktails and cigarettes. I doubted they actually talked about dames but couldn't be sure. Petro was class president and ultimately cool but not a bad guy. A bit stiff with no varsity letter and a certain privileged future, he compensated with an open-minded, pleasing social presence and a dry, if cautious, sense of humor. I liked him, though I think his father's savvy buy—Standard Oil stocks in the mid-forties—did not warrant naming the son Petro. Most people thought it dashing and Italian, but it wasn't Pietro. It was Jewish and oilish.

I resented Petro when he tried to keep up with a Davy Wood blow job story by sharing his recent session with Susan Comings, who choked his chicken on the backseat of his father's Grand Prix. Back then, Grand Prix was a performance luxury car, and young Petro would have hell to pay for dribbling spunk. The story made everyone laugh and boosted Petro's stock in coolness but didn't sit well with me. Susan Comings was an artist, reclusive, shy and beautiful, exotic features over a two-button reveal, a seductive glance and no bra.

I recall soft fingers grasping my own chicken for a sensitive choke. We engaged regularly. She seemed pleased to help out as I examined her breasts yet again. I thought we shared a unique bond, reclusive, artistic and worldlier than cool. To learn that she whacked Petro odd nights was a growth experience.

But benevolence is the nobler part of perspective. What the hell: it was common knowledge that Susan Comings had a boyfriend anyway, a college guy; she was just that advanced. He had to study during the week. Natch, he got the honey pot, the blow jobs, the works, because he was in college, after all.

Petro ended up in LA, not with Davy Wood but a few years later, since Petro first graduated Ivy League and then an Ivier League law school. He affiliated with a huge legal firm in LA and over the decades became a partner. His website bio went on and on with reviews, boards, distinctions, appointments, et al indoors with fixed windows overlooking the urban dynamic.

I would have been curious to say hello to Petro, to laugh and wonder where Susan Comings is now. But he'd done exceedingly, upwardly well in the dry sciences, his stoic smile conveying client confidence and fiduciary trust. He seemed a fur piece from the Petro Hazloff I shared a chicken choker with.

The End, yet again.

Except for another lingering image of Lissa Newtwiler at seventeen, an arabesque, moist, smiling, nubile and innocent, dangling her womanly legs in the park pool. Isn't it great, the way seventeen-year-olds seem mutually suited, and so do fifty-eight-year-olds? I would think no less of her now, with her children twice that age. The same age seems a better fit, not so fragile and less inhibited. Lissa Newtwiler was another classic beauty who could not generate interest like Susan Comings because of her resistance to chicken abuse. Not only that, she blocked advances on her curvature with both elbows and hands. Hey, she was seventeen. Surely in forty years she loosened up. Yes? No?

Except that reverie got disrupted on a quick response from Brigitte Montray, calling my little joke juvenile and inappropriate.

Which dredged up the entire, ugly society I left behind in June of '66, a culture of containment, self-consciousness, inhibition, judgment and embarrassment. I thought to tell Ms.

Montray about appropriate reality, but deferred to silence, fade to black, roll credits and, yet again: The End.

Except that the bitch had the nerve five minutes later to send another email, happy-face babble on a few candid shots her husband took of last night's reunion planning session. There, in low res was the object of my scorn, dashing my rancor on the rocks under time's breaking wave; forty years and many miles off-road had taken Roseanne Markowitz from a pimply, putty-faced, gossip-mongering oaf to a sad, shapeless dilettante, living in an appropriate suburb with a more appropriate name. Brigitte Montray? How about Tamara Press? Or Jabba the Hut? Oy. And to think, I nearly gave her what for.

In blithe, smarmy rhetoric, she asked if you could recognize anyone around the table. The room was a dimly-lit eight by ten, dwarfed by the wall-sized hutch common to a Midwestern suburban lifestyle, where grandeur is displayed in a hutch.

And there she was, Lissa Newtwiler, blocking the Markowitz/Montray horror with the back of her head.

I scrolled down the photos and around the table to her front, thin, poised, still a peach. The story could have faded whimsically once more, had not Petro Hazloff's cousin Randy dominated the shot that should have given Lissa Newtwiler her rightful splendor. Randy was a stuffed shirt in medium starch, sky blue button-down with long sleeves also buttoned, his elbows taking more room on the table than his size or performance merited, smiling wanly over his amazing state of preservation. In a life stifled by privilege, nothing had changed.

In the lap of luxury, albeit suburban Midwest, he thought this situation natural. Self-esteem seethed from his pores. His move on Lissa Newtwiler was apparent in the slant of his eyes, as she guilelessly blinked at the camera.

A story might arise from any three former classmates popping up in a photo, but this trio seemed ironic, possibly onerous. Recollections abounded, leapfrogging the decades. Here's what got my goat:

Way back when, in that spurious world, those who counted in the material, predictable future were different from those who didn't count. Joe Montana and Jerry Rice got picked late in the draft, both lacking dazzle. Two great players had not yet developed, much less reached their prime. Potential and realization are mystically timed—except at Whippet High, with its intellectual neurosis, its stability, security and gifted insight.

To be precise: The girls invited the boys to the Peppers Prom for an airless evening of chiffon, rented tuxes, corsages, any liquor in volume, the ride with the parents, the puking in the bathroom or the parking lot, the see-and-be-seen, the boring teacher chaperones and the odd fingerfuck. I loathed prospects and decided not to go.

Meanwhile, Laura Russell was both "cool" and cool. She was a knockout with great curves, a wit, wild blonde hair and friends running the gamut from "cool" to greasers and hoods. It was rumored that she planned to ask Randy Hazloff to Peppers. High schoolers in the mid-sixties went to hall talk on possible matchups for the Peppers Prom. Who (the fuck) cared?

Long story short, that page would have turned like the rest, had not Judy Wetstone, a shoo-in for Homecoming Queen and captain of the cheerleaders, let it leak that she thought Randy Hazloff was dreamy.

Randy agreed and let it be known through Judy Wetstone's emissary that he would be her date for Peppers, making him the coolest guy in school, his date with Judy Wetstone virtually turning Laura Russell down in short order. How cool was that? Turning Laura Russell down? She was hot. But Randy wanted to be King of the Peppers, which he never got to be, because Meredith Wilkes-Bashford Bush had sucked off both the offense and the defense to claim a come-from-behind victory as Homecoming Queen, virtue intact, making cousin Petro the Pepper King, because, in the spirit of Peppers, the queen picks the king, and Meredith Bush chose Petro.

Forty years later, Randy was still ruled in his own mind.

Meanwhile, Lissa Newtwiler pigeonholed me against my locker to ask if I'd, you know, go with her. I told her we could go anywhere—En . . . ee . . . where, but not to the Peppers Prom. She looked sad. She looked down. She walked away.

Meanwhile, as matchmaker for the "cool" set, Brigitte Montray (nee Roseanne Markowitz) first secured the date between Judy and Randy, then came to me. She hadn't spoken three words to me in three years but one day strode alongside like a secret agent transmitting code. "Laura Russell thinks you're cute. Will you go to Peppers with her?"

That was tough, loathing Peppers on one hand, and on the other hand, Laura Russell and prospects over the top. On the third hand, saying no to Lissa Newtwiler and yes to Laura Russell would be a crime against . . . any chance of getting anywhere with Lissa. I could not commit premeditated rejection of Lissa Newtwiler, the fairest of them all, though a much colder prospect. Teen boys are universally practical, but I loved her a bit and declined the Russell offer. "I can't."

"Whaddaya mean, you can't? She thinks you're cute. She could go with anyone, you know?"

"I mean I can't. I told Lissa Newtwiler I can't. So, I can't."

"What's she got to do with it?"

"If I go with Laura, Lissa will feel . . ." Did I really have to spell this out? Then again, I was naïve. "She'll feel bad."

"What? Lissa Newtwiler? She's nothing! Who cares? I'm offering you Laura Russell."

Forty years later they sat in Roseanne/Brigitte's house spitting distance apart at a chintz dinette, likely the Windsor Estate Collection from Castle Homes Department Store.

Who cares?

The women had revealed their once and eventual selves, one a graceful beauty, the other a lumpy oaf. *She's nothing!* It echoed down the decades. And here the man who would be King, Randy Hazloff, moved on my rightful date. That pissed me off. Worse yet was the nagging suspicion that nothing had changed in Brigitte Montray's frumpy head. Her indictment of a sweet child stuck in my craw. Brigitte Montray had learned values from her grown parents, witless at eighteen and looking like Sister Unfortunate, she seemed unchanged.

I googled a classmate search and in mere minutes got an identity search and with the help of the married name provided by Brigitte Montray, found Lissa Newtwiler, married twice, now living four point two miles from school, our school. Go Whippets. Fuck it: what are you waiting on? I emailed her. *Are you going? Love to see you.*

Of course she was going. She was on the planning committee. Still, you can't just ask for an attached photo in a swimsuit, the one she wore at the Shew Park Pool that summer of '65. A current photo would cut to the chase but might lend the wrong impression, too, that forty years later I'd become a pervert. Or I could still be the same pervert she chose to favor, back when we had potential. You can't very well express interest in someone and ask to see more of her body, to be certain. But you can't beat around the bush either, because we won't likely have another forty years. So, what are we waiting on? Still, a subtle approach is best for both intention and receptivity to jibe. Not that I'm looking. I'm not. I'm married. But what wife would deny her husband a fantasy pursuit, after all these years?

Gotcha. Calm down. That was a test.

But then (as Lloyd Bridges said each week at the dramatic apex of *Sea Hunt*), it happened! In a fell swoop, as if aligned with the planets, two events occurred with synchronous precision. The first was an email from Brigitte Montray nee Markowitz to update the three-day schedule of the greatest reunion ever. Nothing had changed but a simple substitution, replacing the softball game with a tour of the high school.

What? Was softball too physical for the old gang? Was a school tour meant to revisit the wellspring of realization? That would be "cool," except that neither the wellspring nor the realization derived at high school—nothing began there, except a numbing consensus of a forgettable few.

I'd lived on both coasts, as far away as the third world is from a suburb. Life did not begin till five or six years out of high school, life being the dynamic exchange among people of wide-ranging values and experience.

The second event was Allison's entry to my office. Though my wife, she's still a date, a hot one, able to meet my incessant need. Pretty as a picture with lipstick refreshed and a flimsy nightie, she stopped near the floor lamp to outline her great victory over the odds and say that dinner is served: pot roast and tofu sauté to cover our differing tastes. For dessert: fur pie and bratwurst, for further coverage of our differences. Allison is still playful and only fifty-four, and a wedge o' watermelon sounds better any night than time-warped reality, warmed over.

After the update came a plea to complete the questionnaire, tell about your life, spouse, children and grandchildren, provide your address and phone number. Oh, and the softball game still might happen if enough people want to play, so bring your glove! I imagined jowly people aping success with cocktails and cigarettes, like it's still '66 and the catbird seat hasn't changed. Some must have come out okay. Maybe some are health buffs with interesting lives, nice wives or husbands, kids and grandkids and a handicap to be proud of . . . I would let it pass with no doubt.

Except for Lissa Newtwiler—two years out from sixty, but how gone could she be? She'd likely held up like Allison. So what? What would we do, talk about life, children, divorce, remarriage and high school? Would we duck into the janitor's closet on our tour through time and make out? Would I try to cop a feel, maneuvering like a teen around her whimpering elbow blocks? Would I tell her I loved her so much I didn't have enough skin left to blink my eyes? Would she be flattered to know that she still makes my shorts tight, or that I think of her often when I'm alone? She should be, since the difference between a spirited young man and a dirty old man is their ages.

Or would we fast-forward to the tawdry exigencies of modern life, checking in to discreet lodging for an hour or two then parting again, curiosity vanquished? That sounds so base, but I could tell her it was the Peppers I declined, not her, never her, especially with perspective on the toll the years take and the urgent need to maximize our love before it's too late!

I'd go to a Rotary Club luncheon with her, knowing now what's lost with each passing day. I'd join a quilting bee with her or play bingo. I'd meet her at a Republican fundraiser—I'd sign up for the reunion to behold and be with her!

Yes! It's on! I'm going to the Reunion!

Except that . . .

Nah.

Fuck it.

I'm not going. They got a rise on a low-res shot of Lissa Newtwiler, but I'm looking at pot roast and sexual relations with the wife, then a movie with the easy nods and early Zs. It's a sci-fi epic where this guy warps back to 1418. Village folk laugh when he says people will fly in machines and talk long distance on plastic gizmos. Plastic? They'll play golf on the moon— forsooth! He shuts up and tries to fit in with the knights, wizards and dragons. A Maid Marian character is most lovable with very few moods, but then he realizes he's known these people for years at home, like Dorothy with a twist, where he was happy all along, and the dark ages seem passé, once the blush fades, as it must sooner or later.

Late bios drifted in.

Ilene Trimble got all A's. Skinny and quiet she smiled shyly through the halls and decades, becoming a renowned caregiver, coming out with Kate, a life-partner to counterbalance the vapid years of Villager outfits.

Opposite on the teen spectrum, Renee Rollover was every Whippet buck's dream, with her full figure and wild eyes. One Halloween as Little Bo Peep in a sweatshirt with no collar or sleeves and mostly no sweatshirt, she stooped to tie her pink-bowed shoes and make my tongue numb. Looking up, she laughed; I'd never get a piece of that if I couldn't get tough in the clutch. After three marriages it got "pretty wild, even for me, my life got completely out of hand." She gave no details, except for a stint at the state penitentiary—as a drug and alcohol counselor. In a fourth marriage she is fulfilled for now.

Richard Levitt was a caricature in khaki, shuffling his Weejuns. Forty years later, in a photo by an old truck, he wore a big hat and moustache—a western scene with a cutout for his head. He looked stuck, the shit-eater still pasted on his pie hole.

An email flurry argued over waiting five years or ten till the next reunion, because ten would only fatten the deceased column. I hope it's five. We'll only be sixty-three. I wouldn't bitch-slap Ritchie Levitt, though he still makes me itch.

Seeing Lissa Newtwiler might be lively, too, especially if that codger she lives with croaks by then.

Yeah, I might go to that one.

A Strong, Lasting Experience

At forty-six, Lisa Morell denied the years more aggressively, as they gained momentum. Like a cool breeze, she wafted through beautiful days, looking great and loving life. Cornflake-fed, she munched a bowl of Special K every day, spiritually linked to the hard-body woman on the box. Did that woman look great or what? Sometimes Lisa had two bowls.

Lisa Morell could stand sideways in the mirror, square her torso for top thrust and minimum belly and get a wowie zowie every time. She could arch against a pillar at the post office, parting her pout over brilliantly bleached teeth and profile fortyish. She could last and felt good about it.

She smiled at a man passing by, a man observing from the periphery. He returned the warmth, like the guy on TV in the ad for male performance. The woman in that ad put a rise in many Levi's, and Lisa she did, too. That gal put her needs on the table. *Do you want a strong, lasting experience?* Who wouldn't?

Lisa was only checking for a pulse, but return on investment felt heady.

Odds were, the man on the street or in the living room was just as keen on strength and stamina. The hard reality on TV was that every man could drive the wild rooster into *this* henhouse.

Lisa Morell had sensuality in spades and would for a few years yet. Still, she liked to dabble in high voltage power and wanted the current sustained. For fun. Like the good old days were only a few days ago, she flaunted her shape. She hinted potential. She could handle strong and lasting and wanted nothing less. Slam-bam and sleep? Get outa here!

If a man had the delivery system for a nuclear payload, then she was a primary target. She feared that stamina was age-related with a youth prerequisite; youth coming in under forty-five and over eighteen, or over eleven, but legality can be a bitch. And then a woman has to assess the double-edged sword, with youth, poverty, stupidity, no manners or poise on the one hand, and affluence, mobility and fatigue on the other.

 Some older men stay virile through diet and exercise, or so she'd heard. And the money thing could make all the difference, like 5-Star digs with room service or some joker's cheap flat with gritty sheets.

More to the point, I was the passerby, and we read each other as programmed by TV. She'd imagined herself in the role often enough to play it, and yes, I, too, had pondered the TV woman in acts of fabulous indiscretion. The story played out many times everywhere every day and ended on brief exchange and mutual fantasy. But I stopped short on my random passing, having realized long ago that passing on a lead most often leads to the nagging replay, the should-have-said and regret. I smiled back because romance begins best on simple terms, and at our age, it could only be romance, briefly, casually, indelibly or eternally. She seemed friendly, and I said, "Hello. If you're free, I'd love to buy you a coffee." Coffee is predictable and popular.

She blushed and sputtered, "I'm married!"

I shrugged and she hurried down the steps to the coffee shop next door, as if for safety. Discretion seemed the better part of pursuit at that point. I didn't follow. So how did I learn her name? It was easy. I came back for another try, on a hunch and a need that hadn't yet faded.

Or maybe it had faded, even as I denied those days of transition. I imagined her instead of her TV woman, often and alone. They became interchangeable. I owned no stock in Levitra, the boner pill vying for market share against Viagra and Cialis. I owned Icos, maker of Cialis, because my broker urged a strong, lasting position. "It's at 22 on its way to 70." He assured terrific gains, once it cleared FDA testing. "It's a no-brainer," he added, explaining that Levitra was merely a copy of Viagra, looking for a market share by virtue of massive advertising in primetime, with a virtually identical product. Both were ten bucks a dose. Both pumped a ramrod woody within the hour, depending on metabolism. Both had blood pressure ramifications. Both could cause blue vision, and both could turn a pedestrian into pole-vaulter looking for a high bar to clear for hours on end.

It was a helluva thing, when all a guy wants is sexual relations with his wife or other consenting adult. Cialis raised the bar with no blue vision and no coronary complexity. The better option was an on-call stiffy to be proud of, any time in a thirty-six-hour period, which should be time enough for a man to get laid, if he has any chance at all. Cialis could put him right back into play, the way it used to be, and the market would demand the very best.

"The French call it the weekend pill. The French!" George was excited. George is my broker, taking his material from Tom, his stock analyst. George and Tom agreed that a pill good for an on-call Hebrew National Salami at only two bucks a dose with no nasty disclaimers, except, of course, on the emergency exigencies of a four-hour boner, would rule the roost, not share it. Besides that, the thirty-six-hour effect was the low end of the range; it could go to forty-eight. "Forty-eight hours!" George exclaimed.

"Have you tried it?"

"No," he laughed; George was just fifty. "But Tom has."

On his wife? I didn't ask, because broker/client relations call for sober intelligence.

I bought into Icos/Cialis at 22, and it surged in mere days to 25, 28, 34 and 40, swelling with false pride over foresight, intuition and market savvy. "I told you so!" George's cock-a-doodle-do preempted my own, underscoring the natural motivation of men, to seek money and recognition, once absolved of hormonal build-up. George stayed admirably nonplussed as we slumped back to 38, 27, 22, 19 and then 15, saying the market had misread the FDA's call for elaboration of the data, which takes only weeks, not the years required by more data. No more data would be required, only more analysis of existing data.

"Yes, George, I can see you're right by simply reading the FDA report."

"Yes! Exactly!"

"So how did the entire freaking market fail to read the same thing? It's not hard to read. I mean, 15?"

"Yeah," George said softly but with confidence. "Isn't it great? Now we buy more. We dollar-cost average and get you down to . . . Let's see . . . how does nineteen dollars a share sound for five thousand shares? Huh? Are we making money?"

Well, not quite. Yet we shared certainty on growth potential; our stock had only taken a rest, like anyman's weenie will duck for cover on a cold dip. That's self-preservation by instinct, hardly to be confused with failure.

We flexed briefly to 21, deflated to 16 and seemed lifeless back at 15. George was sanguine. "The FDA is dragging its feet on the testing issue. Now they want more field tests, and people still think field tests are data that'll take another ten years, but that's not it at all. I told you: they only need another reading of the data, not new data. We'll come out of this in sixty days. This is *tuh-riffic!*" That is, I could now buy even more stock and dollar-cost average to get even further ahead of the curve—now that we'd found our bottom. George asked, "How many times in life can you look back and wish you'd done something and then actually have the chance to go back and do it?"

"You mean it's like in Vegas, where you can't win if you don't play?"

"No! This isn't Vegas! Man, this is real!" He meant that this was one of those times in life, in the game, which is different than a casino, which is gambling. I didn't press the fine point but bought deeper into the concept, tried-and-true, of dollar-cost averaging. Sure enough, we swelled to 18, 22, 27, 32 and alas, back down to 26. "That's only because we got some bad press on the ad budget. Give me a break. We got a product here profiling monolithic, a market Goliath! What do they expect, a minimal ad budget? What would you rather have, the word out right now on the superior benefits of this product, or holding back the dollars?"

This ad budget miscue was also deemed *tuh-riffic*, as if cleverly scripted, another giant step in the right direction, actually, a step that would allow us, unbelievably, yet another dollar-cost average that would comp admirably as any DCA in the textbooks. So? What do you want to do?

What I didn't want to do was buy in to a losing proposition one more time. I conceded that our company's product delivered far more steak than the other two. However, I recognized the possibility of failure in the marketplace from weak sizzle. "George, please. The Viagra ads look like cola ads, with familiar association. They show a fat, homely guy leading the parade down the street of his tract house neighborhood, waving a baton! What does this have to do with the drug's performance and potential side effects? A baton is going up and down! And the guy is grinning. The Viagra ads beat us, hands down. The numbers don't lie. The Viagra ad targets and profiles the market. It's lumpy suburban guys who eat meat and potatoes and sweat the mortgage and get fat and can't see their wives as sex objects anymore than they can see their peepees without a hand mirror. They need to feel something, and those ads assure them of who they are and tell them it's okay; help is on the way.

"Our company's ads show a middle-aged schlump in a bathtub, a guy who looks well-to-do, marginally bored and mostly impotent, with an announcer asking if you're ready. George, I've been ready. I am ready. But can we get it on? No, because the wife is in a separate tub. A separate tub, George, so if the guy wants to play up periscope, where does it get him? She'd have to reach four feet across the valley to grab the grouper. As if the images aren't enough, our ads alone among all the boner pill ads use the phrase *erectile dysfunction*. It's negative, George. It defines users as impotent. The other drugs are imaging with turbo sportfucking in the suburbs, and we're calling our market impotent. It's a losing proposition, George, a non-sell, a downer, nowhere. The images don't motivate. The message is wrong. The other spot for *our* drug shows the schlump poking his wife's back in the kitchen. He's in work khakis and she's in a *shmata*, getting a cattle prod in her lumbar. These ads fail."

George sighed in resignation; advertising is my game.

"Now look at the Levitra ad," I continued. "The product is strictly average, a copy of a second-rate performer—but! They got this gal every man can imagine on top or bottom. *That* is feel-good imagery to connect the dots and win market share. Ergo, *that* is the stock to buy."

"But . . ."

"George!"

I'd seen art mimic life from time to time but had not yet felt an investment based on reality, as portrayed on TV, which is what we'd come to. Things changed that year, the year I passed the point of sexual acuity. Don't get me wrong; the cock still crowed at sunrise, but that's hardly the same as standing up in company to urge a point. Given my days, weeks and months of solitary sleeping, a twosome would have felt strange and pressured from the outside. Morning wood is often self-defense from bed wetting; by the time a guy gets his other joints coordinated for the bathroom trek, the old ramrod is ready to relax for a leak. Sex at sunrise became an amusing recollection.

I chalked up diminished libido to short-term stress. Allison and I had finally agreed to disagree. We further agreed that life is long, and the years remaining should be joyful and occasionally thrilling rather than tolerant, strained, tedious and gray. Allison agreed that I was not to blame, provided that I would not blame her. Blame? What's blame got to do with enhancing the joy of our remaining days? What's to gain with blame?

The romance went away, yet we'd sustained the charade for an imaginary audience. We further agreed to get back together or not, allowing nature to play out. Letting go was a relief, but the old drives don't die in solitude—especially at night. Prospects can seem loathsome on the common pattern, dating, until the ultimatum forms up: solitude or contact. Prospects seemed grim, with scheduling, chitchat, nice, nice and the whole sugary panoply or walks in the rain, movies and hiking, yadda yadda. An honest personal ad would read: *no diseases, good teeth, strong pulse, below average body fat, hygienic, hetero, sexually motivated.* Nothing wrong with biological need, but people want to dress it up. Getting pesky hormones calmed could well open the door to more meaningful dialogue. Or maybe I'm hopeless.

Then Ruby died, aka My One True Love. She came the same year as Allison but seemed more present, loving, devoted, uncritical, and so on, et al, infinitum. Ruby slept beside me, belly up, head on the pillow, front paws over the cover since the first night two decades prior. She'd get up for snacks in the night and return to bed, touching her whiskers to my cheek and purring. Could any love be purer? Maybe Allison's departure was a blessing, distracting from greater loss.

Into the senior discount, a man can remain virile, though drive and frequency needs may vary. I sustained my fantasies, however, imagining women with no clothing and random acts of perversion once every thirty-seven seconds, in conformance with the national average, accelerating to every twelve seconds during primetime TV. I would not attribute diminished appetite to hormonal deficiency but to general fatigue. That, too, seemed honest and natural; I'd earned the right to be tired and, moreover, tired of it. Hookers made sense, but for the tawdry, risky, public nature of the thing. Wouldn't it be great if you could call a housewife for an hour or so in the afternoon for some . . . There you go: thirty-seven seconds on the dot.

I won't belabor the first time I got lucky PA, Post-Allison, because it was generic; a high-end bar where a well-shaped woman in a skimpy black dress engaged me in reasonably intelligent conversation, leading to a few shared values, mostly political and nature-based, and a common personal experience: recent divorce from a long-standing spouse. We were there for the same thing, which thing remains immutably unspoken in keeping with good taste. Her name was Claire, which felt redeeming. Or maybe I only hoped so.

She confided that forty-nine and single wasn't easy. I nearly blew prospects on a glib refrain that no, I bet it hadn't been. But discretion seemed best, so I let it lie, pegging her at a hard-earned, svelte fifty-three, a woman who'd worked for minimal BMI with dietary diligence and workout rigor.

What the hell, just as vain as anyone, I felt the body-fat issue running nip and tuck with the money issue. Sitting in a swank pub and grill, swilling pop at ten bucks a go got me qualified on the money front. I sat up like a lead dog to show the body-fat front. She could see; I made the cut. Besides that, she had a winning smile, a warm demeanor and what seemed a brief list of needs. Truth was, I loved her concession to age—not that I believed her, but that forty-nine was the new thirty-nine. We all have little proofs and denials; I still felt game and randy like at nineteen, not so long ago. I avoided the mirror first thing in the morning, but who doesn't?

We went to Claire's place to get familiar and maybe squish our sorrows away. It seemed basic in a good way; we wanted to have and to hold the old times once again, however briefly. Dead people can't do that, and we weren't there yet.

I won't belabor my failure or her generosity in helping me, even though we'd only just met. It worked as long as she helped but failed again when she stopped. It seemed one-sided and pitiful, and I offered alleviation in kind, but no. Worse yet, along the way came time for a prophylactic, the mechanical installation of which on an iffy situation allowed for or perhaps facilitated deflation. It became a moment of growth, so to speak.

Lying back, accepting life as it came, Claire called them condoms. "What a nuisance."

My memory of this device was from teen years, when we said, *strapping on a rubber*, and giggled.

Her nightstand drawer had a gross of condoms in a box, two-thirds full, which basics in math put her at forty-eight squishes since the box got opened. Background context fuzzed on doubt and her anxiety over "helping a guy out" without said condom. "I mean . . . You know? What if . . ."

I assured her that probability on deadly contagion could not be greater than zero, that my single life had been monkish. "You're it," I consoled.

By that time, it was a salvage operation, sinking on her reminder that sex with a spouse can be as hazardous as any.

I didn't argue. What could I gain, a point?

With the iffy stiffy, ramification, doubt and risk, she'd had enough of all of the above. Why play in the mud with vast grassy meadow out front? I lay there, as she dressed and drenched me with the pitiful sentiment for a man who can't. *Don't worry about it. It can happen to anyone. We'll try again, another time.*

It can happen to anyone and will, and a man catches himself saying: *This never happened to me before.* Which is like denying the moment of passing. Failing to stand and salute constitutes insubordination to the superior officers of life, love and the pursuit of happiness.

The long walk home was longer and colder that cold, damp night. A few couples passed, arm in arm. I checked out the females, fantasizing perhaps, down to four-minute intervals and inner scorn, as if to assure others that I was no threat.

But I wasn't yet dead; the miracle of homeostasis got me back in the running, slower with age but getting there. I fantasized Claire with some success and soon fantasized a visit. She had promised another try. I didn't have her number but knew where she worked. That seemed obtrusive or too forward. I could sleuth her number, but that seemed like stalking. Besides, what would I say? Let's try again? I ran into her at the grocery store for a grand reunion, warm and huggy. "Let's try again."

With a big smile she said, "I already am. I may be in love. He doesn't have a problem—far from it, and he's so . . . I just can't believe how things work out sometimes. I shouldn't tell you this, but I will; life is such a mystery, and we keep so many secrets. I went to get you that night—I mean, I knew which direction you were headed and I followed to bring you back, thinking you are a very nice man, and the next day was Saturday, and, well, you know. I got a half block down and this man was lost, looking for his cousin's place or something, and it was late, and I don't know what I was thinking, but he slept over, in the living room, of course. But the next day was Saturday, and we had such a lovely time, and it seems surreal. I mean, if you'd, you know . . . I might never have. Isn't it amazing?"

In the living room, of course?

I learned long ago to accept the things we cannot change, chief among them, death and taxes, but she was selling a butterfly flap in China that caused a hurricane in Booneville. I could sooner see my limp noodle keeping me unlaid forever. Did she freshen her lipstick before heading out on that cold, damp night to find me?

With investment strategy on the table, I asked Kenny—Dr. Rhys—for a sample of one of those new boner pills. He didn't press but cut to the choice. "Which would I like?"

"The one with the foxy woman arching her back on the porch post. You know?"

"Yes," Kenny laughed. He knew.

"I'm looking at the company." Investment was to save face for Lord Jim, but Kenny laughed on. He hadn't heard the investment research ploy. I thought it sounded good.

I felt better on the way out, loaded for bear. Well, I wasn't loaded yet, but the scrip in hand was good for a cross-chest bandoleer of fifty-millimeter shells. I swaggered like a suicide bomber willing to fuck all to smithereens. It was downtown Fallujah, crawling with infidels (women in need), and I'd take them on with my flame-thrower. Couples beware; I was armed and dangerous.

I needed psychiatric help on the macho military delusion, but it was only a game, compensating for impotence, for assault with a dead weapon, for being outa ammo. It was foolish, that's all, not pathological. It was boner pills: glory, glory hallelujah.

I passed Lisa Morell on my way home from the pharmacy in a second synchronous scene of this insistent play. She came on strong before shying. That's what they do, sometimes, taken at face value, as if things aren't as playfully presented.

She wasn't married—I could tell. She had high standards and required a man of merit, worthy of relationship, which I could be.

I'd returned to the scene, which isn't the same as stalking. I wanted to get something straight between us. Sure enough, she had a pattern, visiting the coffee shop by the post office at the same hour only five days hence. Spotting me, she could have thought the same, until I preempted further thought on a smile. "You're not married."

She corrected, "I am."

I paused for chagrin.

"Separated." She looked aside. "Over a year."

"Can I buy you a cup?"

"Why not? Can you stand a triple espresso?"

If only she knew. "I can now."

She glanced again to measure weirdness and led the way. "You can now?"

"Yes, I can."

She looked perplexed but amused. I could swing with repartee all day long. No rush here, so we talked leisurely of world events, politics, personal summaries, interests, pets, marriages, solitude, the death of nature and so on, offering the mutual twinkle of common drive.

Time flew to dusk and twilight with patience and interest, my heart sensing love beyond sexual liaison. We seemed bound for intimacy, as every woman wants, unless it was caffeine overdose beating my chest. Triple espressos? Where the hell did that come from? And why? I suffered the fantasy/fear, vagina/angina matrix—till Lisa Morell said, "Okay, do this."

"Do what?"

"Close your eyes halfway."

I did.

"Okay. Now, imagine me naked." She laughed, when my eyes reopened. "Come on. It's a game." Oh, how well I knew it. "Okay. You got me in focus? I'll give you a hint. I look better naked than I do with clothes on. Scratch that—than I do with most clothes. I look great in a bikini. I have great hips, a flat tummy, tits to die for—naturals—great legs and the rest. I've tried Italian cuts, French cuts, Brazilian. They come out . . . not exactly wrong, but not as good as plain naked."

"You look great," I said.

"Well, I look better naked, except for one little dress I want. You wouldn't think it should cost eighteen hundred; it's so skimpy and only black. It brings out my features. I gotta tell you: it's the single dress that makes me look better than naked—I take that back. It makes me look as good as naked. I don't mean it makes me look naked, and naked would look better, but it makes me look great. You wanna see it?"

Wait a minute, I thought. *What's-her-name, the one I met in the bar who helped me out right before her Prince came along wore a skimpy black dress. Come to think of it, nearly every woman in that bar wore a skimpy black dress. And yes, they shouldn't run eighteen hundred. Two hundred maybe or four hundred for a great design. But what . . .*

"Come on." Lisa took my hand. I resisted so we wouldn't get arrested, so I could pay our coffee tab, only forty-eight bucks but steep for a bad case of jitters with chest pain and acid stomach. Symptoms vanished as I signed the voucher, and she whisked me away, whispering playfully that we could go to her place and she'd model, and I could compare to see which looked best. That got the horses galloping again, so at the risk of resisting once too often, I stopped for a glass of water and a discreet reach and pop, pocket to talk hole, of my tiny nuclear device. Oh, I'd be ready to defend our borders with honor.

We walked briskly, in pursuit of love and retail therapy, on caffeine and expectation, sharing at last the richest vision known to man and woman: our happily discovered selves going in, out with thrilling gratification in the moment and beyond, to love, which is all you need, as the song assures. I didn't think for one moment that eighteen hundred was exorbitant for such potential, or eighteen forty-eight with the coffee, or eighteen-sixty with the twelve-dollar tip; we'd tied up the table for so long.

Yes, she modeled the dress there at *The Chic Boutique*, changing in the dressing room, showering us and our evening with giggles. I couldn't see the difference between this dress and many skimpy black dresses at fractional prices, but she looked scrumptious, head to toe, edible and then some, so yes, I bought her the dress and hurriedly, since the boutique actually closed seven minutes prior, which timing seemed like one more incredibly lucky stroke.

We stopped on the way to her place for a libation more suitable to the hour and prospects at hand. *The Swan's Down* was her favorite little bistro, charming, cozy and a crossroads for celebrities. She could hardly pass it without stopping in for *some*thing. Besides that, we were both adults, seasoned, to say the least. We knew—or should have by then—the golden value of that precious interval prior to confirmation/consummation, in the heady atmosphere of anticipation that we would never have back but would soon recall with laughter and longing, just before another round of exhaustive love, to be sure. I told her I hadn't felt so ready in a long time. She snuggled on my arm.

I concede: the first red flag went up when she ordered a bottle of Dom, but it *was* an occasion after all, but then she proceeded to the *Lobster Thermidor Swan's for Four*. Why not? We had to eat. It was *delish*, and we could take the leftovers home. "Oh, you're going to *luuuv* Fatboy." Fatboy was her cat, who would die for some lobster thermidor and who, really—once you get to know him, you'll see—was the only reason to order heavy cream, butter and cheese. My God, it was thick enough to put a good man down, present company excluded, of course, we hoped. A beer calmed me, dulled the caffeine and got me primed for Dom.

She went to the bathroom, buffering her profile by not calling it the little girl's room but saying she had to pee. I'd take an earthy woman any day over a thrifty woman with cutesy speech patterns. Cliché is bad enough without gagging diminutives: little girl's room, tinkle, tush and so on. We could gear down on spending later, post-celebration, when a Moet Chandon would do at a fraction of the cost, thank you very much.

Fat content would be another bridge to cross, a four-laner, also down the road. For the moment, what the hell, Lisa Morell: let the good times roll. I was up to it, not at peak condition—that was twenty years ago or twenty-five. Fuck it; I felt giddy, good and bad. A guy should feel casual, relaxed. It's not like fifty-eight is the new eighteen. But Christ on a crutch . . .

Unless it was. Out of the blue, from under the table, lo and behold, up rose the signpost of triumph. Eyes closed, I envisioned her naked, *et voila!* Flags up was not red, white and blue but white—tablecloth unfurling for a nation unbowed. The eagle had landed! The Phoenix had risen. We had liftoff!

I knew this stuff was on call; add stimulation and *'Ten hut!*But hell's bells, I'd downed a handful of triple espressos, a couple brewskies and a pint o' Dom—and Lord Jim towered beneficently over his subjects.

She returned on a laugh, not at Jack in the Box but at the mystery of nature and random events. She touched my hand. Silence was a new phase, a good one, an interlude for dinner, which was delish and very nearly worthy of the two-hundred-ninety-dollar tab. Make that four-eighty with the Dom, and take it up a notch to an even six bills with the beers, cordials and tip.

She laughed again; we could cheat Mr. Death by surviving the *Swamp Mud Fudge Sludge Suicide*, which might help buffer the dollop of *man-tapioca* to come, if I could catch her drift. Catch her drift; we nearly capsized on that breaker. Well, I loved her spirit, and flat didn't care about another hun for sweets or anything except growing anxiety to get it on. Monumental milestones would be plentiful enough in the near term.

She leaned in so I could better see her tongue rimming her lips, shifting the drug to overdrive. When I was twelve, a broomstick rose over my belt on the school bus, and another kid yelled and pointed, and everyone saw, mortifying me in proclaiming adolescence. *Full circle*, I thought, with pride.

Lisa sparkled, her spirit also restored. Sprightly as a nymph she said, "Excuse me again." An eyebrow rose over distance traveled and heights to be scaled. She hurried off again with the skimpy black dress, to preview what could only look better naked, I thought.

I never saw her again, not that night, at any rate, which felt like forever. I thought she'd gone to change. I thought that was foolish; home would be better than a restroom. Maybe she wanted to wipe her chin or check her teeth for fennel or her chest for dribbles. But she left with the skimpy black dress.

I knew the score but denied it an hour, counting it as the first of four, at the end of which I would need emergency assistance. I'd laughed at the warnings on TV, never suspecting I'd be timing the wood. But there I was, pinned down behind enemy lines, eight thirty. This was the fifty-millimeter cannon I'd longed for, and I had no target.

Well, I could take care of myself. I'd get up and head down to the ER if I couldn't get some deflation in three hours, much less four. I contemplated a hooker, for emergency use only, or going manual, but the thing morphed from heavy artillery to intercontinental ballistic to a beast unto itself, an entity unconventional, invader from Uranus. Make that Pluto.

Experience took a break on reflections of well-being and romance thrashed, on deflation in the second hour, on thoughts adequately horrid to bring the thing down.

Yes, the drug played havoc for two more days and a third night. I would have visited our coffee shop, to show her what she'd missed; but I suspected she'd worked our corner before and knew what she'd missed and was glad of it.

I arrived at last at what would have been impulsive forty years ago. Hell, I had nothing better to do. At least giving in to chance would put me out in public where something might happen. I knew what would happen at home.

I ordered herb tea and sipped. She walked past the window at a quarter to three, looked inside and grinned. What could I do, pursue? For what?

Offering a lame smile in return, I imagined her naked. Jack languidly nudged the lid, too sleepy to care, much less jump.

But nature and women conspire to keep the game alive. A woman seeing a man with a good-looking woman wants that man. Not always but often. A woman saw our brief window play and took the seat across from me. "I saw that."

I shrugged.

"Is she an ex?"

"You could say that."

She nodded, as if commiserating on common experience and pain. She hoped I didn't mind, but she was weak for a sad-looking man drinking herb tea. Did she mean in comparison to the macho meatballs and fay milquetoasts surrounding her? Her silky skin held up when she leaned in to confide. I knew I was meant to look at her rare cleavage but shouldn't stare. She lit up, as my hand slipped into my jacket pocket for the little pill bottle resting there.

I think it's okay to mess a thing up and come out smarter. This time I'd wait until safely indoors, my place or hers. Then again, waiting could make me late. Then again, women like a slow, deliberate man. But they won't wait too long. "Waitress. Could I have a glass of water, please?"

She said, "That's sensible, drinking water instead of alcohol. Hydration is so important."

She watched me pop a magic pill. "Allergies," I said.

"Oh, God!" Stuck in the headlights of coincidence, she blurted, "I thought you were . . . I mean . . . I'm an account executive, and I have this new client. We shot a *bazillion* commercials, so many takes, I thought you were putting me on."

"Putting you on? With a vitamin?"

"No. I love a man who takes care of himself. I thought you said it was an allergy pill."

"Organic antihistamine."

"Ah! I thought you recognized me. I thought you were going to ask, 'Do you have stubborn, lumpy stool?'"

"I beg your pardon."

"Not you. That's my account. It's a laxative in pill form, no more chocolate or chewing gum, and the thing is, you take it like a vitamin! Once a day after lunch, and you'll never worry again. About regularity. My challenge is words and images to go double-digit market share on diameter, grease and taper. Give me a break, wouldja." She sighed. "Sorry. That's why we get the big bucks, but it's the worst spot ever, this guy taking a pill to have a nice BM. Nobody says BM anymore, except for my grandmother and the dork down in creative. I'm not complaining. Sorry. I thought you recognized me and were putting me on."

"No. No shit. I'm not putting you on. I'm just grateful to control the sniffles. For a while anyway."

Honor Among Men

The Wailuku Aikido Club was more than a club to its members. It was a way of life, far beyond the basics of throwing and taking falls.

We took pride in our Sensei, the only aikidoist in the world listed in the *Black Belt* magazine Hall of Fame. His status saved us from esoteric obscurity, from a pursuit more suitable to the aerie fairy crowd with their auras and cosmic vibrations, more suitable to pussies, such as they were. We weren't perceived as fay, but then the soft arts weren't nearly as blood 'n guts as Tae Kwon Do or other schools keen on grappling. Those schools taught sparring, punching and kicking, which rough contact was most often machismo and brutal. Brutality did not make for effectiveness in the short run or value in life. What could benefit everyday life in a punch or a kick? A beautiful fall, on the other hand, with *ki*, in friendship with the mat, weight underside, one point set, no bumps or surges? That could engender lasting grace in essence that could apply at street level.

A Tae Kwon Do teacher killed a guy outside a bar on Lower Main with a single kick to the chest, because the guy had insulted him, likely on something obscure that lit the short fuse. Maybe the guy mentioned a tree and a mud puddle in the same sentence. Sensei would have counseled, "Do nothing!" He would elaborate now and then that doing nothing is not the same as not doing anything but requires posture and ki.

Sensei would have walked away, which was our onus to bear among more macho martial arts students, but his listing in *Black Belt* magazine made us bad, in the colloquial sense.

One of our highest-ranking members was fifty-four when I was thirty-eight, the year I began. David Wade, a known operator in real estate and commodities, played it close to the chest on his operations and commodities, but tall tales got spun. David cast risk to the wind in a cavalier approach to life and business. Hardly cautious, he stayed cool, cheerful and indifferent to embroidery going over the edge. He enjoyed the stories of Wild West spirit as much as anyone. David Wade was not a Rotarian. Civic-minded in a loose sense, he now and then took us lower-ranking men for drinks after class, elucidating on the breeding and social status of one person or another, and on his wife's true beauty. Nearly twenty years his junior, she could keep up with his blistering pace. Colorful and likable in a rich, seedy way, David went against the grain, never overbearing, tedious, condescending or dull.

In a move discussed widely in town, he'd optioned a thousand acres of mountainside and basked in public perception of crazy and worse: foolish. The mountainside optioned was inaccessible, and roads would not be built in our lifetime. The slopes were thick with *koa*, a reddish rich heartwood then selling at fourteen dollars a board foot, but the trees were endangered and couldn't be harvested. The steep grade ranged between ten and twenty percent. The mountain was volcanic, dormant perhaps but far from dead. And each of the thousand acres faced howling tradewinds gusting to fifty knots daily. Yet he beamed that the option was only a million dollars, huge money then, with only ten grand down and another ninety grand in sixty days, balance due in six months.

Within a week David had sold the land for four million more than the price of his option, sold it to Japanese speculators for the freshwater aquifer rising to a hundred-foot depth below the surface in the center of these acres. The Japanese were invincible then, not like they aspired in WWII but the Second Invincibility, when golf club membership in Tokyo ran two million dollars and benchmarked the Values of the Empire in general. The Japanese wanted it all and then some, revealing again their appetite for global ingestion, beginning with all of nature. The Japanese called their plan Optimum Resource Utilization. In their inimitable, insatiable way, they would leave no stone unturned.

The mountain acreage went hand on hilt with all the resorts on South Maui, resorts purchased at Japanese and science fiction value, resorts that couldn't pencil out in thirty years, but only because the pencils weren't Japanese.

David asked Sensei the week after his big sale if he could please teach the Wednesday night adult class. Sensei, open-minded as a teacher could be, didn't ask why or what would be taught, but took David at face value, assessing his posture and intention, easing into the single nod. David had trained nearly twenty years by then, demonstrating his diligence and ki, as if four mill counted for nothing. Sensei said, in his own inimitable detachment, "Okay, you teach. Wednesday."

Word got around, and it seemed like a good time for old members to convene at this milestone of sorts, this edification of our training and values and the good times we shared. The club was packed, the atmosphere charged, alertness and awareness elevated in ultimate calmness. With so many people throwing in such limited space, self-preservation required vigilance in all directions, like life. The heightened social aspect was foregone, with the old-timers on hand, including Sam, Watanabe, Tengan, Nobu, Larry and Olive, all past seventy, some pressing eighty.

Then, like icing on cake, Sergio Tortolini showed up, just arrived from Italy for an indefinite stay. As visitors often do, Sergio assumed that the heightened spirit was the nature of the place, that it was just another Wednesday around here, so he effused commensurate love and jolly good cheer, his world-class jocularity letting him laugh along with everyone at the size of his feet. We trained barefoot. His feet went fifty-four centimeters, size sixteen. A small crowd stared at his feet, so he asked if they knew what was said about big feet. They played along, asking what. Sergio blushed and glanced at Sensei, who also waited. Then he blurted, "They give better traction!" Everybody laughed briefly, because class was ready to begin.

Our unspoken credo required humility in all things, thereby precluding David from mentioning his glory. He began with a short review on the soft arts we practiced, and on the aggressive, bloodthirsty nature of these same arts. "We don't practice blocks or punches or kicks. We practice movement, throwing and being thrown. Most of you get the basics in a year or two. But the second thing takes, what, Sensei, ten years?"

"Forty-four years I train!" Sensei called from behind the counter in back, where he observed. "I still train. I still have plenty to learn!"

"Forty-four years and then some. The second thing is seeing what your partner will do before he sees it, before he does it. We don't block. The very nature of a block means that you've allowed the attack to begin. *Shin Shin Toitsu* teaches us to go inside before an attack begins. That's what we practice. I want you to be clear on this. This isn't nice. What we do here is the nastiest, dirtiest, most aggressive martial art in the world."

Adept at the dramatic pause, David waited to let his words sink in, to give us time to glance back for Sensei's reaction, since, after all, it was a regular love fest with Sensei teaching. Sho nuff, the old man nodded slowly. "Am I right, Sensei?"

Sensei continued nodding. "This is why we have side discipline training. This is why we meditate. This is why we breathe."

We paired up and faced off in *hanmi*, a non-frontal body position of less exposure. The exercise called for *nage*, the defender, to lunge for the larynx of *uke*, the aggressor, before the aggressor moved but not until the aggressor intended to move. Esoteric with a point, the object was sensitivity to the dominance of no dominance, cohering mind and body and vice versa, or to use the popular jargon, honing the killer instinct to invisibility.

Sweat poured, and in thirty minutes we took a break, during which David told a story of these skills applied only last week, when three bruddas confronted him on a, let's just say on a job site, to redress their grievances. "You can tell everything by a person's stance, and these guys were an open book. All I did was step forward, like this." David was very good here, too. Hardly a big or powerful man he stepped up, hands down, palms forward, with a smile on his face and in his eyes, like Jesus, kind of, but without another cheek to turn. David could kill and justify it, and it showed eminently with a strange voltage, perhaps a short circuit somewhere along the line, but oh, he had some crazy stuff to share.

Moreover, he was on his way to victory, to a successful session of teaching the Wednesday night adult class and blowing his own horn without mentioning his killer deal, so far. For what it's worth, the Japanese investors lost their money, lost the land, lost the suburbs in Honolulu, the resorts on South Maui and the golf club memberships, too. But that was a year or so later. As it was, we had an hour yet to go.

Which comes to the juncture relative to our training, our personal development and, that night, to David's extraordinary ability to close the deal, get the money and then tell us all about it without actually mentioning it, making it a night of entertainment, insight and good cheer for those of us who liked David and his antics.

Among those who resented such displays were Hank Raushe and Russ Struic. Hank was Sandan by then, a third-degree blackbelt thoroughly indifferent to rank or degree but striving for perfection in the void, more or less. Hank was a jerk to some, because he flat refused the social effusions common to a club; Hank was there to train, train, train; to lose his self, insofar as self underscores ego and obstructs flow. He was not there to lollygag. Often accused of Germanic ancestry, he supported the contention with his totalitarian view of things. Hank wanted to personify the invisible gem. Free of physical encumbrance, he would float like a butterfly, sting like a bee, in the spiritual sense. Hank was different, willing to chase the spirit, tackle it by the knees, then stand on its throat till it said uncle.

Not really. I exaggerate to make a point. Few people in the world sensed the ether like Hank did. Like a fluke of nature, Hank trained with a vengeance. At six-one, two-ten, his movement approached ultimate softness, nearly transcending feeling on contact and throw. He was the best aikidoist the club had ever seen, in a different league from those who put in the years and wore their tenure on their sleeves, as if the years automatically yielded development. This spurious concept was Hank's great test, especially at seminars, where the clans gathered from around the country and the world. Hank could bow to the very best, or, tougher still, the very worst, and lead and follow through the paces gracefully.

Most people sensed his skill, but nobody spoke of it, except for Sensei, who constantly critiqued Hank's movement, so perfection wouldn't go to his head. Egotism is the death of selflessness and tantamount to life imprisonment, no less a burden than visibility, muscle mass or brute force, harsh sentences indeed.

Hank taught the beginners, sharing the figurative sense in a blistering pace, opening the book on what he knew. Hank held the invisible gem. He showed it at all times for all to see, because it was a sacred thing to share, not to garner for personal advantage. This became the rub.

David got along with Hank as well as anyone, which was marginal. David was Hank's first teacher, demonstrating his streetwise version of ki, combined with agility and speed. David had a coin trick, in which he could snatch it from an open palm quicker than the palm could close, because he could see the intention of closing before the closing occurred. He called this the essence of aikido. Hank caught on, closing his palm with no visible intention.

But Hank had no time for tricks, stories, fluff or happy games. Hank sought attainment. He would not discuss his objective for fear of sounding foolish, and because mentioning a thing undermines the magic, which should be obvious to anyone. Hank could feel vibrations and considered them ordinary rather than extraordinary. He visited Stonehenge on a Sunday, when ten thousand tourists quelled the magic. So, he went back late on a Monday night, jumped the fence, found a spot and sat for an hour of magic restored, as it rolled down the aeons into he who could receive it. The invisibility Hank sought was the essence of pure power.

He worked as a landscaper, but mostly he trained. He meditated an hour in the morning and an hour in the evening, like Sensei. Through the day, driving down the road, he counted breaths, in slowly through the nose to the sacrum and down to the toes, inflating the calves, knees, thighs, hips, on up the trunk to the torso, into the arms and shoulders and up the neck to the head and crown of being. Then he exhaled, emptying the vessel just as methodically. He trained on the job site with his *jo* and *ken* (staff and sword). Marking a leaf in a cluster, he'd back up, hone in and advance, slow but fast, fast but slow, his ken swooping from overhead quick and quiet as muted lighting. Stopping an inch past the tiny cut, he would extend a hand under the marked leaf in its descent, then examine the cut dispassionately for frays.

Hank taught when I began. He tried to teach the proper feeling a big opponent requires—that is, the magic that transcends physical force. Otherwise, physical force will predicate victory to the bigger, stronger person every time. We could not grasp the concept. So, he took the beginners outside to the edge of the lawn where weeds grew and asked each student to pull a weed. Each weed broke at the surface, proving a physical approach. He grasped a weed gently and said that putting his mind at the tips of the roots and coordinating his breathing would facilitate his and the weed's letting go—just so, up came the roots. We tried again and got the roots, amazed, though still wary of big opponents.

Meditation in movement was Hank's standard. Mostly humorless, he stood one step back from the void, spine straight, chest open, arms down, palms out, floating, or maybe coiled. He could matte and frame you for his scrapbook of inanimate attackers. He chided himself bitterly for throwing someone physically. If a bone broke, well, that was your fault, too. He wanted to feel like nothing and throw like a force of nature, irrepressible as an ocean swell, unavoidable as a spring breeze, without impact or friction, and he could. Oh, you didn't want to mess with Hank; here comes the floor, or a wall, or a post, or somebody else's frikkin' head.

Unless of course you were Russ Struic, who was already *Godan*, fourth-degree blackbelt and much higher in the political hierarchy, equal in rank to David Wade. Russ hated David, or maybe it was only the idea of David, because David was slick and fast and could tell a gut-wrenching story in a half minute and had electric energy and a former babe for a wife and millions of dollars and public recognition and all like that. Worse yet, David began training a month before Russ, so he would always rank higher, which seemed unfair to one so acutely conscious of status, one who ached in his heart to rise above all others and do good from the summit. That is, Russ nurtured aspirations so visibly as to embarrass those around him, maintaining that his objective was lofty all along.

The bigger problem of his professed loftiness was its intimacy with the material world of three dimensions. He sought dominance within the club and recognition from the international organization. If lower-ranking members revered him, he could demonstrate compassion and warmth, what the world sorely needed. With presumed good taste and intelligence on display at all times, he clearly disapproved of David's burlesque. David had so much as deprived the club of more meaningful training available under his own, more spiritual tutelage. Russ Struic rose every morning at four a.m. to meditate for an hour. This practice also deferred to Sensei. If you didn't know Russ's meditation regimen, he would tell you. He reminded someone every day. "I meditate every day at four a.m. Every day! I made a promise to Sensei . . ." And so on, ending his service-oriented profile with a disclaimer: "I'm not bragging. I only want to show you what you can do," which never sounded selfless.

The not-bragging disclaimer was Sensei's line, but then new members didn't know. Russ commonly struck a pose with a suburban Buddha smile, and with soft intonation he would remind: "Sensei has trained for forty years and still thinks he has much to learn. You'll *never* be as good as Sensei. So you have no choice but to train, train, train." Inferred was that we would never be as good as he was, which felt ridiculous to belabor.

Allowing his vast humility to absorb in the hardheads sitting before him, he could change pace in a blink, often with a sprightly anecdote of himself training with the leaders of the organization in Japan, gaining insight at the highest levels on a first-name basis. In that way, we mortals could sense the divine connection arcing before our very eyes, if we believed.

Russ Struic often advised on dojo etiquette, with soft reminders to call him Sensei in class. That bone stuck in my craw. I wanted to tell him that I knew Sensei; Sensei was a friend of mine, and he was no Sensei. We all had needs and shortfalls that kept us coming back to the mat. Maybe that was mine. Besides, it was only a clever thing to say, a snippet from media history, an expression unworthy of my own aspiration, which was correction of the reactive self.

Russ was big, and size mattered, because he most often took advantage in any form available and called it ki. It was plain to those of us under six-two, two-thirty, that personal development could easily take a hike with a hulk coming at you. Physical violence was anathema at the club, a dishonor tantamount to cowardice, thievery, disgrace and worse, but accidents did happen. I soon figured the proper defense to this buffoon. I smiled and stood my ground. What could he do? Brain me?

I simplify; Russ could maim as quick as Hank could, but they were different. I'd follow Hank into a throw, because he knew things very few people knew, beyond sentient knowing but rather in a developed intuition on the ethereal plane that surrounds all things at all times. Hank put in the hours and years to become what he wanted, reclusive and esoteric as that may seem. My resentment of Russ Struic's gregarious, hail-fellow presumption stemmed from his chronic superiority; he so obviously lacked in social fundamentals. He was a very big guy who could fuck up in a blink, slam you into the wall, then rush in with concern for your broken and/or dislocated bones, with a lecture on ki, its proper extension and where, exactly, you'd failed.

Confiding my deep resentment to Hank, I gained his own concession that he, too, along with most everyone else, also resented the stink of ambition imposed by our mutual friend. Hank advised more meditation. I assured Hank that Russ hated him, hated what he was becoming, felt threatened by him and tried to undermine him, calling him a rough, young student behind his back, downgrading him to Sensei.

Hank smiled in his own Buddha rendition and said, "Of course he does. But you can't stay here if you let that stuff or any stuff get in your way. It's a gift, all of it. How much better can you or anyone be, with a force like that to reckon?" He let the idea sink in, advising, "His ego is only one more fall to take."

I liked that, and you can't get along bearing a grudge. I vented my frustration by capturing the jungle fowl roosters who came to my henhouse for the two squares daily and a bevy of hens. Most of the wild roosters were gentle as pups, dazzling, with brilliant red combs, blue-black tail plumes and iridescent greens, but they had to go, on account of my pet rooster Peewee, a cocky little silky with an ego as big as Russ Struic's, though more purely motivated. I followed the cocks into the coop, closed the door and bagged them gently in fifty-pound feed sacks.

Rats came, too, what with the chicken scratch and straw. I caught them live in a Have-a-Heart trap, and they went with the roosters over to Russ Struic's house at night, to live happily ever after, humping, gnawing, scurrying around corners and across eaves, pecking, claiming dominion and cock-a-doodle-doing to their hearts content. But a petty prank could not scratch the itch.

I meditated more, sometimes easing into my own smile.

Meanwhile, Hank alienated more members with his sanctimonious approach to each and every thing a person can do. Eat, sleep, wash, defecate, work, talk, walk—you name it; you were doing it wrong, all wrong, until you got it right. I liked Hank's unique critique of everything as wrong, because he wasn't perfect, and his seemingly pure motivation made him easy to discount when he was off base or, dare we say wrong. That was okay, too. He could take it. Sometimes he smiled. His occasionally unfounded criticism felt like a small price to pay for his gems of growth and development.

And there we were, with David extolling the virtues of ki in life and business, up-front, center stage, with Russ resenting him for personal reasons, Hank resenting the subject matter for practical reasons, as I tried to maintain meditative repose in diligent observation.

The scene flowed with familiar current, with known eddies and undertows and something more. I couldn't tell where the evening would lead to but felt the brimful energy of the place verge to overflow. Dynamic ions felt palpable, indelible, the grist we'd come for, and that would be enough. Perhaps I, too, was gaining contact with ethereal potential at last.

Never mind; let a scene play out. Wended our way on a memorable, provocative class, we watched and learned, as David Wade basked in the pride of no pride, borrowing successfully from Yamaoka Tesshu's sword of no sword. Hank, meditatively aloof as a pure student of the gentle arts should be, spent his break time in meditation, like a battery restoring its charge, for more juice when the body is next engaged.

The more philistine among us schmoozed, catching up socially, as lay people will do.

Russ Struic murmured disapproval to a small group of beginners, seeking devotees to his brand, doubting something or other in this strange, odd, peculiar situation. He often mentioned selling pot to kids and something about a pimp and a thief, not to be trusted, not the time or the place and so on and so forth, in regard to David Wade. Only David Wade and Sensei were higher rank that Russ, who rumbled into a lull, "He shouldn't be allowed in here, much less allowed to teach." This was the fart of no fart; we all heard it; we all smelled it; we all pretended otherwise.

Move to David, who took that throw and offered one of his own, calling out, "Look at Hank!" Naturally, everyone looked at Hank. "He's pissed off, Sensei, that we're having too much fun. And Russ is pissed off that he's not up here in the spotlight! I never dreamed I'd bring these two together. Ha!"

Sensei laughed tentatively at this apparent good humor, this all too real connecting of confrontational dots in a ragged thin line, smiling eyes on one end, do-or-die hearts on the other.

Hank didn't twitch. Russ glared at David, presumably with ki, trying to throw the glove of no glove but only managing to throw no glove. "I don't know, Sensei," David went on. "Russ is bigger, but he only meditates an hour a day. I think Hank could take him."

"No!" Sensei bellowed. "We have no taking. No winners or losers in aikido! No competition of any kind! You beat nobody but yourself here! That's what we train!"

"Hai, Sensei!" David bowed and held. He rose and called mellifluously, "But wouldn't it be great to see your two top students go free-form, you know, off-the-cuff, just to show everybody how it ought to be done?"

Sensei stared, which was the no of no-no, or to put it more directly, yes, it would be great. "Okay!" David called, clapping his hands twice, so everyone would form up again in rows, sitting *seiza* (legs under) and ready for what might come next, though the realpolitik of synchronicity rendered the veterans acutely mindful of the potential that Wadesan was about to tap.

That is, David Wade's performance was randomly timed, till he'd clapped his hands at the moment Russ Struic strode toward the window to check the parking lot or watch traffic or otherwise demonstrate his interest elsewhere. You can't break etiquette; we sit *seiza* immediately when the teacher claps, so Russ sat, coincidentally as it seemed, in the rare placement adjacent to the other one of Sensei's two top students. Beside each other, at the deep end of the pool, they waited. So it was that Wadesan set up a dazzling display of glory and glittering humility. What a show.

"*Taigi* One!" David called, drawing the evening toward perfection. Because an art or series of arts called out by the teacher is followed by rigorous response, all students rising, pairing off, bowing and moving with alacrity into throws.

Each taigi is a series of five or six throws to be completed with utmost poise, posture, ki, grace and the whole enchilada in a given time, precisely, usually thirty seconds but sometimes twenty-nine or thirty-one. One person attacks, over and over with full speed and intention. Yes, the throws are known in advance, but the objective is blending and movement in the eye of the storm, not kicking ass. Once through the series, the roles of thrower and thrown are reversed.

Taigi Thirty is the exception; more a state of being than a series of throws, it demands perfection in body, mind and spirit and must never be attempted by anyone other than Oyeah, top dog, or in more appropriate terms, The Master in Japan. Oyeah was tenth *dan*, dan meaning rank, tenth being perfect. Only one person in the world had a ranking of perfectly perfect perfection; such was the flaw of the doctrine or dogma, feeding egomania in a trickle-down hierarchy. Some high-ranking teachers derived meaning and identity from it. It felt rigid and cultish and could be embarrassing and a certain factor when, from time to time, a student may ponder an easy drift. Oh, but the training was something else, reflecting sheer genius in movement.

Anyway, David Wade calling for Taigi One could have been coincidence, which we knew goddamn good and well was not possible. Hank and Russ never sat beside each other. They avoided training together, to better spread their beneficence to the less developed, they said, because it was awkward, given the appearance/reality, relative/absolute, socio/political scheme of things. Yet there they were, faced off like good students. They bowed, and Hank attacked.

What made the Wednesday night adult class so popular among seasoned members was Sensei's tradition of letting loose the reins, allowing those who could to move freely at high speed in big air. Bodies flying, flipping, meeting the mat from altitude at maximum velocity yet light as feathers, we filled the little room and made it smaller still, like the whole world in maximum population density on spin cycle. I loved Wednesday night for the distraction available.

Unlike anarchy, it required precision, with no stray thoughts or worries distracting from the feeling, the approach, contact, blending, opening, leading by following the hardwired laws of flight, the landing and continuation to up and ready again, as if a fall was in fact an attack, into the approach, and so on.

Bullets never sweated so freely, and the sheer, lovely pump of blood through veins was the cleanest symptom of life a human ever felt.

Russ Struic had a peculiar approach to the basics, often abbreviating his movements or accompanying them with a shrill, otherworldly whine. This strange behavior was meant to set him apart, I suppose, underscoring his advanced, never-to-be-equaled, no-matter-how-hard-you-tried status. With everyone thoroughly engaged otherwise, he took a breather on showmanship and went through the throws, as he should.

Hank, as usual, was by the book, at one with universal time, down to the second. We, too, knew he had it honed to a fine edge, or he would have told us how miserably he'd done.

Suffice to say that this rare exchange between Russ and Hank could have nothing but a neutral result. Either one hurting the other or in any way gaining advantage could threaten severe loss to the apparent winner, who would be the certain loser. This, too, complied with the victory of no victory and assured the highest standards of neutrality, non-dissension, non-confrontation and going with the flow.

Yet David's choreography was tighter than most scripts. He had by chance, it seemed, selected Sergio Tortolini to partner for Taigi One. Moving through *Kirikaeshi* with no seams showing, into *Zenpo*, he spread his wings like a chrysalis. Opening ever so large to meet and greet Sergio for a most dramatic *Kaiten Nage*, he led the game guinea around and around, strumming the banjo, as it were, to the ally-oop! And up . . .

Fore!

Wait a minute! Did David just make a subtle bow to Hank?

Did Hank actually take Russ to the airborne plateau, into the ozone of mastery, where Russ could really show his stuff? Did Hank simply yet unbelievably turn aside, away from his opponent to stand in perfect posture and stillness?

And whaaa . . . *KABLAM*!

As if served on a platter to the emperor, all fifty-four centimeters of Sergio' right foot soared majestically skyward and leveled decisively, just as it had in scoring the winning goal back in the Brindisi district soccer finals as a youth. *Che bello! Evviva! Fantastico!*

This score, also a game-ender to remember, was a clean shot, arch to temple, turning knees to jelly as the wobbles rose to Struicsan's face that still smiled, though wanly, melting to mere slits in the supreme visage, ambition reigned in, benign at last, for the would-be master. Perhaps in knee-jerk denial, Russ held posture until fading beautifully to the inevitable master, Gravity Sensei. Songbirds warbled on a perfectly pruned branch of a stunning bonsai in a tranquil Zen garden, as our pal fell like a mighty oak.

Cuckoo. Cuckoo. Cuckoo.

A hush fell over the room. A crowd rushed in to kneel around the cold-cocked countenance. Two students of the vibratory school placed hands above the fallen one to channel healing energy from the Universe to Wailuku. Some closed their eyes. Some mumbled vibrations.

David Wade said, "Holy Christ. What was he doing there?" Nobody called it a knockout, though it stared us in the face.

Hank stood still as a post in wakeful meditation.

Sensei busied himself with paperwork, checking attendance, reading the yellow pages upside down, anything but worry, ultimate anathema to the *Budo* code. Sergio went for a glass of cold water and drank it but then refilled and walked back to pour the second glass onto Russ's face. "Hey. Wake up, you."

Blinking, the great one pressed for drama, noble warrior struck down at the height of glorious battle. Laughing like a terrific sport, he asked, "What are you trying to do, kill me? Ha, ha, ha. Well, you'll have to do better than that." He stood to yet another posture, scanning the crowd with a glint, in control, coherent. And he smiled at light applause, then slumped to another swoon.

"Close the class," Sensei called.

Everyone scrambled to *seiza* but Hank, who was already there, having read the movement prior to its conception and so on and so forth. We sat in even rows as David W sat, facing the class, waiting for calm before announcing evenly, "Officially, a TKO." Pivoting on one knee to face the *shokshu*, he bowed. Everyone followed suit—except for Meesta Struic, splayed like roadkill and obviously excused.

The newer students renewed ethereal ministrations as the more seasoned enjoyed our third or fourth beer just up the street, reviewing the play, as sports fans will do.

David Wade returned to the club infrequently after that, retiring to his small estate on the mountainside, coming down for Sensei's birthdays, odd holidays and the occasional deal.

Hank moved to Japan, to approach the source of perfect time. I, too, drifted away, having reached the plateau on which benefit balanced cost.

Russ Struic successfully explained to Sensei that by promoting him, Russ, to fifth dan, and then sixth straight away, he, Russ, would gain greater recognition and respect, which would benefit everyone, and he, Russ, could more effectively campaign for funding and recruit new students with more credibility and therefore less effort gone to waste.

Sensei saw the reasoning or at least went along. And everyone lived happily ever after, honor intact.

Athena & Buck

Moose grew up with the People, who were only called Apache by the Zunis, whose word *apachu* means enemy. They called themselves *Dineh*, the People, and some generations after their last migration and final constraint on a reservation, a few of them showed Moose how to express Spirit using bones, wings, beaks, feet and other animal parts in tribute to nature's gifts.

He got his start when his older brother got a gun and used it on birds in the foothills near the White Mountains, not too far from Phoenix. What the brother killed, Moose took to the reservation as raw materials for art.

Moose would become a gifted artisan of medicine shields, native sculpture, figurines and trinkets. He lived hand-to-mouth, annoyed with making ends meet, never doubting that things would play out as necessary. The brother went west to become the Number One Hummer Salesman in Southern California.

In those early days the brother wounded as many birds as he killed, also leaving the maimed to Moose, who took those birds to the reservation as well, where he learned avian healing arts. In his prime, he could splint a leg or wing or otherwise manipulate a bird toward recovery, returning many birds to the wild, birds who would have died on their own or left to others.

He gave me the Indian name Snow Eagle the second year I knew him, when I drew the eagle card from the animal spirit deck. "Oh, God! Eagle!" he whimpered. Moose back then went a burly six-two, two-fifty with a mountain-man shag and beard. "I've only seen it once before, ever."

What did it mean? His face scrunched; the answer was so painfully obvious. "You'll soar."

I let that news sink in, as if Moose had just knocked on my door to tell me I'd won the Publisher's Clearing House Sweepstakes. Moose delivering news from the animal spirit cards could be taken at face value. It was money in the bank, not on the material plane, but currency that would survive the flesh, that could be taken along the journey. Nobody wants to call a gift horse long in the tooth, but I felt within the bounds of etiquette to question what seemed curious. "Why Snow Eagle? What's snow got to do with it?"

Moose shrugged, his face arching in equal perplexity. "I just read the cards and tell you what I'm told."

The following ten years took their toll on Moose, with two quarts of coffee and a pack of smokes daily. At fifty-three, his heart condition, blood pressure and joint pain had him strung out and worn out on Vicodin and hydrocodone. Down to one-ninety, he needed a new doctor, one who could cobble some simple relief without the opioids that were killing him. He could feel it.

Still urgent when I visited one Saturday, he said he'd interviewed two more doctors, but both defaulted to pain pills, according to protocol. He was exasperated; he'd fumbled with the fates and felt that drug addiction threatened his connection to the great spirits. But the pain was real, and difficulty compounded on official policy of the American Medical Association, beholden to Big Pharma. Through this troubling time, he remained sensitive to messages from the ether, including notice of impending death, if his pill diet didn't change soon.

Out on a scooter ride, I wanted a fifty-mile loop to change my mind, so I headed over to see Moose and whoever was hanging out there—always a wayward, colorful crowd who profiled on a popular bumper sticker in that neck of the woods: *All who wander are not lost.*

I often accepted Moose's peace pipe but planned to avoid it that day, not even noon, and I'd never make three more stops on the ceremonial reefer Moose kept on hand.

Two local boys sat at the kitchen table, Two Trees and Greg, or rather Two Trees and Snake Jumper. Snake Jumper, like me, had to go, bidding adieu with the local handshake, a double-clasp hand jive. During these ablutions to etiquette, Snake Jumper put a small bag of buds in the cookie jar.

Two Trees at the head of the table held court, as it were, neither rising nor moving any part of himself but his head. Of massive volume in the native way, with huge melon calves and the general girth of a beached marine mammal, he lolled his head in a fat man's rendition of affirmation and meditation. With less discretion, he pulled the plastic bag from the cookie jar to roll, or rather construct, a cigarillo joint. Beginning with cuticle scissors and surgical excision of sparkling bud tips that pulsed with life of their own, he said, "Excellent chrome." He snipped, piled, sprinkled and separated into two small mounds on the paper, then massaged the little bundle to perfect roundness.

Moose shared Two Tree's credits. "Two Trees has had five different buds in *High Times* magazine. He took the shots himself."

"That you grew yourself?" I asked foolishly.

Two Trees looked halfway up from his task with a tolerant half smile, so much as asking back: Who else's buds would I have in *High Times*?

I nodded in sanguine recognition of *High Times* high standards and the skills required to qualify for those pages five times. *High Times* not only demanded excellent chrome; it challenged perfection. Dazzling glow-in-the-dark chrome with electric red veins, gold nuance and iridescent chartreuse glow, a *High Times* bud must speak to its readers—or rather its viewers.

As the joint in progress swelled and lengthened, I projected a roll out of six inches by a half inch in diameter. I put Two Trees at a few hundred pounds, give or take on both counts. The jumbo spliff would look tiny in his big mitts. When he caught me staring and assessing, I asked, "Where do you get those papers?"

He smiled, lolling his head again, more forward and back than side to side. Ah, that was where.

"Come on back to my room, Snow Eagle. I want to show you something." Moose seemed corny using my Indian name in the clubhouse, such as it was. But nobody looked twice or blinked, and Indian names were all I knew of them.

He wanted to show me his owl. He called her Athena after the blind Greek goddess who carried an owl on her shoulder to tell her what was seen. The comparison was a stretch. Athena the owl was found on a roadside in trauma, likely hit by a car. She got a ride to the Humane Society and another ride to Moose, who looked and sensed; she was blind.

Moose was a birdman from way back by choice and avocation. I don't know what drew him to Hawaii, except for the gravitational pull of the place, mystically drawing those of whom services may be required. "The state of" Hawaii has always been different, commercially motivated, without spirit, and had warned him to cease and desist his illegal keeping, treating or engaging wild animals in any way without a permit. The state is notorious for its Department of Land & Natural Resources, a sundown and payday outfit that manages and protects nothing but payroll, political consolidation and campaign donations by controlling permits. DLNR is not natural or informed and is often dangerous.

He couldn't get a permit because appropriate authorities would not appropriately authorize him. Why should they? How could they, after all? He was suspect as a civilian and subject to fine and/or imprisonment. He stopped. During that hiatus, all road kills, injuries and maiming went to the Humane Society, where Gail, the director, called Moose, to find out what to do, till

Gail stopped calling and simply sent the injured birds to Moose, till the state of Hawaii called Moose to inform him that a special permit to keep, treat and otherwise engage wild animals would be forthcoming directly, requiring him to proceed as necessary according to the statutory guidelines pursuant to the blah, blah, blah. Or else he would face the blah blah blah.

Moose wrapped a three-foot stick with a leather strip, colored beads, conchos, whip tails and feathers and lashed the last two inches of a steak knife blade to the end. He used this stick to feed his baby owls so they wouldn't imprint with a human. He fed them meatballs, sometimes using the rounded end of the stick to cram the meat down the gullet, when the babies wouldn't take meat so long dead. When he had the money, he sent away for frozen mice and used the blade end.

He'd also housed injured chameleons. Jacksons got introduced in recent decades, someone smuggling in a few and either releasing or losing them to the wild, where they adapted. School kids caught and sold them to tourists, who couldn't take them home, but didn't know that till the airport, where they were euthanized, the lizards, not the tourists, not yet.

The male Jackson has three horns like a triceratops, and ninety percent of those males in captivity were named Michael. With popularity came abuse; again, the injured came to Moose, who applied first aid and sent them into rehab on the lizard highway, hand-width planks hung end to end around the perimeter of his room where the walls met the vaulted ceiling. Sticks and small limbs along the route served as rehab challenges or detours leading to larger branches with foliage. The lizard highway ran the length of all four walls with an arched bridge over the center and served as a training course for reintroduction to the wild. A support population lived among the water dishes: stray mealworms, wingless flies and assorted baits to attract new flies, so that rehab would also reinvigorate hunting skills. But how did he feed his infant or injured lizards in rehab to avoid the warm and fuzzy imprint? With a Godzilla hand puppet. They took to it, recognizing family who cared.

Athena the owl had a broken leg and remained blind. In two weeks, he felt the leg had begun to knit; she wouldn't put pressure on it, but at least she rested that foot on the perch. At six weeks the foot knuckles were calcified, stuck in the closed position, which could support her body weight, and she soon demonstrated that the leg bone had healed. But the claws were growing into the skin on the bottom of the foot. Moose trimmed them once, but they grew back quickly. He wanted that foot declawed by a veterinarian, who wanted five hundred dollars.

The blindness hadn't changed. She'd learned his scent early and loved the aroma combo, Moose and mouse. She fluffed up in his presence. He felt certain, however, that she'd leave the body soon, if she couldn't fly and hunt. He crooked a finger and put it near her beak. She tilted her head for a neck scratch and cooed.

"Sometimes I think she can make it in the wild. I put her out in her cage every night with a few mice, and she cocks her head to hear where they are, and she'll try to pounce on one by sound, and sometimes she gets it. She can stand on her club foot and use the other foot to eat it, and I know when she's caught one, because she won't eat her morning mouse if she had one the night before." Still, he worried.

She'd made contact with several owls who flew over at night, one of whom came in low a few nights and eventually perched overhead. He and Athena would coo and hoot for hours.

"What's his name?" I kidded.

"I call him Buck."

"Buck and Athena."

"Yeah. I got to tell you, I bring her into my room to perch every morning, and she stays here all day, and I love having her here, but I got to believe her sight is coming back. She preens now. She didn't do that for weeks. It's a strong sign of recovery, and she turns her head three-sixty. That's got to stretch the tendons and nerves and all that other stuff in there. I think she'll see again. It's the only thing that could keep her from making it."

Two Trees called down the hallway from the kitchen. "Hey! Smoke 'um!"

I told Moose I wouldn't get high because I had a few stops, and it wasn't even noon. I didn't want to be rude, but I'd go ahead and make my apologies on the way out. He said he wouldn't smoke either, because he couldn't smoke that shit.

"What shit? You mean in general?"

"No. The shit Snake Jumper brings over."

"You mean two hits and out?"

"I mean you never had anything like it."

"You say that every time."

"Check it out."

I didn't want to check it out but did. Any doper knows that etiquette works on several levels, and any random gathering may include a lifelong friend, just met. Here, too, was a rare presentation of hybrid buds. Growers crave approval no less than any artist. And it was Saturday, so what difference could it make, before noon, after noon? The spliff was lit and offered, and though some people said no, thanks, I only said thanks, thinking it a pretend session, two hits, maybe three, little bitty with hardly any inhale. It got similar in a hurry to a freight train speeding past with barely a touch. It tasted unusually fresh and mild with no hint of chokers.

Moose said no, thanks, and took his own pretend hits.

A connoisseur also knows that buds of fortitude and attitude will melt reality like cheese fondue. Projects, errands, phone calls, tasks, points on the threshold of speaking, sentences not yet finished—anything relying on neural connectors will short-circuit. Moorings loosened, and I thought to leave while I could. Motion is more easily sustained than initiated. Couch lock is no joke. Tilting ten degrees, I leaned onward and thought of up.

It was so long, farewell, adieu, auf Wiedersehn, aloha, a hui hou and mahalos. I rose. Brief talk of Two Trees' uncle who used to have a scooter followed me to the door, where Moose said, "We ought to call you Two Wheels."

We stared into thin air, until I broke the trance. "Snow Eagle on Two Wheels?"

On that note I got out, leaving the boys laughing into the next story about this guy who couldn't get a ride to work one day in the rain, so he . . .

To describe the dope stumbled onto that bright, rippling day as psychedelic could not capture the surreality. Physical dimensions varied directly and conversely, as equilibrium flexed in a universe geared to relative north. Nothing seemed fixed on horizontal or vertical, uphill or down, which didn't matter, really, with rubber on the road, and it was, on subtle crosscheck. The ether tingled. Color effused from small pools, rising and breaking in waves, till the eyes shot the gap to elsewhere. Sorted planes of existence attempted coherence but failed beautifully, as two lanes between two ditches followed a dividing line in the center. Drift was minimal with two hands who felt like vague familiars, changed from the good old days when we really knew each other, not that we couldn't still get along, but who knew how receptive they'd be to our former chain of command. I wouldn't challenge them for performance in the clutch, as it were, but they did seem keen on muscle memory, up to convergence of speed and curve, motivating them to do the right thing. They seemed to have a mind of their own; I told them so little.

A blustery tailwind made for easy speed to sixty with lifts to sixty-five. The seasoned scooterist will distrust a tailwind. It can swing fifteen degrees for involuntary lane change or the ditch. It can come around for a header like a fifty-pound pillow. But intuition and the soaring spirit prevailed on a brilliant day, flying downwind invincibly, optimal conditions for quick death for very stoned riders.

Knowing demons helps to avoid their mischief. The seasoned rider often differs from the dead rider in seeing through the lovely feeling to the tricks it can play. We soared, spirits, demons, hands, heart and life, until wings could spread for flight—briefly, until a young demon shot the cross gust, fluky header combo. An exit could hardly be improved, stoned tingly in profound clarity, at altitude with no regret. It felt like twenty years ago when . . .

Whoa! Red light! Brake time. Ease on in, back to the lanes, ditches and centerline. Where was I? Where am I? Isn't it beautiful? On a scooter under the sun, all systems go, hands and eyes and equilibrium choreographed to move the show down the road with nary a wobble or miscue. "Ho! Motherfucker! Stay in your own lane!"

The world overpopulates with demons, too many to watch, but a ride rises above. A survivor stays mindful of encroachment, ambush and so on through two errands, both lost on recall, confirmed by receipts, and on to home to raid the fridge and a nap, slogging at four in a daze, arms and legs heavy as George Forman's in the fourteenth, a long time ago when they went fifteen. Those were the days.

Arrgghh. The crash and burn aren't pretty, but caffeine and ibuprofen ease reentry. Dope gets stronger, as if enough isn't enough, as if AK-47 didn't make for enough smithereens or Crush didn't crush enough. Train Wreck will end a working day, which would be perfect for humanity on Earth, three hits at first light for seven days to give peace a chance, a reprieve from church, school and shopping, manufacturing and deal making and more, on the way to much, much more.

The dope is too strong for anyone's good. Can it catalyze mundane thought to searing insight? Maybe. Sometimes.

Thoughts struggled, as I pressed the numbers for Moose's house. He laughed when he heard me ask for a small bag of Train Wreck for home use, not for cocktails but for special occasions among friends.

"You're preaching to the choir. I can't have the stuff around."

"Because you'd smoke it all and be stupid all the time?"

"Yes. But listen: I was sitting here with Athena for about two hours. I think she saw the light."

"You mean she's listening to reason?"

"I held a penlight out to the side and flashed it on. When I pointed away from her, she didn't respond, but when I put it on her eyes, she turned to it."

"How do you know it's improvement? Many blind people are sensitive to light."

"Yes. But I tried it last week and got nothing. Not only that, I left the light on and put a frozen mouse in front of her. She wouldn't move on it. Then I turned the light off, and she took it."

"Maybe it just thawed out."

"No, not cold frozen. The mice are freeze-dried. She loves them right out of the box, but not with the light on this week. I think she's getting her sight back, Snow Eagle."

"You'll be sad to lose her, Moose."

"I won't be losing her. I'll be gaining her."

"Pardon me. I measured gain as a function of possession there for a minute, which brings me back to my need."

Moose said he'd call Two Trees and get the train rolling, so it should be on hand for a wreck by tomorrow night. I didn't look forward to another trip up the hill so soon, but then a man has to move when he can. Besides that, I could take the car and Lulu, which would make her happy, though she fears Moose yelling when she chases his cats to sniff their asses. The world is complex in layers of need, and the outing shaped up.

When I told her, she leaped for a nose lick.

Moose died about thirty minutes after dinner the following night—Two Trees' famous three-meat chili, with beef, buffalo and elk. Two Trees wanted to make it four meats and had a connection on moose meat, but Moose begged off, unwilling to eat his namesake and spirit guide.

I begged off for other reasons, like the nature hike I'd promised Lulu, which would take until way past dinnertime. And I didn't believe like Moose and Two Trees, that animals give their lives so that we might feed. The world is ill with vanishing habitat for every other species and factory farms killing the countryside. We kill animals to eat them, as if converting them to human sewage makes it right.

I challenged Moose often enough on eating wildlife—he challenged back on the importance of preserving the old ways, what little remained of them.

With no moose meat in the chili, he had four bowls, calling it the best chili yet from Two Trees' kitchen. Two Trees and Walks Upright retired to the living room to roll a number and watch a movie, a Hollywood thriller with sleazy terrorists and mayhem. Moose watched a few minutes but didn't feel well and went to his chair for comfort, to let the discomfort pass. He often used a cola on ice and a cigarette to bide time. Ten minutes later, the phone rang. Moose yelled down the hall, "Mike! It's for you."

Mike was aka Walks Upright, but the caller asked for Mike. Mike took it on the living room phone and in a few minutes went to see if Moose would mind a few people coming over. He found Moose in the chair, mouth and eyes open, a cold cola sweating on his table and a cigarette in the ashtray, lit.

Moose was dead and looked it, but EMS got called in anyway. They roughed him up on the jump start, but Moose had gone blue. Just that quick, word was out, up and down the street, that the Moose man had begun his journey.

Lulu and I arrived to neighbors milling in the yard and the street, neighbors who'd lived there thirty years, before Moose moved in, neighbors who'd brought Moose their problems as kids. Moose had comforted when their parents passed and counseled their children, who came to the Owl Man of Makawao with injured pets. The neighborhood convened on hearing EMS, and the gathering felt like a revelation, not exactly like a white buffalo birth but along that order. The idea of death marking the beginning of a journey was not local but Native American, an idea Moose taught them. They seemed uncertain what was taking place or would happen next but soon enough found out.

Moose left on a gurney, fifty-five, under a cover, in an undercurrent of lore and healing skills. His passing made the airwaves in minutes.

Most people die with their friends unprepared. Moose left suddenly, what should have been no surprise, with his caffeine, nicotine and pain pill habits. He'd been weak for years. We thought he'd continue that way.

We hung out in his room for company and to feed the lizards. I asked where Athena might go.

Two Trees said, "She went. Earlier tonight, just before dark."

Moose had taken her out to the night cage but stopped on the way to see what she might try. She took off, a surprise and a worry, since taking flight is up into space, but landing must be precise. She landed easily in the tree over the night cage and waited for Buck. She followed him in a few low circles around the yard, then he went high, but she wasn't ready, so she came back and landed again.

Moose said she was taking it slowly, and she looked down before touching down.

We could hear her outside, calling from her branch, ruffling her wings. Buck called back, first on high, then swooping low.

I suggested putting a mouse out for her.

Two Trees agreed. The mice would only go to waste otherwise. I did not suggest that they go into the chili, though Moose's passing was full of crying and laughter, silent and talkative, life without seams, one phase to the next.

A true friend lingers. We sensed Moose, near his chair, before Athena's perch, under the lizard highway.

Two Trees said only a few mice remained, and that was good, better to throw them out than get Athena and Buck on a bad habit. I regretted Moose's bad habits, and Two Trees shuddered, like an ax had hit his base. He broke down and cried.

In a minute, I asked if he had any idea why Moose had come up with Walks Upright for Mike. Two Trees sobbed into a short laugh, "So he would."

Athena called again, leaving her branch, taking to the heights.

Snapdragon

Fact: grocery store pork marked down twice for quick sale, unwrapped and circled on a kitchen counter, will move out of the circle in less than an hour. Even so, Terryl Boyington Ratchford hated to pass on that bargain.

T.B. Ratchford's ancestors settled in what was then called the lower half of The Carolinas. He was the modern heir to a 25,000-acre King's Grant, commonly awarded to those families who asked for it through proper channels. Several centuries of liquidation as necessary, had left a modest plantation as the Ratchford legacy. The family still owned controlling interest in a buggy whip company, but sales were down, and most of the war bonds bequeathed were secured by the wrong American government. T.B. held on anyway, just in case.

In harsh terms, T.B. Ratchford was a foolish old man, land-poor. A kinder phrase was gentleman, old school. He asked for nothing but courtesy, wanted nothing but good weather for his garden. Yams and goobers saw him through.

In addition to his forty acres and a garden, he had a strong lineage. That is to say, his forebears had been integral to the character and fortunes of the region. Friends included a man whose family founded a printing company two hundred years prior and printed treasury notes for the Confederacy. Another friend was a silversmith, eleventh generation in the same shop, renown for crested chalices and prosperous until crystal came into vogue, just before the turn of the current century. His peer group rounded out with a ship's chandler, a furniture maker, a tailor and a tanner. Most of his friends owned cars, but to him and his friends, few things had changed.

T.B. Ratchford was a thinker. Summertime was best, when limited movement appeased unconscionable heat. On a stool, chin in hand, he'd been watching a side of circled pork on the kitchen counter when Cousin Owens walked in.

Owens dusted around the house. "Only benefit of the heat," he said, wiping his brow with his dust cloth. "Piece of meat at a decent price."

"Ultimate speed is imperceptible, relative to magnitude," T.B said. "Only two things move faster than the eye can follow." On summary assessment, he settled again.

Cousin Owens went along. "I'm game. What are they?"

T.B. looked up. "Light. And old pork."

"You make no sense," Owens said. "Light is too fast for the eye to follow. Old pork is imperceptible for the opposite reason. It's slow, T.B. Too slow to see. Like an hour hand, for example, or blooming flowers. Too slow." Owens reached up to dust the brass ring hanging from the ceiling, clanging the pots and pans. A younger man, not yet fifty, Owens had come to visit some years earlier. When his weekend became a month, he assumed a useful posture, a veiled and tasteful suggestion that he stay on, gardening, feeding the cats, keeping the place tidy.

T.B. accepted the new order in his way, though assurance got rationed. Owens rarely disagreed without a punctual dusting.

"Many things move beneath the low limits of perception, as you say. Hour hands, blooming flowers. But old pork? All we know is that it leaves the circle." T.B. hunched down for the point. "Who's to say if it crawls or jumps?"

"Who's to say time doesn't fly. Or flowers don't pop open. Nobody says these things, T.B. We accept things as they are each morning, so that another day can begin."

T.B. pounced. "You prove my point! We accept, because we're lazy. Miracles surround us. Time does fly, Owens! It gains speed! And snapdragons pop open!"

On a concessional nod, Cousin Owens sidestepped to the counter for more pressing business. He couldn't win against T.B. but could circumvent, if he saw the opening. He thought he did and said, "I found a horse."

"Ribs or roast?" T.B. was curt on his cousin's specialty. Owens called himself a horseman, though in the years he'd stayed on, he'd only run his mouth on symmetry, haunch, back, stance, composure, spirit, sweat, coat and on and on for any nag shuffling by. In the last year, T.B. had discouraged equine critiques by recalling a woman who'd called herself a writer but never wrote. He knew a fellow who travelled with an expensive camera but came home pictureless. A Rutledge girl who lived down in Darlington visited New York City for a week and came home in ballet slippers and leg warmers, talking about "the dance," but nobody ever saw her try to tackle the box step.

Cousin Owens hated looking T.B. in the eye; direct contact set the curmudgeon to thinking, to clouding the issue at hand. But on certain ocular contact, for conviction, he said, "Gelding. Three years old. By rights, he should be priceless."

"Ah, rights!" T.B. warmed to a well-worn topic.

Owens persevered. "Sired by Falmouth Champion, foaled by Queen o' Sheba. He's never run. He has one eye and they say . . . no heart. He's for sale."

"He's on sale, I would think."

"Go ahead, blot the ray of hope, if it helps you," Owens parried. "I've offered five hundred dollars. Cash."

"You don't have five hundred dollars, cash or otherwise."

Cousin Owens held him, eye-to-eye. "I have a mind to race him."

Staring at cross-purposes on that note, T.B. cleared and mumbled, "Ignorance." He slid off his stool and reached up to the brass ring for a cleaver. Raising it high on a stride—Owens jumped back—he chopped the pork to six pieces and set them in a row. He drew a line across the counter. "My money is on the loin. Care to bet?"

Cousin Owens, dabbing his dust cloth to his cheek, felt obligated to bet and chose the cutlet. Pulling up another stool, he stupidly watched nearly rancid pork, waiting for it to race, wondering when stupidity had become a dominant force at Ratchfordshire. Ah, but he knew the game.

T.B. thought it clever, intimidating through logic.

Owens called it rent, to himself.

They watched until sweat trickled and T.B. asked if Owens would care for a julep. "We'll make a day of it, at the track." He nodded assent and stepped to the parlor for the bourbon.

Owens shoved the cutlet across the line. T.B. could fill his days with this nonsense, if Owens took no initiative. When T.B. came back with juleps, Owens pointed. "My pork won."

T.B. looked grave. "Did it jump?"

"It crawled. It struggled. It won."

T.B. inspected and shook his head. "You think you have a winner, but you can't be certain."

"Racing is hell," Owens conceded.

T.B. mounted his stool to sip his julep. "Shall we bet on place and show?"

"No." Owens pulled down a carving knife. "Race your dinner too long, you lose it."

T.B. watched, sipping, shifting, as if to freshen perspective.

Owens didn't think him senile but merely perverse, superior, a gamesman. Owens knew the reward for playing along and the penalty for sitting out.

T.B. finally asked, "Who'll jockey?"

"I'll jockey," Owens said.

"Who'll train?"

"I'll train."

"What am I? Tits on a bull?"

Owens played his ace. "You'll manage, sideboard and bar."

T.B. twitched. Reality warped to the realm of consequence. "You mean . . . the Cup?"

"I do. How many men dream, never to waken? Or accept what comes at first light?" On eye contact yet again, Owens murmured. "He's thoroughly bred."

"I like it, Owens. I like it very much."

Owens beamed. He'd won on method.

But victory vanished. "We'll call him Old Pork. No! One-Eyed Heartless Old Pork! That should get us some odds."

"Why wallow in the mud?" Owens asked. "Come out of it. Come up. Let life change for the better."

"You're not happy?"

"We'll call him Snapdragon. We have a chance."

T.B. downed his julep and stood, trembling, pulled back against his will to something long gone and happily so. "Damn it, Owens! If not for me, you'd be a public ward. A racehorse with one eye? The Cup?"

Owens turned to profile, "We may not win, but winning is a probability greater than zero, unless we don't enter."

T.B. stared through his imbalanced cousin, hunched his shoulders, slid back onto his stool and settled into a think.

The Cup was heart and soul of the lower half of the Carolinas, the course itself unspectacular. Low jumps over white-washed fences, high jumps over slovenly hedges, long jumps over swamp bog called water hazards. But society came out, came down, came over, sometimes from the Mother Country, that island, that rock, that England. Social legacy prevailed.

The track and paddock, rough and earthy in a rural mode, sat apart but not too far from the men's latrine, a fifty-foot trough behind a cinderblock wall. The women's facility, equally rustic, rose to comfort, sit down, bench style, each opening walled and doored, with clean tissue on a shelf. Pissing outdoors, in the dirt, in good company from good families, was communion, historical in the moment, natural in nature and plentifully imbibed. The Cup was old as good money and memories, and people had lined the track for centuries with buggies and sideboards. Now they came in cars, station wagons and old Mercedes mostly.

Tables were set with linen, plates, utensils and goblets to support lavish buffet and bar, end-to-end around the track, once everyone arrived. Those who merely loved horses or talked horses or used horses as a social vehicle thought the Cup a must do. Those who raced enjoyed celebrity status. They viewed the Cup as involuntary, like drinking or death.

Seven races through the afternoon led to the finale, a two-lap run for Grand Champion.

Limited betting trackside went to a dollar or five in the spirit of harmless distraction. But like most fêtes embedded in tradition, drawing those clans, interests and fortunes disparate from the rest, the Cup was alive with prospects far greater than two-dollar fun. The Cup was a daytime drunk crowded with rich people, and it was behind the paddocks or off in the trees where bigger odds were met, where fortunes could be made or restored.

"The Cup," T.B. ruminated, chewing on it like Elsie Borden.

Cousin Owens trimmed fat, first with the cleaver, then the carving knife, sculpting the lean, iffy pork. He stopped to sharpen his blade and rambled over social access to big wheels, meaning financial access. "The five hundred is nothing, T.B. Nothing. Let's not get constipated over the money. We can borrow against the place, probably eight hundred if we wanted. Back taxes couldn't begin to match the value of the place, probably. Eight hundred would be better, considering sideboard and bar." Owens sold upstream, against T.B.'s unraveling thoughts.

T.B. half heard Owens' din, half watched his surgery, as he remembered. Harking back was acute in the region, and the Cup recalled the season of youth, heir to a vast tract with a future of equal potential.

The Cup of '46 saw young men just returned from the World War as it had played out at the training base in Beaufort. T.B., unblemished, had felt ready for life when R. Harold Smythe, land agent, put an arm on his shoulders and said, "Son . . ." R. Harold tolled the virtues of land. R. Harold Smythe, bunghole buddies with the governor, himself, had interstate highway routing in his pocket and wanted to die a wealthy man. "You can, too," he said. "Call me up."

T.B. stared off.

Owens pierced the reverie. "Smythe'll be there," he said. "He knows you." Smythe had become Woodrow, son of R. Harold, who had achieved the plushest coffin money could buy.

"He must be seventy," T.B. said.

"Sixty-eight," Owens said. "He has a horse this year—Prufrock or Crotchrot or some such."

"Sure he knows me," T.B. said. "Like his father did."

"He still calls you the man who did nothing." Owens twisted the knife.

"Yes." T.B. gazed out his kitchen window at the land he'd clung to for comfort, in lieu of different comfort.

Owens rambled over horses and their weaknesses.

T.B. scanned the scrub and littered yard for the peace of mind he'd misplaced long ago. "It couldn't be much greater than zero," he said, glancing at Owens. "Our chance of winning."

Owens slashed at thin air. "Unless we win!" Pausing, knife at eye level, he opened the drawer for his cuticle set. Paring green flecks and grease gobs with tiny picks and scythes, he speculated on a new probability, that untrimmed old pork was slow, but leaned out, it would jump and run.

Oh, they had a chance alright. Firmed, trained, trimmed down in the rump and belly, Snapdragon would be formidable as Lightning Sal, Runamock, or President Rutledge. Or Othello!

T.B.'s head ticked up and down, more like a piston short on compression than a nod of conviction. Suddenly still, he stared again, another point at hand. He asked why. Why had the horse one eye and a reputation for no heart?

Owens exclaimed, emphatic as a senator guaranteeing exoneration, "Those charges are nothing! Nothing! Nothing!" The eye was lost to infection, he said, an oversight. The vet had been dismissed. The reputation followed with no reason.

"*Rumorous nonsequiturous*," Owens said, "what the region is known for. He lost the eye. The reputation for no heart derived from not racing and eventually for not winning those races he hadn't run. He hasn't run! His heart is unmeasured, T.B.!"

T.B. sat motionless, indicating absorption.

Owens followed through deductively: within their grasp was an unknown commodity, just as a possibly round world had sprawled before Chris Columbus. Owens was certain of heart. More importantly, the good eye was on the right-hand side, which was not the eye needed for racing.

T.B. moaned, "Bully."

Owens cried, "He's a thirty-thousand-dollar animal!"

T.B. squinted at the sense of it.

Owens held his hands up like goggles. "I have eyes!" he insisted. "I can see!"

T.B. sat back as if to view dinner. "Well done," he said.

Owens stood tall, face like a beacon in victory.

"The pork, Owens. Cook it well done."

Owens dimmed. But things were moving along, better than expected. He'd keep the spirit lively with his specialty, hominy and yams, to shore up the old pork.

By brunch the next day, with nary a nay say, momentum belonged to Owens. The Cup drew near. T.B. did not say no. What was that sound? Little gears and cogs turning inexorably onward. Owens smiled.

"What?" T.B. asked.

Owens shrugged. "I love hominy and yams."

Bristling among the years, in the rub and reminiscence of it all, Alisia Petigru lingered. She'd married well, a rich man whose heavenly aspiration included a chat with God, Himself, for Whom he would stand a round of top-drawer spirits and a round for the heavenly minions, too, because he could. He had the money and would spend it, to show his stuff.

Mrs. Stalworth Grimsley-Hayse, widowed at an early age, became the countess to her friends by request, her request, to reflect "royal antecedents," her phrase. The title would infer direct descent from rule by Divine Right.

They'd spoken last winter in passing. T.B. had stood by a ditch bounding his property, where the interstate highway could have been. Taking a leak into the ditch, he looked up.

Mrs. Grimsley-Hayse had paused in onerous deliberation, rendering the verdict at last, "My word!"

T.B. called, "Cow pies! Steam in your ear!" Turning away too fast, he dribbled on a boot. "Damn you!"

She watched, either perversely or to sear the infraction, an indelible misfortune in the memory archive, as if suffering an offense of social magnitude.

Nonplussed but puzzled, T.B. could not ascertain the source of her apparent discomfort. A man took a whiz in the country. He'd turned around, after all . . . Ah! That was it! He'd turned his back on the Grimsley-Hayse.

She remained obtusely observant, uncivil as when their discourse devolved forty years prior. T.B. had asked why a man needed a name like Stalworth instead of, say, Harry, and why that man would retain his mother's maiden name for any reason but hifalutin hyphenism on a top layer of crust. T.B. had answered the question in asking, as per habit.

Grimsley had been around, landed, tenured and revered.

Alas, Hayse had been more recent and outlandish, immigrating from a neighboring country, such as it was, descended from due north, well-heeled but not original. Stalworth Hayse installed the maternal maiden name to remind and exalt.

Why had T.B. Ratchford asked?

The reason, simple if not obvious: Alisia Petigru, Terryl Boyington Ratchford's first white love, at twenty-two for him, twenty for her. Her farewell sentiment a tearful flurry of harsh reality: Terryl was too close to terrible, and T.B. suggested a horrid disease. She took her leave for betrothal to the House of Grimsley-Hayse forthwith.

Did she mellow over time with money? She summered on the continent but came home in autumn for the Cup. Othello, King of Rook, flew from Antibes to Atlanta and on to Greenville. The last hundred miles to the Cub had him strapped fore and aft under the belly and tethered to a helicopter, delivering him safe if not sound, in a dither and a sweat. "He luuves to fly!" The countess proclaimed their love, falling into his ear with horsey goo goo.

People talked but didn't complain, not with the countess' spread and overwhelming wet bar. Othello won last year, distressed as he was. The countess had gone all in on steroids, banned at once; the horse made such a fuss.

T.B. had shunned the Cup. It represented exclusion of him, his family and his honor. Perceived as reclusive and moody, he was said to have dipped into principal to stay afloat. That was nobody's business but his own, and T.B. Ratchford knew the Cup and excess. He'd belched like broken bellows on too much food and drink, and he'd laughed! That was then. Now was apart.

Also apart, his memory of Alisia Petigru, a fulsome, giggly girl of twenty who got thick by sixty.

And now came the horse with one eye and no heart, out of the blue, unsummoned, heralding a new season. Why? He knew not, but would snatch redemption from the vainglorious society of his subconscious gloom.

Word got around: the Ratchford cousins had a horse. "Derelict" drifted across the county. The Ratchfords or the horse? The standing joke got old like all else.

T.B. felt adrift, without reason or rationale. He'd heard her raucous drivel, dropping names like a foolish woman. She'd come home urgently and would leave again soon or later.

Woody Smythe arranged a homecoming and farewell reception. T.B. wasn't invited. He could attend and let them snigger. But why? Was he the greater fool? Had Owens drawn him in? Would they crawl together up and out of the mud?

Hail Mary, full of doubt, he crossed days from his calendar, three weeks to go. Owens, the naïve drifter on a hapless gelding, reaching for the gold ring. Were they so desperate?

Owens, less encumbered, spirit unbridled, leaned into
training. Or wanted to. The sale stalled when the seller refused a
mortgage on Ratchfordshire as collateral, even for the humble
sum of five hundred dollars.

"Is that place an asset or a liability?"

Owens had no more to offer but honor.

The seller chuckled. The impasse resolved when Owens
threw his hands in the air to mutter soap, glue, Jell-O from the
hooves and walked away.

The seller called him back to document the transaction,
detailing a long list of failures from the buyer.

T.B. called it the modern Magna Carta.

Owens said flexibility was the better part of hope, and T.B.'s
wit was arid as the south greensward, or what used to be.

They had no funding for sideboard and wet bar, both critical
to a Cup campaign, especially in the event of loss.

T.B. rose to the occasion. They would approach the Cup like
artists, from need. Loss was incomprehensible. As sideboard
manager, T.B. would determine funding and betting strategy.
Owens shouldn't worry. "Train him to win, Owens. The rest will
take care of itself." Owens wondered and leaned further in.

The horse, a tall dapple gray, had his mane bobbed and tied.
Unlike most thoroughbreds, he followed a lead gently, perhaps
realizing that someone at last saw him. He'd suffered the slings
and arrows of his handicap but stood to spectacular height and
stance, formidable. Owens said, "His heart is strong."

Dragon snorted and shied.

Training began on garden produce, liberating the grocery budget, twenty-four dollars weekly. Owens wanted to shed a few pounds anyway, but delay and diet were minor.

Snapdragon shied from his blind side, the rail side. Owens tried scaring him into a left turn with the help of a barn tom in a cage on the right. Dragon pulled back in fear.

T.B. thought it over in the shed, among the anvils, hoops, stays, bungs, mallets and other tools of antebellum function. Emerging two hours hence with an odd, glistening harness, he strapped it into place and moved around for perspective.

Owens shook his head. An oval mirror covered the empty socket. Another mirror hung from baling wire and straps acutely angled to the first mirror and six inches out front. Cheek to cheek, as if to tango, T.B. eyeballed the mirror out front, adjusting the angle and stepping back to see the pleasing point of proof.

Snapdragon saw it, too; rolling his good eye over his nose could reveal the counterclockwise direction of the Cup.

Owens mounted up, inspired when the horse cantered wrong way around the yard. Whinnying and bobbing, Dragon spoke to a side of life too long in the dark.

T.B. removed the harness for refinement and reinforcement.

But problems solved bore problems anew. Finally harnessed to the gift of left-hand vision, the horse could not choose which hurdle to judge and jump, the one out front or the one in the mirror. The solution was for Owens to reach forward and cover the socket mirror with his hand at the moment of reckoning.

Although sacrificing a majority interest in stability, he conceded the small price to pay to clear the jump ahead.

Next up: strength and endurance. Owens requested and was granted twelve dollars weekly for extra oats and vitamins.

T.B. allocated funds from the wet-bar budget and covered the deficit with two cases of forty-year-old bourbon bottles. Washing them inside and out and cleaning the labels, he refilled with a funnel and new bourbon, saving thirty-two dollars weekly, after oats and vitamins. Seasoned corks were plentiful.

The two weeks remaining felt historic with T.B. on board, bearing up, stretching dollars with imagination.

He traded a new bourbon to Ellis Brown for catfish. Skinned, dressed, diced and spiced for a light meunière sauté, they went to sterling trays as catfish canapés. A crumbling cookbook from a recent century provided the recipe and helpful hints.

"Flavor with fennel to taste." T.B. and Owens felt diligent, settling in to simple repast, bourbon, string beans and fennel. T.B. said he'd loved green beans ever since when.

Though relieved on a cheerful note, Owens had hit the dirt too often on the jumps. He thought failure occurred in the reach, just prior. "Uncovering the mirror screws me up. If I let go too soon, he changes his measure, I think. If I wait too long, he lands fine, but I don't do so well."

T.B. reflected aloud on a shutter, cockpit controlled.

Owens said he had no cockpit.

"Like a camera shutter," T.B. said.

Owens pushed his string beans aside and sipped bourbon. "You can fix it, so I won't fall off?"

"I'll try," T.B. said, bolstering morale by unveiling sideboard samples of catfish canapés and candied yams on crackers.

Owens tried each. "Candied yams for crackers," he said. They chuckled, rednecks to the core. Crackerdom, however, was anathema, white trash, sometimes poor. Owens asked how the sideboard would keep for ten days to the Cup.

T.B. had fired up the deep-freeze his Great Aunt Mayrose left him in 1957, her only bequeathal to anyone, though she did return everyone's peace of mind when she croaked. They toasted Mayrose on another round, on an enjoyable evening of stories.

T.B. designed the shutter in a day and took two more to build it. Owens jumped and landed smoothly. The shutter was a slat, formerly a cypress shingle, spring-loaded with steel wire, controlled with a rawhide cord. Owens apologized, saying he'd never felt better for a prospect, and it was daunting.

"Yes," T.B. said. "We'll likely win the Cup." He stared off. "Tomorrow is Woody Smythe's reception. I'd be such a cad for crashing. All that sort of thing goes away if you win the Cup. But what if we lose?"

"I saw Woody Smythe at the tack shop yesterday." Owens said. "I told him I was afraid our invitation got lost in the mail. He said he was afraid it had not."

"I'm glad you told me that."

"Sorry."

"I mean it, Cuz. I think we'll attend together."

They gazed in parallel. "We haven't done a social outing."

"No," T.B. said. "I think we haven't."

Woody Smythe's reception was anticipated, imagined, inflated with glittering promise. "Not certain why we bother," T.B. said on the way. "Crusty farts getting drunk."

Owen shrugged. "We'll try to fit in."

They wore vintage tails from rum time, when importation paid those whose property bordered a river. The mothball smell faded on airing, pockets stuffed with rabbit tobacco and mint. They seemed taller under shoulder pads, in vogue then. Sherry bolstered spirits, a half pint for courage.

Anticipating the tepid welcome reserved for crashers, they walked into the lantern-lit crowd tittering across the greensward of Smythehaven, hardly noticing two more. Johnny Mack noticed, as a servant should. Well-known on the circuit for ancestry, Johnny Mack descended from Daddy Ancrum, known for an honest day's work. Those were the days, prior to an honest day's pay. Johnny Mack shone, offering sherry on a tray. "Mr. T.B., sir. Mr. Owens."

Owens took one. "They say to drink the good stuff first."

T.B. said, "Too late. Not to worry. We'll make do."

Johnny Mack belonged to the countess in the figurative sense and was loaned out for entertainments. Standing by as the cousins drained the little goblets, he prescribed another, advising that a crowd this big could take a while between rounds.

The newcomers agreed, easing into arrival. Meandering the great lawn, they drifted to raucous laughter on the far side, near the punch bowl. Garbled praise for Othello's landing and survival would continue until the last crumpet got smashed in the sodden tracks of the last car leaving the Cup. Or until he was beaten. "The Grimsley-Hayes is here," T.B. said.

Owens pointed. "The Grimsley-Snowdens, too. Remember their horse, President Rutledge? He can't win."

"He can hardly run."

"But the Grimsley-Snowdens throw a party to celebrate their being. We haven't been invited."

"Have we gone?"

The cousins chortled, above that little world. Those who competed enjoyed elevation, after all, with stakes so high. A Cup winner was sacrosanct. Consequence was real. Anxiety prevailed.

The Ellisons and Pringles commiserated on the responsibility of position, both families original, both sustaining total loss on Sherman's march to the sea, not so long ago. Honor intact, they'd restored nobility to the region in the last century, Mercedes, a black Lab retriever and entry to the Cup filled the bill. They agreed on love of tradition and the regal, rural sense of the thing. That was to say, the plantation sentiment, damn the expense. The show set them apart, and they loved that, too. The Pringles and Ellisons doubted Cupcakes or Hop'n John stood a chance, but they'd have a go.

The DuRants and Rutledges stood a chance, each family winning this century.

Miss Marguerite Kanapeaux also mingled. Barely forty, in her twenty-third year of eligibility but hardly a spinster, her beauty served as a resource. Sadly, Marguerite's parents had died suddenly from bad oysters, typhus, three decades prior, leaving Marguerite millions for a life of happiness. She came forth, greeting the cousins with a touch, leaning in for a kiss.

They blushed.

She said, "You have a horse!"

T.B. looked sheepish, like a boy caught in a prank.

Owens nodded.

"I'm so happy for you! I hope you win!" Marguerite's horse, Lightning Sal, had won two years running, two years ago. "We're taking it easy this year, Sal and I."

Owens' eyebrow rose; Lightning Sal was a threat.

"I heard he's swayback, one eye and can't hear."

"No," Owens said. "Not swayback. His hearing is perfect."

"I knew it," she said, asking if she might have a gander.

Owens would have said yes but said, "Horse's ass."

Huguenot was the other heritage of note in the region besides English. Huguenots suffer nobly from too many letters and odd charm, after a fashion. Huger is spoken as yu•GEE and could be a first, last or middle name. They'd intermarried freely with Anglicans, and among the Cup crowd: Rutledge Reid and Reid Rutledge, Pringle Smythe and Smythe Pringle and in extreme unction, Huger Huger, who owned of last year's winner and defending champ Jehosaphat. "Hey!" Huger called from twenty paces and "Hey!" again from ten and two, "Hey!"

"Come again?" Owens asked.

"Hey!" Huger said. "I heard he was deaf!"

"Huger!" Marguerite scolded, giggling, leaning in to peck his cheek.

"Yes," Owens said. "Deaf and lame. Can you imagine how worthless he'd render any horse he beat?"

"Now looka here!" Huger stood straighter. "You can't come in here and . . ."

"But they can," Marguerite said. "They're not outlanders. They been here long as you or me. Longer. Come. Buy me a drink." She led him off, glancing back.

T.B. watched as if unruffled.

The murmuring crowd moved to the punch bowl, where Woody Smythe announced his new horse Prufrock.

T.B. shook it off. "Must we?"

"Private reserve?" Johnny Mack offered brandy.

"Why, thank you, Johnny," Owens said. "I believe we will."

"Yes, sir, Mr. Owens. I believe I will, too." Serving two, Johnny Mack retreated with the last one.

"Come," Owens said, joining the flow. "Scouting report."

T.B. followed like a drogue anchor.

Woody Smythe slurred, too proud too early in the evening, a caricature by rights.

Johnny Mack found the Ratchfords on the edge with two more snifters, too full for the drawing room.

"Thank you," T.B. said.

Owens leaned in for the tip: "Snapdragon to win it all."

Johnny Mack said he'd borrowed against his IRA and would factor Snapdragon in his wagering strategy.

Woody Smythe finally reached Prufrock from four generations back in equine lineage.

The horse came forward.

Owens weaved through the crowd for a closer look.

T.B. eased back for comfort.

She looked up, missing a beat but recovering quickly.

So the evening wound down on a superb port after a fine brandy. The cousins headed out, past a table laden with blueberry pies and apple tortes. A few wouldn't be missed and could add nicely to their sideboard only three days hence. Would they be recognized, the pies? Nah.

On stolen pies and a buzz, they hiked home under the stars, snifters half full.

T.B. said Woody Smythe was too tedious for comfort.

"He sweats too much," Owens said. "And Woody paid twenty-eight grand."

But in the moment of assessing Prufrock's cost and sweat, they stopped when a hitherto raucous voice softly accused, "The boys are at it again. Stealing pies."

T.B., his back to her, said, "Knows all, hears all, sees all."

"Knows all and hears all, perhaps. I heard he sees only half."

"Ah, caught out," he said.

"Some things don't change," she said.

"I'd rather steal pies than kill time."

"Touché," she said. "I'm wagering a great deal on Othello. For fun." She walked off.

In the morning, two days out over silent brunch, Owens wished he could take the day off. But he could not. Returning near dusk, he said training had gone well.

T.B. smiled dimly into the night and despaired by morning the day before the race.

Owens cracked a bottle of cheap bourbon and poured two shorts, to bolster the glory of victory.

T.B. rasped like the cellar door. "Glory?" He poured it back. "Is that us, Owens? Claiming our rightful due? I think not!"

"What about not accepting what's been ours? What about invincibility in the face of all odds?"

"Yes, ignorance and bliss. We lost it."

Owens knew these depths.

Holding steady on the oblique plane, T.B. was stuck.

"Should we quit?" Owens asked.

"Mm," T.B. nodded.

Owens drank. "You're right. Better quit than be humiliated. Embarrassment wouldn't be the half of it. The butt of it to Kingdom Come; that's what. Defeat is one thing. We could live with that, if we were normal and had a normal horse. Nobody could say we didn't try. As it is, we set ourselves up. You can't fuck with history!" He drank.

"You rarely express my feelings so succinctly, Owens." T.B. sighed. "Can you imagine? Catfish canapés?"

"The butt of it," Owens said.

They brooded, defeated for the best, sooner rather than later.

"Private fools are better than public," Owens said. "What about the horse?"

"Give it back." T.B. said.

"We can give it back, but we'll owe the money."

"It won't be the first money we owe."

"I think he'll sue."

"He can sue. He can go to hell." T.B. laughed at his own insolence, refilled and drank.

Owens looked out the window. He could enter alone, but it wouldn't do. A transient with a horse couldn't enter the Cup. Well, he was a Ratchford, and he'd been around, but losing alone on a heartless one-eyed gelding with mirrors and baling wire would banish him from marginal fringes, much less the kingdom.

T.B. was off, muttering old age, caution, contentment and value, trailing further off to ridicule and the butt of it.

Owens left the eulogy. He came back with a carpetbag, packed, the one left by Uncle Allston Greely Ratchford, lieutenant governor, '81-'85, would-be governor but dead by '86. Uncle Allston had beat George Washington Green for lieutenant governor and won the bet, too, the bag against Ratchfordshire in the election of '81.

The bag would leave as it had come, half empty in the hands of a desperado trying to be somebody.

Owens faced his mentor as he'd imagined he would one day. He'd envisioned humble thanks in subtle irony for the work he'd been allowed to do. He filled T.B.'s tumbler to the brim, so no sip would come before a spill. "There you are, T.B. I doubt your life will be so full. Enjoy it while you can."

T.B. suffered, had played a losing hand close to the chest for too long. His face slumped, as if showing cards.

It would have ended there, the Cup and chance, but for a probability greater than zero delivering a rap to the front door, quaking foundations at Ratchfordshire: a visitor.

"The world comes to those who live in it," Owens said. "I'm sure this kind of nuisance will cease." He went to answer the call.

Marguerite Kanapeaux, blushing as a trysting wife, framed in the glare of her orange Mercedes sedan, looked back as if for the jealous wife and rushed in.

Looking side to side, she asked, "Who died?"

"T.B.," Owens said. "He lost his nerve."

"Well, he better get it back. Do you know what the horse's ass is doing? He's called the Rules Committee to stop entries at noon. He can do that. You're the only ones not entered. Get your things. I'll take you over."

"He's worried about us?"

"That's what I said," she said. "He found out that your horse's great grandfather was Prince Valiant, and his mother was Queen of Sheba. He's posted an open bet, honor bound."

T.B. raised the short, slurping to minimize the spill.

"Open bet on Jehosaphat to win, fifty thousand," she said.

Weary, T.B. whined, "You can't bet fifty thousand unless you have fifty thousand."

"I'll buy your horse now for fifty thousand dollars."

T.B. squinted. "He has one eye!"

"Yes, but you've fixed that. And, frankly, I'm attracted to that sort of thing, you know."

"Well . . . then . . ." T.B. bobbed, nodding off or spending vicariously.

"Might I have a minute with my cousin?" Owens asked.

"Certainly," she said, stepping out.

As the door clicked shut, Owens thundered, "No!" On that negative note, his life began again, in the future. "We race!"

"I can't," T.B. said, matter-of-fact.

"You must." Owens gripped his arm.

"I can't!"

"You won't! If you'll neither jump nor crawl, then you're too far gone!" T.B. looked away, reaching for the whiskey, but Owens backhanded the bottle. T.B. hung his head, also shattered.

Owens strode to the sink, filled a pot with water and strode back to douse his cousin, his mentor.

Marguerite came back in, invisible as life to T.B. Ratchford, dripping in a chair.

She offered her flask. "Here. Try some of mine."

He tilted it back.

Owens filled the pot.

T.B. sputtered, "Owens. I can't."

Owens poured again.

"But I will."

"We must hurry," she said.

T.B. said, "I only have my tuxedo."

"Put it on," she said.

Odds narrowed.

Owens paced. He asked Marguerite to take the old man over; he had so much to do.

She hesitated but asked if the Snapdragon Syndicate might want to borrow fifty thousand against the horse. "The horse would be worthless on a loss, but like I say, I'm attracted to that sort of thing. I think you'll win, and I do want Huger in the loser's circle. Why is he despondent?"

Owens shrugged. "He carries the torch for the countess."

"Oh God. Kinky."

Owens stayed behind for grooming and communion.

On the way to registration, Marguerite asked if T.B. could keep a confidence.

Glazed as a mummy, he said, "I will."

"I've been sent on strict confidence, she said. "Mrs. Grimsley-Hayes."

He turned, undead.

She shivered in a way heretofore reserved for critical moments. This year's odd Cup was paying out.

On the surface, the Cup shone golden, reflecting high society at play. Without a victory last year, Huger Huger could have been dismissed, a bore with bad breath. The win, however, put him on everyone's A list. Sudden glory did not help his manners. He yelled at the orange sedan. "Too late, old man, you lose!"

T.B. signed at the registrar's table.

"Do you have a hundred dollars?" the registrar asked.

Marguerite gave him the money.

He paid it.

"I didn't know it was a hundred dollars," he said.

"You didn't have a hundred dollars!" Huger yelled.

T.B. turned to Huger. "I knew your father,"

"He knew about you!"

"You remind me of him. Incredible likeness."

Huger huffed and puffed, as if holding back.

"You've issued a bet, Huger?"

"That's right. Fifty thousand," the registrar affirmed.

"I'll see your fifty thousand and raise you ten cents."

"That's not how we do things around here," Huger said.

"Put up or shut up," T.B. said.

"You don't have fifty dollars! Much less fifty thousand!"

"He has fifty thousand," Marguerite said.

"Oh, Fricassee . . ." Huger moaned.

"I asked you not to call me that, Huger. I can't go into it. It's an old debt. I had no idea T.B. would call it in now. But he has. I'm honor bound."

T.B. smiled at the volley and said, "Your money please."

She wrote a check.

He added a dime.

Huger dug for his dime, grumbling, "Goddamn Cup ain't what it used to was."

The registrar, Allston Huger Rutledge, held the bet.

On the drive back, T.B. asked, "Where was she?"

Marguerite wondered if she might one day piss away all her money so foolishly. "Saving herself for tomorrow night, I'd bet."

"Oh, God," T.B. said.

At home, T.B. said thank you.

With a hug, she gave him a bottle of blended whiskey from the case in her trunk. "For the stretch." And she was off.

He found Owens in the barn, grooming, coaching on the will to win, attitude, ability, destiny and family honor, both Ratchford and equine. He interrupted, "Owens."

"Yes."

T.B. related his exchange with Huger and the wager.

Owens said he'd tried to insult T.B. out of his funk and failed. They owed that much to Huger Huger. They spent the afternoon in the barn, on a bale, in a comfort meant for kings.

Near dusk, T.B. said he hadn't cowered to failure but to fear of losing what took so long to gain: solitary contentment.

Stars twinkled where the tin roof had failed.

"Solitary?" Owens asked. "What am I? A kitchen utensil?"

"You know what I meant, Owens."

"I'm not sure I do. You're not the only one who's spent years on a way of life. I call mine poverty. I didn't hate it at thirty and dirt poor. But now? The place is good, T.B. But a voice told me this morning that some of the boys were planning a breakout, and I could come along, if I have the balls. You know, conning towers, spotlights, machine guns. I told that little voice I wouldn't miss it for the world."

"I suppose money would be nice," T.B. allowed. Night fell on another drink, another thought on the longest shot of their lives, another apple and a carrot, good night and sweet dreams.

Owens whispered in his ear.

Snapdragon snorted agreement.

In lantern light, T.B. ferreted a hay pile for a package and presented it.

Owens unwrapped to silks, breeches and a blouse in emerald green with pink and gray side stripes down the legs and sleeves. The Ratchford crest embroidered on back showed two rats in waistcoats, one with a white mane, the other smaller, not yet fifty, standing on either side of a stream, forepaws locked on the same barbecued rib.

"I've never seen the Ratchford crest," Owens said.

"Me neither. I made it up a few weeks ago, when I was full of piss and vinegar. Do you like it?"

Owens held it up. "Yes." A matching head cowl and saddle blanket filled the bill.

"Where did you get the money?"

"They say I spent the principal," T.B. said. "But I didn't spend it all." They laughed, spending more in their heads until falling asleep in the hay.

By the time Woody Smythe learned that all fifty thousand of Huger Huger's open wager was taken, he'd secured another mortgage on Smythehaven to take the bet himself. Had Woody dipped into principal? The Cup crowd sensed it: a situation worse than terminal. Death with honor was one thing, profligate waste another. The interstate highway had bounded Smythehaven since way back on a federal lease/option with acceleration clauses to support future Smythe generations. R. Harold Smythe had doubled his right-of-way revenue on kickbacks from other distinguished families, whose property the great pavement swerved to touch, endearing the Smythe patron to the region and its heirs. Inheriting wealth, however, Woody Smythe was born to spending, foreign to earning.

He bought oil wells in Mississippi on a tip: Libyans were shopping Mississippi. He owned majority shares in a nuclear device to cure tooth decay. He'd drained two swamps and sodded over for croquet and par three pitch and putt, both with water hazards. He'd excavated for eel ponds when eels were bullish in Tokyo. He drove a car with doors hinged on top.

His remaining asset, FIRECRACKER CITY! still boomed on the interstate highway. Sales were down in rubber tomahawks, giant combs, T-shirts, back scratchers and foot-long hot dogs, but cherry bombs were up.

Prufrock would restore greatness in the Cup.

Finding Huger at home early on race day, Woody Smythe asked for another bet. Huger agreed, and each wrote a check to the other for fifty grand. The checks were tacked to a porte cochere pillar of Hugerland.

The countess declined the offer. "Of course not. If Prufrock wins, I lose fifty thousand. If Othello wins, I put you out of Smythehaven. It doesn't suit." How did she know?

He said thanks all the same and headed for the DuRants.

They said alright, they supposed they would. Runamock had been looking very well, and a bet made the Cup more exciting. Frankly, they thought they'd win, no offense. Two more nods, another shake, and two more personal checks @ fifty grand were tacked to a front pillar of DuRantwood.

The Ellisons and Pringles chuckled in constrained embarrassment; neither could stand the bet. But Marguerite Kanapeaux said yes.

Woody Smythe turned for Ratchfordshire, feeling lucky.

"Hallo!" he yelled, pounding the door. "My God," he mumbled, around back. He'd heard poor whites lived like this but never believed it. He found the cousins snoring in the hay beside the bottle, so he tiptoed in to see the mystery mount. A stranger on the blind side got a whinny and naysay, waking the cousins, who grasped at who and what.

"Wha?"

"Who?"

"Hell of a day for a hangover!" Woody yelled.

The horse jolted and kicked, too skittish.

Woody doubted these crackers would pay up, but he wouldn't fare so bad on a loss. What could they do? "Hey now. Ah enjoy yo type o' livin'. Ah sholey do. The infamality of it all. You wanna make a bet?"

T.B. deferred, "Owens?"

"What do we have to lose?" Owens asked.

"Good then," Woody offered his hand.

T.B. shook it, pulling himself up.

"Personal checks?" Woody asked.

"Don't use them."

"Personal notes then?"

T.B. agreed.

Woody drafted: IOU fifty thousand dollars if Prufrock beats Snapdragon in the Cup or vice versa. Each signed both, and Woody Smythe called it a morning, make that a two-hundred-grand day. Converted to pesos and invested in Guanajuato treasury bonds, already discounted eighty percent, that would make two and a quarter in borrowing power by tomorrow. If that wouldn't guarantee Jefferson Rutledge Simmons to the Senate of the United States of America, then what? A military airstrip on the far side of Smythehaven opposite the interstate highway would make jobs for the people! Look away!

Meanwhile, the countess had sent her man, Longstreet, to those owners she proposed to bet. He carried a half dozen signed checks and a pad of thumbtacks. He came home with three checks unused and one inscribed on the back from Marguerite Kanapeaux, wagering champagne luncheon for fifty. The other two checks got posted with the DuRants and Huger Huger, for a total wager of a hundred thousand. "All for the best," she told Longstreet. "Some years we go easy. Othello appears to be tired."

"Yes Ma'am," Longstreet said, headed to the track for Othello's arrival by helicopter. Longstreet would jockey.

The countess emerged from her boudoir shortly after breakfast to review preparations for the Cup Ball, a Grimsley-Haysemont tradition. The countess chortled; she could call the place Buckingham Palace, given its grandeur. But that would tease presumption, even for herself.

Reaching for the old lucky feeling, Huger Huger headed over to the track via Miss Marguerite's place to see if she might share a need down south. A woman sees luck on a man. And what better way to relax for the Cup?

She came forth in a negligee, sipping a morning cup. Huger Huger said, "Hey. Jist stopped on by."

She offered coffee and turned to get it, knowing he'd follow.

He sipped and asked, "Wanna make a bet?"

She thought Lightning Sal a fair match for Jehosaphat and said, yes, fifty thousand, if he'd spot her a length.

He said he'd spot her a length if she'd lay him some odds.

She said fair enough, five to four.

He nodded, she nodded, they shook, wrote checks for forty and fifty grand and tacked them to a front post of Villa de Kanapeaux; pillars were overdone and obtrusive.

Huger said, "Well . . . er, uh . . ."

She said, "Not likely. And your breath. You may be unwell."

He chuckled and left, ending first-round betting.

T.B. made the track by ten, bruised but intact, catfish canapés and candied yams on crackers in tow, thawing nicely. He also took the early lead in hospitality, backing Johnny Mack's hot coffee with blueberry pies and apple tortes. A hangover needs sugar, and the early crowd was humbled in gratitude. T.B. took kudos in silence, staring off from the linen-covered tailgate of Ratchfordshire's old truck.

Owens was up early ironing silks, grooming and dressing himself and the horse, walking to the track to loosen up, get some air, let the mirrors and shutter settle in.

Horses were seeded according to wagers to assure the best finale. Seven seeds for seven heats and the final for winners. With a hundred thousand wagered, Snapdragon got the seventh and last seed over horses with smaller or no bets.

Runamock drew sixth, Othello fifth, Lightning Sal fourth. Tenure tipped the scale on equal bets. Jehosaphat got third, and Prufrock, also at two hundred thousand, drew second. President Rutledge got first seed for no heat on no wagers by special dispensation to honor his name or tradition or something. Too old to win, he'd shuffle across the finish on his way to the finale.

The first race filled out with no-chances, primarily Hop'n John and Cupcakes. Allston Pringle, staid and dull as a bank VP, felt anarchy in the air, ditching his jacket and loosening his tie before lunch. Despairing for a win, maybe cracking up, he saw hope as a flicker in the gloom and laughed aloud for confidence.

Allston Pringle showed negative net on the bottom line, his Mercedes and black Lab past middle age and Pringleberry Glenn leveraged to a tilt. A Cupcakes win in the first heat could justify a noble wager on the finale. Tipping his flask, he, too, drifted, longing, wondering if the vague shape in the distance was landfall or mirage. He'd made an unsecured loan to a bank VP on a signature, hardly more than a small farm loan with no risk on weather. He'd made the loan to himself and spared Althea the worry. He would surprise her with the win. Seven hundred people at the Cup. Allston Pringle was one of those stories.

By noon, the Cup grounds thrummed: horses, jockeys, cars and trucks, sideboards end-to-end from starting gate to first turn, around for the backstretch and the clubhouse to the homestretch. The crowd flowed past whiskies, wines, bubblies, meats, fishes, fowls and fancy dishes. This was the Cup, serene country silence cleaved by the hiss of bicarbonates and low moans of relief, building to effervescence, ready to go again. "Hello!"

By a quarter past noon, Cupcakes had won the first race, which meant nothing, except to Allston Pringle, whose clenched fists and twisted face showed hope in a restoration and history in the making. Cupcakes beat President Rutledge, five-time winner.

T.B. spotted the banker in the shade, punching a calculator. T.B. thought to propose a wager, but Woody Smythe spotted, swooped and made the kill for twenty-five thou, a hefty sum for Allston Pringle, in whom a glimmer rose to dazzling shine.

Woody laid him three to one and threw in two lengths for goodwill with a slap on the back to boot.

T.B. winced at the miss, as Woody gazed with vague familiarity at the last apple torte. T.B. suggested upping their bet.

Woody said, "Sho, fo two to one."

"Three to one might be better for a horse with one eye."

Woody Smythe agreed that the poor beast had not much of a chance, so they upped their bet to seventy-five.

T.B. had already won two dollars in the first.

The countess arrived at twelve thirty with an entourage, drivers, coordinators, cooler bearers, ice porters, assistants and valets. Not slaves; that was over. In a dither and a sweat, she cried, "Othello? Has he arrived? Othello?" The *chop, chop, chop, chop, chop* came on cue from the northwest, the horse squirming into view. "He's here!" The countess hurried to Othello's descent.

Huger Huger and the DuRants asked to raise their bets.

But the countess scolded, "Can't you see he's upset!" She stopped at Johnny Mack's sideboard for review.

Johnny Mack had set up next to T.B.

She demanded more champagne, adjusting the roasts, dips, nuts and fruits and fromage.

T.B. called, "Alisia. Thank you."

"Not at all." But seeing his sideboard and bar she headed to the registrar for seedings and wagers. "A hundred thousand dollars," she said on return.

"A hundred twenty-five."

"You've been funded." It sounded like indictment.

"Alisia . . ." The name didn't wear well. She further feared her other former label, the lowly Petigru. "I've been . . . I could have . . . And you . . ." At a loss, far from home, he turned his palms up, as he'd seen the Pope do.

"Your presumption here today . . . Your . . ." She showed subtle disgust. "Your familiarity . . ."

The crowd rose to howling crescendo. Prufrock had won the second. Woody Smythe howled loudest, second across the finish.

Many moans regretted his near trampling.

She spun on an exit.

Filling two tumblers with Woody Smythe's private reserve, Johnny Mack advised no worries; "It won't be but a peck of races till times change for Mr. T.B."

T.B. joined the toast but churned.

Johnny Mack said, "Come on, man. Esprit de coe don't mean shit, you ain't got some joy de viver, too. Don'chou worry'bout her majesty. She come around."

T.B. nodded and asked for the bottle.

Johnny Mack complied.

T.B. sought consolation with his cousin and his horse.

Huger Huger stood at the finish, legs spread, arms folded. The bell rang, third race, and he got out of the way. The crowd gained momentum on drink and good cheer.

Owens and Snapdragon rested under a tree near the paddock, chewing grass. Well-bred children at the fence stared at the one-eyed horse and poor cousins.

T.B. sat. "How much longer you reckon till good times?"

"Is the hundred thousand to invest, or will we spend it?

"It's a hundred twenty-five. I upped it with Smythe when he upped his with Pringle."

"We'll get retail ribs and decent brandy." Owens took the Smythe reserve and turned it up. "I've acquired a taste for this in a very short time."

"Yes. We oughta be livin' the dream by sundown."

Owens smiled, lay back and closed his eyes.

T.B. took over the watch.

Jehosaphat won easily in the third, Lightning Sal in the fourth. Othello lost in the fifth to Henry IX, an upset blamed on Johnny Mack, who failed to press.

Worse yet, Henry IX was owner-ridden. Gaillard Cabriolet-Pinckney had married Courtenay LeFleur of the Red Hills LeFleurs, but had no jockey. What? Unspeakable is what. Cabriolet-Pinckney's gray matter never gelled, they said. Henrys I through III missed jumps to roll on their shoulders. Cabriolet-Pinckney shot each with his Great, Great, Great, Great Grandfather Simons Smythe-Pinckney's dueling pistol, point-blank to the head.

Why, when injection was available and tasteful? Cabriolet-Pinckney said, "Whom do you think forgets!"

Henry IV, or Bolingbroke, sole exception, survived two jumps but failed the third. Pinckney had conceded to injection. Executions resumed for Henry's V through VIII.

Henry IX marked history, completing the course intact, his advance to the finale a wild card, unforeseen.

The cousins shared a bracer.

By then, Dragon's lineage had gained currency. People laughed. A one-eyed horse? Win the Cup? But jocularity submerged to slur and misty recollection, such as it was.

Snapdragon odds improved, as top-drawer folk, tipsy, heart-burned and hoarse, agreed on the best Cup ever. Last heat coming up, the crowd murmuring, tension rose.

T.B. Owens and Dragon marched to destiny in color and pomp. Mirrors sparkled, and they drew cheers of rebellion and scorn. The cousins shook hands at the gate, their trembling unseen to a thousand eyes.

Owens leaned in. "I plan to save him. It's only an hour to the finale, so don't worry if it's close."

T.B. said no, he wouldn't worry. He stepped back in reverie that got smashed to smithereens on a gunshot.

And they were off.

Snapdragon won it, walking away.

The crowd remaining at five was hard-core, drunk, talked out, anxious to go home for a nap before the Ball. Yet they knew this finale would be different, not in the tradition of great horse races through history but more or less, different.

The fun was over. The horses sensed it, too, the blue bloods among them skittish at the gate.

Prufrock bolted and Woody Smythe yelled, "No! No! No!"

The registrar called time and tide and no man. He fired the gun, and once again, this time for keeps, they were off.

Owens maneuvered to put Gaillard Cabriolet-Pinckney on Snapdragon's mirror side out of the first turn. With the lowering sun behind them in the back stretch, shutter open, Cabriolet-Pinckney would see the light. The move would be recalled for years as that of an expert horseman.

Henry IX missed the far hazard, taking Runamock and Prufrock into the shrubs with him.

Jehosaphat came on near the clubhouse, with Cupcakes surprisingly close, but Owens' gentle nudge to Dragon's flank showed the difference in breeding and class. The second lap was a formality, and history was written, Snapdragon, Cup Champion.

Shadows reached over the weakened crowd, momentum waning, a boisterous toast here, a depressed rave there.

Woody Smythe sobbed at the gate.

Huger Huger threatened to geld him if his check bounced.

T.B. and Owens shared a toast with a new bottle of Smythe reserve. The crowd dispersed, trucks and cars pulling out, leaving the sodden, trampled track in weary aftermath and two men basking in silent glory.

The Cup wedded winners to history. They alone in the thundering herd remained unvanquished. Their names lingered on the lips of many and the breeze. It rustled the mossy oaks.

Presenting his card, one Gervais Haupt-Manigault, attorney at law, informed the cousins, personally and confidentially, that he could represent the Ratchfords in fiduciary matters and legal what not with particular regard to collection from Smythe et al, and in the event of default, liquidation of the aforementioned Smythehaven. "Gentlemen." The sun set to horizontal, putting the countryside in a blaze.

Haupt-Manigault wanted to chat in the lovely twilight ahead, but Mrs. Simons LeCompte Simmons interrupted to hope that the Ratchford biographies and memoirs would soon be part of the State Historical Society's permanent archive.

She, too, got preempted, when Mrs. Florence Rutledge-LeGare (luh•GREE), of the Queen Street LeGares, said indeed, the Snapdragon Archives were best bound for the State Library Society. Not to be outspoken, Elizabeth Windsor-Riley urged the cousins to share recipes with the State Culinary Society.

Marguerite Kanapeaux awarded each cousin with a peck on a cheek, lingering to tell Owens she'd never seen horseflesh handled so well. She said winning looked good on him, and so would she, as escort to the Ball, if he liked.

Dumbfounded, he stared.

"I love it with a winner. I'm attracted to that sort of thing, you know. Do you think me odd?"

Owens thought to say he hadn't been invited. But speaking gave way to realizing: those words, like all else in the realm of past consideration, no longer applied. "Yes. I would like you on my arm. And yes, I think you odd."

Marguerite said toodles; they would meet again soon.

T.B. asked, "Did the countess send you?"

"She meant no harm," Marguerite said. "And besides, the winner must attend. It's not the Ball otherwise. It would be a terrible snub. I think it's never been done!"

"No. I can't imagine," T.B. said, shuffling off to the truck.

He woke in the dark from a dream of watching races not run. He looked in Owens' room and the kitchen, craving a cold beer and supper. He showered, dressed comfortably in dungarees and for the occasion spray starched his shirt and put in collar stays.

Outside, under the stars, he knew it was no dream. They'd won the Cup. He found five dollars in his pocket and drove down the road for a sandwich and a beer. He came home to lamplight and undressed, crawled into bed and slept like a victorious man.

Owens called next morning. He'd been told he was no longer peculiar or shiftless. He'd been transformed to eccentric, prudent and independent. He'd been told he looked like an heir and complimented on formidable sexual durability.

"Congratulations, Owens."

Owens said Snapdragon also slept well, in Marguerite's stable, and that he, Owens, had picked up Huger's check from the registrar and would cash it first thing Monday. Until then, he supposed he'd stay put.

T.B. said, "I understand."

Owens said, "T.B., I think she was humbled."

"You must have been quite something, Owens."

"Not her. The Grimsley-Hayse. She tried to make light of it but couldn't. The victor has never not been to the Ball. The old girl was shook, T.B."

"I think you should call on her," Marguerite said, nearby. "I think flowers would sit her down."

"I'll think it over," T.B. said. "Goodbye."

And he did, on the front porch that day. He thought the next day in the garden, mostly weeds. He thought in the barn and the kitchen, prepping retail roast.

Owens came home Tuesday for a few things and said, "You know, T.B., she's quite a woman. I think she likes me."

"We'd all like to think so." T.B. advised taking time.

"I do," Owens said. "I like it slow, but sometimes I go fast, like a race, with strategy and all. She says I'm sensitive." He left.

T.B. relaxed. Soon, the Cup and the Ball were stories told so many times they were part of what everyone already knew.

Allston Pringle moved to Spartanburg the following month, banished as it were, trading his Mercedes for a domestic wagon, for the kids and groceries. He got enough for his horse and Pringleberry Glenn to pay debts and secure a little place near his new hometown, convenient to church, schools and shopping.

The State Humane Society reported in its monthly newsletter that Gaillard Cabriolet-Pinckney had broken both legs in the Cup and waited a painless injection.

Smythehaven went to probate, where Woody Smythe could keep it for his lifetime, because Judge Gerard Huger Smythe was a Smythe first and a young man, and Smythes stuck together.

T.B. Ratchford finally rounded the clubhouse turn late one afternoon when the florist arrived with a single rose and an invitation to tea at Grimsley-Haysemont. He thought he'd go but maybe not. He might head to town for the fall special on mums and glads or call for delivery. The world would come to him, if he wanted it. He'd won the Cup, spawning talk of an era, a dynasty, an astonishing horse called Ratchford's Snapdragon. It suited T.B., the man to beat.

He needed more time to think but picked out a black smoking jacket in velvet, semi-zoot, left behind in '49 by Uncle Greely Grimble-Ratchford, who rode Slowpoke to Savannah and into the Carriage Inn lobby, where he shot up the chandelier with his sidearm, for fun. "I come this far," was Uncle Greely's epitaph but hardly his last hoot.

T.B. remembered him as a bigger man, but the fit was good. So he took it off, hung it up to air, ironed his shirt and put stays in the collar, in case he might decide on a social call.

Resolution loomed in the stretch.

The Luck of the Draw

A love story in drag

I once believed that greatness would be recognized. How could it not, if truly great? But truth gets skewed, leaving greatness as its own fulfillment, often as not.

Great minds and works through history are mostly unknown. Anonymity may be requisite to purest greatness. Knee jerks will recall Mahatma Gandhi or Mother Teresa, claiming anonymity implausible, recognition inevitable, celebrity eventual, which is rarely great. But that's a quibble. Greatness endures on humility, the amateur spirit and inner satisfaction of a job well done.

I qualify.

Or I did, until motivation morphed to revenge. Getting even cannot be great, but for the sweetness, which can be profound. Initial greatness is rarely natural. It's developed from inspiration and in time measurable. My greatness is tainted, as I am known. That's how it goes, with media exposure, compromise, agents, scheduling and other impurities. I sought vengeance and became a household word, but I get ahead of myself.

An author once wrote a book about dunces in the deep South and couldn't get it published, because nobody in New York saw fit to "champion" his cause. He killed himself.

His mother persuaded a well-known author that her late son had written a great book. The well-known author made a few calls and got the book out. It won a Pulitzer Prize. I couldn't finish it, but it showed what a "champion" might achieve on a call. The well-known author had a few prizes himself, his opinion far weightier than chaff on a breeze. The well-known author's assessment was deemed more correct.

My mother wouldn't do that. She wouldn't know whom to browbeat for starters, or what to tell them, short of the sheer, natural genius her son showed as a child, into adolescence and beyond, where he had a tough row to hoe and paid his own way. Even if I dropped a necktie from a rafter, and she followed through, her effort wouldn't take, because "champions" have given way to "platforms." Greatness needs a platform.

The challenge to potential? Who the fuck are you?

I'm nobody, on the ground, no longer moving forward. I would complete the task with minimal pain and mess, leaving only a corpse and nominal clean up. This decision wasn't casual but devastating. Human inclination is social, not solitary. A person who chooses suicide opts for ultimate solitude.

Take hundreds of suicide jumpers from the Golden Gate Bridge. All but one leapt from the city side. The oddball jumped from the west side, facing the deep blue sea. All but one jumped back in, such as it was, briefly.

Suicide represents relief, but for the time between awareness and completion, between the unbearable and eternity. On a practical level, quick and painless with minor bother seemed best to me, until I saw the great efficiency of two birds, one stone. Practicality can be a factor in life decisions, and consequence is good to savor. That is, I would cancel the source of my depression along with myself, making life worthwhile, briefly.

Revenge is self-defeating, unless defeat is foregone. Just as society is meant to help, hope springs that another demise might compensate the ultimate loss.

I got panned and worse. A bad review is tough, but a personal attack that cancels advance sales is severe. Dirty play, blows below the belt, bitterness and contempt are common to a writer's failure. The reviewer could have perched on a bell tower with an assault weapon. He called me "unwashed," an "aging hippie" who apparently participated in "a seedy club, where unwashed miscreants . . ."

"Unwashed" appeared six times in fourteen column inches. A failing writer having a bad day wrote the review. Like many industry periodicals, *Books Biweekly* is gossipy but influential, integral at the wholesale level. A bad review in *Books Biweekly* can erase many months of work. A review earns a couple hundred bucks and remain anonymous. That is, a flunky turned a few bags of groceries for a mercenary-literary rag to appease failures of her own, taking comfort in killing my chance. Did I know her? Why?

These questions led to thoughts of revenge. A brief exchange with Senior Editor Sylvia Silverberg yielded a concession, that the reviewer had no basis for "aging hippie" or "unwashed." The book contained no sex in the street. Would Sylvia run a retraction and apology for the personal attack? No, she couldn't do that. Retractions are not practical or allowed by editorial policy. Would she mind forwarding the name of the reviewer, so we might correspond?

I reminded Ms. Silverberg of devastating consequence, depriving me of income, present and future. The "facts" stated had no basis, the places, dates and critical references incorrect. My book, though masculine was not macho and therefore not fair game for slur from an unstable reviewer.

Sylvia Silverberg would not disclose the reviewer's name but promised to affirm the substance of my complaints with her managing editor, who would present those complaints to the reviewer. I was copied in, with the reviewer's name reduced to "V". Many paragraphs of drivel concluded that I was wrong: V was not woman but man, a man's man to be sure, a man who lived by the pen and knew how to treat a lady. Beyond that, a retraction would appear in the next six months.

It sounded grim. She'd proven my theory that the reviewer was female—or homosexual, transsexual or transvestite; not that it mattered, but the publisher had unwittingly given the first clue of a long and arduous sleuthing. *Knows how to treat a lady?* Who talks like that but a New York publishing chippy, deluded that anything she says can fool whoever she chooses?

Oh, I would find this reviewer. Call him X. No, that's racist. Call him Y. It doesn't matter—call him Elemenopee for all I care. The hard reality was: this motherfucker's going down. I would find her. I would engage her. It would seem serendipitous. We would imbibe and let down our guards through cocktails, unwinding for a nice wallow in what we held self-evident. I would learn why she spilled my blood on a petty kill. I would learn her worst fear, like in *Brave New World* with rats. I would give her poison oak. I would show her photos of her ex in acts of submission with a huge other, one hung like a rhinoceros, like *The Magus* with his young initiate. Or a Latino, Bosnian, Sherpa or Sikh, one right out of a taxi after a double shift, dirty and downtown scented with matching syntax, grammar and usage.

The hours and days were not a healing meditation but were bent on orchestration, building to crescendo in a perfect score for pain and suffering.

Sylvia's sophistry would not get this problem slipped under the rug. The greater problem fleshed out: merely killing myself would resolve nothing. I'd already been assassinated. I still lived and breathed on a single motive, to blot the failed reviewer at BB: V. I fomented, far from greatness. It felt unnatural but good. I savored an accounting but had less to go on than foolish Jack, who traded the family cow for magic beans.

Never mind. I went to New York and took a cab to Manhattan and walked into *Books Biweekly*.

Yes, in, past security with penultimate New York superiority, dominance, importance, world-shaping urgency and the rest. I'd considered a disguise, say, a pizza delivery uniform or a jumpsuit and a tool belt but in the end cloaked myself in confidence and clarity. Just that easily, in and up to the second floor, I realized that the building had many tenants, and BB security began just off the elevator.

Downshifting for traction, I strode boldly to security. "Joaquin Mismaloya. Seelvia Seelvarbarg ees expect of me." Security nodded and picked up a house phone, keeping me in peripheral vision until doors opened on two fay fellows sprightly engaged in the pros and cons of subtext played to prevalence, when interior monologue outweighs exterior action. "¡Hola, hombres!" Out-faying them, I hugged one in passing, warm and sinewy as required.

He blushed, perhaps afraid to admit he'd forgotten us.

I strode in and onward. "Escuse. Luego. A este noche." A duck left, jog right, a zig and a zag and into a cubicle cum closet, I waited. My ingress lingered at security. As luck would have it, a young author with budding greatness on a fabulous platform arrived, and in no time, calm and relaxed, I proceeded to a phone on a desk. I pressed 0 and asked for V.

"Who?"

"Never mind." I hung up. I wandered carefully, checking desks and bulletin boards in passing for letters or memos, nodding with condescension at others glancing my way, navigating to a far corner and feeling failed again. What could I do? Noting the absence of a V anywhere, I further noted no names whatsoever, except for victims waiting review.

Stuck on doubt, I looked up, as a homely woman rounded the corner. I nodded with superiority, as a voice called, "Oh, D!" She turned, acknowledged a meeting later in the day and turned back to me, assessing.

I said, "Do you perhaps know V?"

She flushed. "I was V. Now I'm D."

I chortled in highbrow bemusement, "It is quite confusing, you know."

"I know. But you can imagine the hazards, this business of ending people's literary hopes."

"Oh, yes. I can imagine. Perilous, I think so, yes."

"No. You can't. Can I . . . help you with something?"

"I want not to make for you bother. But if you no mind, please, terribly, showing the way to me out?"

She relaxed; what harm in an exit on awkward English?

"Not at all. Won't you follow me?"

"Do you mind? I . . . The elevators. I do not ride."

She stopped to scan, head to foot. "Are you CIA?"

"I am afraid that I am not. I have some of the, as you say, claustaro phobia. That is all. In my country, we have these things, but my village is, how you say, ah . . . primitivo."

She nodded, stepping in to whisper, "I get it, too. From heights. Sh. Our secret. Come." She took my hand.

"This is very good service. I cannot complain."

"We try to please. Why are you here?"

"Well . . ." I gasped, blushing at will. "I cannot expect anyone to take me seriously, so I perhaps should not elaborate for now. Let me say I would be honored to join ranks, as a reviewer of books."

"I for one do not review books," she said. "I review literature. Books could be telephone books, cookbooks, celebrity books, pop culture books, coffee-table books, handbooks, self-help and reference books. It's important now, with so many books, to safeguard the idea of literature. It's under pressure, you know." She turned with a curt smile. "Where do you live?"

"I am in what you call transition for now."

"Ah. I know it well. I'm in Colorado."

"I thought this was New York."

"Ha!"

"Ha, ha!" We chuckled over droll geography, on our way down the back steps. "Of course, this is New York. I'm . . . sojourning, you know, shoring up foundations and the like. BB generally reviews out of house. We're all independent. But surely you know that. That's why it's so secretive and secure. You wouldn't believe the nut cases coming around for their little ounce of satisfaction. But enough of me. What about you? Where do you live? Where will you live?"

"Tell me" I said. "Where is in Colorado that you live?"

She shrugged. "Outside Denver."

I nodded vigorously. "That is amazing; that is exactly where I will live. Once I find a place."

"And what will bring you to our fair town?"

"I have a . . . let us say I have known people from my country who have moved there and felt a community, because of, well, it is simple, because of a, you know, *las cucinas* . . . and also as well *por la gente*, for speak the mother tongue to. I mean people, with whom to speak the mother tongue."

She smiled at my self-edit.

I smiled back. "I must say that I have anticipate a solitary pilgrimage, until now. Now I will have a friend in D. *Mais oui*?"

Putting fingertips to lips, she tittered, "That's French."

"Yes. That is French."

"But you're . . ."

"Argentine, if you please. I speak seven language."

"How romantic. I love that in a man. I mean . . ." She turned to face me. "Please. Call me Ferne. I'm Ferne DePieux." She opened a door onto a short passage. "This feels clandestine, you know." She tittered again over our little adventure and its mysterious potential. Turning back, she asked, "What's your name?" She faced me again, her pirouette a question mark on another double eyeful. Her impulse disarmed me.

I stood mute, as if not knowing my own name.

She lit up, self-consciousness giving way to fantasy, taking her from homely, forty-something to ballerina in a jazz step for one, going to two.

I also beamed, though my interior monologue felt diabolically different than the romance churning in Ferne DePieux. "My name? I am Alexis Gutierrez." I bowed semi-majestically, just shy of over the top, lifting her hand to my lips, barely kissing it in surrender: exotic Argentine reviewer lost in the BB byways, a macho gaucho at home with dominance, going submissive.

Flushing again, as if short-circuited, she said, "Oh, my. What a lovely name. Latin and . . . literary."

I acquiesced. "Thank you, I am certain."

"Do you? Write?" She hovered, imperceptibly closing the gap, as if for a kiss.

I nodded, lowering my gaze. "You may call me A, if you please."

She liked that; a first name basis was social and friendly; first initials closer still, like Marlon Brando and what's-her-name in *Last Tango in Paris*, when Marlon said, "No. No names," then reamed what's-her-name with a stick of butter and drove the Chevy home. We sensed the muse between us. Ferne tittered again, giddy with life on a gray day in the city.

"I have not heard such a name as yours. It is, how to say, different. Do you have exotic etymologic?"

She repeated, "Different." She gazed off. "I like that. It's better than funny. That's what most people say. They say it's funny. They can be so mean."

"Yes. Mean and cruel. Numb to the harm they bring."

"My name is different, perhaps odd. But not funny." She gazed up. "I'll tell you something I haven't told anyone. I'd appreciate it staying between us. My name isn't D-e-p-i-e-u-x. It's D-e-p-u-e. I changed it. D-e-p-u-e is so bad. It looks like De puey. That's what they called me."

"You mean . . . in school? The children. The mean children."

"Yes. When I was young."

"Mm. It must have been difficult. Very difficult."

"That's why I changed it." She giggled like a girl who changed her name when nobody was looking, till she faltered, her voice growing husky, nearly constricting. She looked down at something else, so I touched her shoulder, then stroked it, till the eyes and smile came back up for the wonders in store. I told her I would love—loff—to have this thing between us. Twinkles restored, she agreed that a coffee break might be nice.

Just so, Alexis Gutierrez cleared the first hurdle with nine inches to spare. The hurdles ahead looked like curb height. I had penetrated the Fort Knox of literary destruction and careers undermined, past a security system designed to Keep Out the kooks, cranks and half-wits who fail to accept the failure granted by *Books Biweekly*.

The next six days felt like a sentence, life without parole, but revenge slogged onward. Alexis Gutierrez worked the journeyman's role, wining and dining if not sixty-nining Ms. DePieux. Two strangers in a strange land bonded on the streets of New York. The only home turf between us was getting to know each other. Two more nights with meals ran two grand for average accommodations, slightly better fare and aggressive society. She clung, a babe in the woods with a literary ax. We flew home to Denver, two reviewers for BB.

"All is well that ends for us," I said,

She gazed off, a reflexive pattern. "I love you . . ." Stifling a gasp, she came back. "I mean, I love it that we're waiting. You know?" In hour three of the five-hour flight, she held my hand. Hers was rough and clammy. I felt like a time-lapse flower, blossom to wilt, from sexual indifference to disgust. We'd kissed that first night, for her an awkward lipping of my lower face. When I shied, she forced a giggle and asked if I didn't like to make out.

She let it be until night two. Advancing again, rubbing my nub, breathing hard till I chafed, she shied again, into a gasp that she wanted me to have it.

She gave it. I got it, the mighty oak reduced to pudding and whimpers. I could only watch in shock and awe, as she made it go away, a bit toothy but slowly. I like it slow, yet I laughed, pondering my knife slipped into her neck, fearing for the sword in deleting the sword swallower. Eruption seemed unavoidable. "Yes!" She cried like a child, triumphant at last.

I patted her head, not to worry. "Any girl can choke up."

Self-conscious but eager to please, she got the hang of it. She seemed anxious when I hesitated on conventional conjugation, but went along, proud of her power, pursing her lips to keep the teeth back, out of play.

Soon indifferent, as man will get, I felt on track, though satisfaction was still incomplete. Biding time, I foreswore any repository but piehole and bunghole. Never a pederast or tonsil fanatic, I simply adhered to literary guidelines. She called it waiting, to be sure.

"Are you one of those, how do you say, Mennonites?"

She looked down and murmured, "Was."

Four days later, she said patience in the mating act reflects love. She seemed abnormal, a terribly sad person wandering Earth. I couldn't hate her anymore than, say, a cockroach. Would I crush it? No, until remembering that she would condemn books as yet unwritten, to compensate her failures. I could ask for a different reviewer and likely get one. But the clocktower sniper would still destroy novels beyond her barren view.

Slumped on the edge of the bed, she belched. She wanted a Coke to settle her stomach. "The taste that comes alive," she joked halfheartedly.

"That's Pepsi," I corrected, headed to the fridge for a cola, any cola. Tossing her an Acme soda, I commiserated. "Too much of the mayonnaise. To me, it is disgusting."

She looked up. "Tomorrow's Sunday. I go to church. I'd like to . . . Do you want to go?"

"No." She stared wistfully. I pondered another anal plunge, this one with expanding foam. No more leaks. But hateful thoughts only simmered, failing to boil.

She nestled in, cheek to thigh, starved for cuddles, as some women are. She nudged the corpse.

"Do you think it wise to suck it, unwashed?" I asked.

Quickly crimson, she scurried to the bathroom for a washcloth. As she tended to hygiene, I questioned my loathing for one so thorough yet gentle, daubing the dong, lifting the nuts for a tidy swipe. How much longer could I continue? After all, a person is only as good or bad as her intentions; after cleaning, she engorged anew, looking up blissfully, straining on a smile, soon victorious again, asking in a hoarse, "How's that?"

"Okay for now. Would you call that washed sex?"

She shrugged it off, wiped down my thighs and worked around to my anus. "Do you like that?"

"Like what?"

"You know, having your anus rubbed."

"No."

She gave up with a sigh and flopped over.

"Ferne," I said.

"Yes?"

"Ferne D. Used to be V." I lay beside her. "I think the bible is stilted. 'Vengeance is mine . . .' It isn't vengeance. It's more like balance. It's mine. Mine and the Lord's. You know?"

"Mm. I do know," she said.

Flies and stray thoughts buzzed overhead. Alexis Gutierrez, macho lump, felt more demanding to me than to Ferne DePieux. The improv had to fit, even as lines and actions teetered on the edge of the cliff. This respite felt safe, till Ferne said she loved a writer who didn't yak all the time, a writer who lived his work, who felt like his narratives read.

You're my narrative. Never mind.

She loved many things about Alex the author. She'd read nothing, not a book or a postcard, not a phone doodle or graffiti.

I said as much.

She said a woman can tell.

For better or worse, Alexis Gutierrez adapted to the pathos of his making. She'd cut my heart out for casual lunch and needed me to cure her loneliness. I applied the cure, oral and the anal, in character, proving love and keeping her chaste, but . . . Could this be revenge? She loved it. I was used to it. We watched it, thinking our separate ways.

She murmured on cue, draping an arm over my midsection, fingers releasing El Generalissimo.

"I am thinking perhaps to change my name. In the United States, a shorter name is what people do. I can leave Alexis Gutierrez and become Alex Guitar? Does it not sound good to you? Perhaps Indian? Indian is in. Is it not? Stop that!" I rolled away. "Enough."

She sobbed; my turn to feel nauseous.

"What do you think? Alex Guitar?"

The sordid tale could end here on a note of triumph, on a last dollop of splooge down the hatch or up the dukey. But she smiled hopefully through her tears, more gratified than me. The story could not end without resolution, and we had none.

Wiping her nose on a shaky inhale, she said, "I like the ring of it. It could define your niche. But be careful. Alex is good but not exotic like Alexis. Alexis could be a woman's name, and that can help. We run the industry, you know. No offense. On the Guitar part, well, it's catchy, maybe corny. Let me chew on it for a while. Okay?"

Make no mistake: Fern DePieux would go home alone from any swinging hot spot in any town on any night, but with her cheap sofa, her gray flat, low light, a six-pack under my belt, her perseverant lip lock and perfect pace, steady as an oil rig, life did seem convenient. Call it the fast-food version of sexual cuisine, but she knew the basics and served up a great burger. Did she develop a pulsating larynx on her own?

Round 2 had seemed impossible, short of a svelte sister on hand, but life was full of surprises in those days. Victory felt cumulative, another slug o' tapioca a shot for the cause. She wasn't exactly ugly and watching the back of her head, I could picture any of the bevy of beauties on the downside.

Round 2 will take longer, and it's tough to stay mum under an evil reviewer who can't talk with her mouth full. I did share a story from the news, however. One Jonathon Simon got arrested for hiring a hit on a book reviewer. He'd paid three grand for a tabloid ad offering another three grand for information leading to the reviewer, by name, who panned his book, *A Gilded Lily in Guadalajara.* Alas, a wealthier author ran a similar ad with a ten grand bounty the same week. The wealthy author was not caught. Three anonymous reviewers got maimed soon after, car wreck, falling debris and food poisoning. Nothing could be proved

Speak of the Devil. "Dios mio! Gracias, *mi amore.*"

She sat up, wiping her chin and beaming again, a regular winner. She got up for a Coke, mumbling that it would be Diet Coke and pronto, or she'd blow up like a balloon. Returning on a belch, ruddy as a girl having fun, she nestled in for a talk. She loved our talks.

She said the BB reviewer tried to finish Jonathon Simon's novel but could not; it was so baaad.

I happened to have that review, which I unfolded and read aloud. "In Simon's latest misguided adventure, an unauthorized Mexican prefers seedy love, replete with hopeless aspiration and unwashed sex at street level."

She giggled, naughty vixen yet again. Yes, Ferne DePieux had burned Jonathon Simon, too. Indeed, *A Gilded Lily in Guadalajara* was junk, the wanton attack was the same as my own mugging and murder. Had she met, heard of or read anything else by Jonathon Simon?

"No need! His book was so bad; it was almost good!"

"No need? But you . . ."

"You know what I mean." She reached Round 3.

I let her have her fun. It shut her up. But the corpse could not rise. She met the challenge with double time, as insight came clear: time to unmask. Like a down home Hoosier, I said, "They got products to rectify your hormonal rage. Midol, Banshee Begone, Hormone Honeymoon, XPMS." The hard-marched soldier fell from grace. She gazed up, tearful, nearly sobbing. "Hey, hey."

Some women don't like it all one way, but not this one. She sputtered something about my denouement—her word, not mine. She blubbered love for our *expressive dynamic*. She called me mysterious, vindictive and multifaceted.

I assured her that I could provide no comment or a denouement and felt confident she was a shot and a half over the former record of all there was to give.

I'd never had four blow jobs in a night. That didn't mean this was love. Or not revenge. It didn't matter. It doesn't matter. She's good. "Hey." I didn't mind a little dialogue. "When are we gonna fuck? I mean, you know, missionary?" I could have suggested autoerotic asphyxiation or animal cruelty.

She huffed. "I don't appreciate that language. I'm . . . I'm not ready for you to . . . touch my vagina."

Your what? Hey, we all saw *The Crying Game*. Some of us read the book. She didn't look like a guy, but I rubbed her cheek both ways. She took it as affection. No nubs, so I stroked her gullet (outside) for the lump.

Pink went to purple. "I'm a woman. All woman in spirit. The body will follow." That is, with one point five literary reviews per week on average, she'd earn the larynx job and gash enhancement in two years. Till then we'd work through it on lip therapy and anal relief. She says I got it made, but in time she'll need her just desserts. We'll see. Revenge takes time, so who knows what she'll get?

We kind of knew it all along but got caught up in appearance/reality. Nothing beats a terrific blow job. She's the best in the west, especially in the dark. As for the brown round byway, well, they got products there, too, that go slick as eel snot on a doorknob. Add some imagination, concentration, resignation, and it all clears the same. I rationalize with lofty concepts, like literature and art. Modern times call for means.

More importantly, what may be the moral of the story, she says she was wrong. She says I'm a great writer, much better than a good writer, and the world will know of my importance on our next review in BB. Now that we're an item in homoerotic context with trans overtones, market potential is grand.

Ain't life strange? I ponder seasons and shrinking intervals between tax time, Yom Kippur, the commercial Xmas load jamming down our throat and oh, the annual prostate exam. We go in August, to remember our hitherto lonely, failing world of literature without love. And understanding.

We live happily ever after. I only called her Vern once—that won't happen again. We settled on Alejandro Guitar Negro for maximum flourish and subtextual cross-sectioning in an optimally dynamic range (NEH•gro, not NEE•gro or NI•gra) with Latino-chic *simpatico*, though she sometimes calls me William. Who's William?

"Would you care for a crumpet?" I might ask.

"No," she often says. "This Diet Classic'll do for now."

Most importantly is steady progress on my next book, a romance with a twist. It's not cricket for a reviewer to help revise and rewrite, but it's all in the family, and this blockbuster reeks of Major Motion Picture Event potential.

Aumakua

I haven't fished in years. So what. Many people never fished or thought twice about it. But I'd fished every day, sometimes twice, when the tide ebbed near dawn or dusk.

Ultimate potential was a big fish, fifty pounds or better. Dead weight seems primitive but lured me to the end of a wet promontory with a light rig, a gentle sea, salt smell and cut shrimp. Friends were first curious at my keen attraction to the rock jetty. They called it need, meat on the table. The staid men waddling down from the resort thought me reclusive and unemployed.

I also found sense in fishing. In the trying time of youth, reason can hinder progress. I could work, for money, for a car, for transportation to more work, for more money, for meat on the table, and in that process grow old. Or, I could walk down to the jetty with a light rig and some cut shrimp, and commune with Mother Ocean, meat on the table included. It felt like genius.

Nearly three years I fished the jetty five days a week, sometimes twice, honing skills, refining technique. The others at the jetty favored six-inch casting reels and ten-foot surf rods with forty-pound test, eight ounces of lead and treble hooks with braided steel leaders, brass crimps, plastic sheathings and red beads. Too much hardware made a numb line that could anchor itself on the bottom or sweep around rocks and snag for keeps.

Not me. An ultralight spinner on a five-foot stick with ten-pound test made magic. A single Eagle Claw on the end and a handspan above that a quarter-ounce split shot made the offer simple and clean, unburdened of tech and hardware, free flowing in the tidal current under and around the rocks, so light that a fish needn't think twice of threat or commitment but could simply take a nibble. I could sense fish near my bait. A bump would test my response. When the bumps got stronger, I set the hook. I hooked at will, pound-and-a-halfers and on special days three- or four-pounders and rarely a fiver. Incredibly strong, a fish is mostly muscle. I played them light with a light drag, two pounds. I let them run and reeled them softly in.

The young men at the rock jetty thought me peculiar for turning away when landing a fish, like taking a leak, hiding my simplicity. The rock jetty was crowded. I didn't need a bunch of tourists aping my style. I was the best. When I walked away, my spot was quickly taken, as if for easy pickin's.

I caught fish nearly every day, good fish that, dressed out for pan sauté with onions and spuds, garnish and spice, could make a man King of the World. Nerve endings welled in goodness, anticipating from within.

It was a lovely time in those senses. But time moved, not so badly back then, between youth and the fullness of life. Lovely feelings give way to curiosity, and I wondered when it would come to me. I'd heard of fish caught nearby going thirty pounds or fifty. I'd seen pictures in the newspaper from time to time and knew, given the odds and my skill, that I'd hook up with a lunker, sooner or later. I anticipated it, learned the bottom and rocks I would need to know to steer the big fish home. I carried a hundred yards of line on my reel. I dreamed of hooking it, the long run, the slack, the give and take and infinite softness of turning a fifty-pound fish on ten-pound test. In my dreams, I reeled him easily in, the great fish turning onto his side in the shallow foam. In my dreams, I unhooked him, as he groaned. And in brief communion, I turned him back to the depths.

Some people say big fish have worms in their flesh. Others say okay, then give your big fish to me. I didn't care about worms. I laughed in my dreams at the thought of a fifty pounder with spuds and onions. I was beyond. Meat on the table seemed crude, cannibalistic.

In my last year of fishing, I released fish, beginning with the loud ones, their complaint was so real, so reasonable, their appreciation so comprehensible. The dream moment of communion and release became the be-all of fishing. The hookup, the runs and turns, the landing became incidental, unnecessary and cruel. I released them all, could no longer eat them. Yet I went for my lunker, perhaps mindful still of the fullness of life and my rich reward.

I hooked him near the end of fishing. On a rare dawn ebb, solitary, still and clear, a faint suggestive movement rippled the water and air. I sensed action in calmness. But I'd cast once right over a rock and snagged. I'd locked my drag down and snapped my line free. I'd tied on a new hook and crimped on a new split shot and eased another cut shrimp onto the hook. I reset my composure to softly cast again. The first bump had lunk in it, down to the last inch on the spool and in, to the marrow. No need to wait, I set the hook.

In amazement and horror, I gripped my little rod as it bent in two, realizing my error as the line popped like a firecracker. I'd forgot to reset the drag, to lighten it so the big fish could run itself tired. I'd lost my chance. The rare dawn became solitary, still and clear with a double shot of adrenaline. I rerigged, reset the drag and got back out there, straining to reconnect. I got nothing, soft as sunrise. I was too young, I think, preoccupied with the mercy I would bestow, too intent on the score, the finesse, the mechanical advantage of a seasoned angler with proven skills.

That was many years ago on the southeast coast, hooking up with spot-tail bass, also known as puppy drum or redfish, the same redfish made media-famous in New Orleans when a chef charred them with lemon and pepper and called it blackened redfish. The species is similar in texture, taste and appearance to a fish living nearly six thousand miles away, *opakapaka*.

Time is distance for a man on the move. Six thousand miles isn't much over twenty years, especially early years, until you count the changes, farewells and friends, failures and lost loves. Among lasting recollections, the electric moment of hooking up on light tackle and wanting more. A person grows older and meat on the table becomes food for thought. Meditation is a form of fishing and vice versa. The lunker will not arrive to longing. Longing will likely lead to longing. Arrivals will come to the receptive mind. Expectation is human and best minimized. Departures are natural and inevitable.

I wasn't envious when Russell caught his fish. I sympathized. How badly I'd wanted a fifty pounder, or a thirty. Russell's went six hundred, a grouper so big and so many years in crystal clear water that local divers knew her. A fish so big was certainly female, at her most fecund, as it is with fish. Old, still, hovering with imposing energy is how they recalled her. Her big black eyes rolled over them, turning to keep them in view, peering to see who or what they might be. She never moved on a diver, never rushed and gulped like her ancestor gulped Jonah.

She took the hook one night off the beach, when Russell and Darryl had set up their rigs, built a fire and sat on the beach drinking beer, roasting *opihi*. She moved like a log in undertow.

Russell said he knew it was a fish, and though the fight was long, the big fish came in as dead weight, side-stroking in the shallows. She died straightaway, her tremendous bulk deprived of oxygen and bearing its own weight out of water.

Darryl said it was obvious at first sight that the fish was a world record. They backed the truck onto the beach and down to the shoreline, taking care not to sink in the sand. By the time they loaded the corpse, it was sluffing slime as if from a spigot. Darryl says slime is heavy, much heavier than water. How did two guys put the load in the bed? On a jury rig of lines and two pulleys set up for gear reduction and help from two other guys to the south and two more guys to the north, all six losing the pleasant buzz and ambient glow to grunts and groans, heaves and sweats.

She slimed and drained into town and the time it took to find the guys to open the icehouse to roll out the scale and wake them up and wait. Still, she would have been a world record, until the *blala* who came down with the guy who had the icehouse key helped himself to a beer from the cooler and sat on the fish to drink it. Darryl estimated ten pounds of shit, maybe twelve, got squeezed out the big fish's asshole. She weighed in six pounds under the world record.

It should have been a strange, sad end to a noble life, but quirks piled up. Strange got perverse. The media showed up in the middle of the night as excited as a major disaster.

Russell hit the wall on questions near sunrise.

Darryl said his phone rang nonstop for three weeks with more media questions, crank callers and strange offers.

Meanwhile, the fish got recruited to ride in the Makawao Rodeo Parade. She got laid out on a bed of ice, so the slime that rolled down her belly for the next two days stayed cool. She got decked in flowers, like a float.

After the parade, a so-so seafood restaurant made a successful bid to put her in the fresh fish bin, so the folks could see. That lasted a half day; she was so far from fresh.

Finally, DeWitt got the go ahead, once the stink and flies drove the media and folks away. DeWitt administered the last desecration, but it was redemption, too, capturing essence at last. DeWitt painted the fish and printed her on cloth. The prints sold for big money, then bigger money. I got mine cheap, a first run, artist's proof, a little rough with some slime blotches in the ink.

I like it best of all.

Every now and then over the years, I noticed a feeling from within, welling to skin level with a chill and a rush that sometimes shakes my head, like after taking a leak when I was a kid. Goose bumps follow the electricity. On the verge of profound movement, molting, awakening. The Japanese call it *Kensho*; new dimensions open or they feel like they will.

A pattern formed, in which the waves went from random arrival to synchronous timing. Moments of communion could bring it on, say, beautiful first notes, a startling landscape or serene confluence, sunrise, birds singing and mist that floats instead of falls.

First thinking it personal development, I then thought no, it's sentiment, symptom of the aging process. Sometimes, in meditation, I could bring it on. I wanted more, further, bigger, like hooking the lunker I wanted badly. I'd laugh as the waves went flat. They came and went and came again.

I grew older and again stopped fishing.

It was the week Phil died, but he hadn't died yet. He went from the hospital back to the Spartan Nursing Home. He'd ditched the urinary infection at last. His skin was clearing miraculously, and though still confused, they thought he'd pull through six or eight months, maybe more.

Phil raged, as best he could, complaining on the phone about the cancers, skin, blood and bone. Depressed, pissed off and whiny, he sensed a mistake in the bureaucracy; and he wouldn't die, not really, not yet. He was only seventy-six, after all, and his father hadn't croaked until three years ago at 104. But the father was a teetotaler, and Phil drank a quart of gin every day for fifteen years, enjoying fine wine, cognacs, aperitifs and liqueurs, too, as a bon vivant of global seasoning might. Phil understood fun in the French, mystical sense; *nous sommes ici. Alors, porquoi pas?*

"Confused" was his official condition at the hospital and the Spartan Home. Death-numb nurses at both places assured me on the phone, "He's confused. He won't know who you are."

He doesn't know up from down, they said, here from there, awake from the dream. They complained that Phil was yelling at everyone, yelling all the time yelling, and only last night he hadn't known his own brother.

But he'd told me a few weeks earlier that he didn't know his own brother then, before the hospital and "confusion." His brother had tricked him into a power of attorney and the Spartan

Home, he said. Phil was gullible that way, easily fooled, assuming honor and face value.

I didn't tell this to the death-numb nurses, who wouldn't tell me why he'd been rushed to the hospital in the first place, or how he was doing or whether he'd survive another day. I said, "Put Phil on please. I sailed some heavy weather with that guy."

It wasn't all that heavy, but it was a storm on the Beaufort Scale, forty-five knots sustained, a hundred miles out to sea near the strange and ghastly beacons called Frying Pan, big spotlights on stilts rising hundreds of feet from stormy seas off the Carolina coast, on the way north to Morehead City. Gusting fifty or sixty, fifteen-foot seas, no moon and no motor made us understand small life, small death on every wave breaking over the bow.

Phil navigated below, already sixty-five then, and he had a hard time on deck in heavy seas, with his gin gut following the pitches and yaws every which way. And he had thirty years of navigation behind him, flying for Pan Am, New York to London and Paris, including the war years, when commercial airlines flew military transport, East coast air bases to North Africa mostly. Sure, we wanted him on the charts down below.

He had us dead-reckoned and parallel-ruled, divided and homed to the radio signal. He apologized on behalf of his engine, who had sluffed her fuel return hose and returned her fuel to the bilge. He asked, please, for another martini, his delicate phrase for another cup of gin.

Phil's old Seawitch ketch was sea kindly, and we felt her maternal cover, even when she fell down bad and bilge swill sloshed up the hull above the berths. "Oh, by the way," Phil said when the new watch headed up some time in the darkness, when the gusts punched more and seas came from three directions. "Please don't go overboard." He shook his head. He shrugged. "No moon. No motor. I'm not sure we'd find you."

Phil was gentlemanly and understated like that. And that was a comfort, his exquisite good manners there in the face of death, which is what it was for me, first storm at sea. We made landfall a few hours after sunrise and the breeze fell off to ten knots or so. Phil came up and said, "Gee, that was exciting. And you guys. You guys are the very best."

It took nearly all day to make the river entrance and the harbor since the breeze nearly died, and Phil was yacht proper and wouldn't take a tow. By the time we finally got tied up and got a guy working on the engine, it was dark, time for dinner.

We slogged up to the Sanitary Fish Market where we let it fall away in layers, big time, with plentiful liquor and Captain's Platters, and Phil finally let the gin sink in. He fell asleep on his Captain's Platter, laid his face right on it and snored, passed out drunk at last, as his young punk crew whooped and drank and grew into the spirit of the moment, survival.

We propped Phil up next to the cashier while we settled up, and he came around. Opening one eye on a saltwater taffy display, fancy boxes stacked on the counter, he grabbed the top box, tore it open and snatched a taffy. Stuffing his mouth, he smiled and staggered out. We paid for the taffy, too. He denied for years that he fell into his Captain's Platter, but the taffy stuck.

"You know I'm glad you told me that," the head nurse at the Spartan Home said. "We often never know who these people are, what they've done."

I told her. After WWII, Phil got discharged with enough money for the downstroke on a new Harley-Davidson that he rode from San Francisco to Miami, a long haul.

When I asked what he did then, he shrugged. "I rode it up to Niagara Falls." Then he turned around, rode around a few states and came back to the falls from the other side. "I don't know," he said. "It just felt good."

She put Phil on and he knew me in a heartbeat, his voice that of a dying man. Between a whisper and a croak, he said, "Hey, buddy. God, it's good to hear you." He asked if I'd stopped by last night.

"Hell no," I said. "I'm in Hawaii."

"You're in Hawaii?" The Spartan Home was in Louisiana. He fell into a ramble then. He'd been thinking it over and felt he'd be better off in London. Yes, London. He would go to London, he wasn't sure why but knew it was a good idea. Wasn't it?

"I been thinking of Paris myself, Phil," I said. "But I had an insight last night. I had two incredibly good red wines, and I got to the best part of the buzz and realized that's where I really want to be. Not necessarily Paris, but drunk."

"God, I'd settle for either one," he said, and we laughed. I had him making jokes three days before he died, which was something for a body so racked and ruined.

He got quiet again and asked, please, if I could lend him some money, just a little money.

"Sure," I said. "What for?"

Because his goddamn brother had his credit cards, and he wanted to check into The Stafford, the nicest hotel in Slidell, LA. "I don't think they'll let me go to London," he said. "But I could go down to The Stafford, if I had some money. Can you come down here?"

"Hey, Phil, they told me you were yelling at everybody all the time."

Phil mumbled a weak complaint.

"I told them I'd yell at them, too, if they didn't start giving me some straight answers. I think they had you pretty drugged there for a few days."

"Yeah. I think so. I don't feel so good."

"They had to drug you up to shut you up. I think they got tired of listening to your shit, Phil. But don't worry I gave them some of mine."

"Thanks, buddy." He trailed off again to mumbles.

I yelled to speak up, I can't hear.

He said, "Hey, can you come down here?"

I said, "Phil. I'm in Hawaii. I'm five thousand miles away, for chrissake."

"Oh, yeah," he said. "Hawaii. I . . . I don't know what to do."

"You got to relax, Phil. Just relax."

He thought it over. "You mean just relax until I die?"

"That's all anybody can ever do, Phil," I said, aware of my own discomfort.

He mumbled off again and came back and said he wanted to get out of that place worse than anything in the world.

I told him he was on the mend.

He said yeah, he thought he was maybe getting better.

And when the time is right, I said, there'd be no holding him down. In a heartbeat he'd be gone out of there. "Just relax. You'll know when it's time to go, Phil. Then you'll go. You won't hang around." I told him I was right there with him. "I'm right there with you, Phil. I'm there with you." I told him I loved him.

The nurse took the phone. "Aw," she said. "You made him cry."

Aimee and I split up a while ago, but I hadn't realized it was nearly a year until I sat there, still and silent, recalling the good times, the good friends. I called her to share the latest adventure, which was helping Phil on his way. It's easy remembering Aimee in the exotic sense some women convey. A year apart made us faraway from what had been. We met in a parking lot many years ago. It began with a double take by me. She swooped past, tall, lanky and fair with healthy round breasts, good hips and a brief glance my way. She walked past, toward the sun so her gauze skirt became a scrim on the oldest play in nature, which is that of ultimate potential, or so a young man thinks.

I know now how much more women know, sensually, on peripheral vision, than most men realize. Still, I can't believe she conscientiously generated that much power. Optimal translucence, the perfect slant of sunlight, her sway and flow delivered insight: magic is real in nature. The graceful line, inner thighs up to the gap between her legs was where I wanted to be, with all my heart. I knew that broken down to components, to fleshy pieces, this magnetism made no sense. Nor did my speechlessness. But I had the wherewithal, or weakness, to run after her, intercept her at her car and ask with shaky humility, "Tell me who you are."

I reached my focal point, by-'n-by, with all my heart. It was a growth lesson, a growing pain. It was everything anticipated, but another small death, like the one ascetics strive for, in which the self, its needs and comforts are no more. We shared an absence afterward, seeking meaning in the carnage.

But nature is bountiful. Nature is love. We die in small ways each day. If we're lucky, we live again, renewed. Luck ran out with Aimee and me. Our story began in a parking lot short of breath, overloaded with hormones. It ended one realistic evening when difference was the word of the hour. Scant images in the physical realm wisp like fading scent on old bones.

The middle of the story was good in parts. We sailed with Phil every year he came through, loving many fine wines and excellent repast under sail. Phil loved the galley, as long as others could tend the rig. We visited Phil in South Florida, when he had *Morning Star* docked at a fancy hotel. Phil came to visit every year when he got too weak to keep his boat.

"It's so sad," she said. I told her what Phil said and what I answered. I told her he was anxious. She said she was glad I was staying in touch like that. I asked if she'd call him. She said in many words that she would not. She'd had difficulty taking care of Phil during his last visits, when he needed much more. He'd shrunk, his skin gave him trouble, he had the shakes. Death at hand felt imposing, more than she could handle in the moment. I didn't press on the moment. She said she loved Phil, but her love could not preempt her difficult schedule, her busy mind.

I realized, listening to her, that I'd learned to love her a long time ago, and that our chemistry could mix but not blend. I realized, describing Phil, that he would soon die, and that his passing gave Aimee and me the transition we'd been lacking.

Phil stopped eating a day later and stopped waking up a couple days after that. He stopped breathing Friday night, but I didn't find out until I called Monday morning, and the head nurse told me he'd passed on without pain. It was a big relief since the cancers promised pain, his greatest apprehension.

All day I asked myself, over and over: how could Phil die Friday night, and I didn't know it, didn't sense it. I figured it out. Racked and ruined, drugged, done and heavily dreaming like Phil, and dying on a Friday night, he may not have known it either until Monday morning.

Hawaiian *kahunas* have a system of magic, system meaning the loose sense of the word: flexible, generally consistent, conforming to patterns. Magic in this system means what is unexplainable in the empirical world. Kahunas perceive humans as comprised of three selves: the conscious or middle self, the subconscious or low self, and the superconscious or high self.

The high self is just that, closer my God to Thee. The single law of this system of belief, this code of life, is that no human should hurt another. People should be good to each other. This is *aloha*. The high self guides and protects. It cannot cause harm. The system is much older than 2,000 years, yet like the land that spawned it, it has been denigrated, stolen, diluted and destroyed.

Still, it exists, for those seeking contact.

The high self cannot be contacted consciously or by the middle self. It cannot be prayed to. It hears no promise, accepts no sacrifice. It must be contacted subconsciously, by the low self, or else it makes contact from without. External contact is through animal forms, since animals are without sin, since animals are purely motivated.

Kahunas call the high self *aumakua*. They recognize owl, lizard, octopus and shark as common bearers of the protective, all good, high self. They say a protector can be any species, the members of a family will share the same aumakua.

I had a recurring dream as a child. I was in a rubber boat or on a small island or treading water, shipwrecked. Sharks circled, circled. I woke in fear every time because of the sharks, circling. It foretold my future. I know that now.

I sailed once into the doldrums with my friend Phil. We drifted two days, no motor, whispering breeze, the ocean so flat it looked absolute, like movement was a dream in stillness. Midafternoon on the second day, we spotted a fin on the surface a quarter mile ahead and aimed for it. Another and another and a dozen more came up, hammerheads, twenty footers lolling on the surface, not seeking or playful or lazy but cruising, just cruising with a subtle slow shimmy side to side. We threw a big silver lure out but they wanted none of it. We threw out a bigger silver spoon with skirts and feathers and a slimy hunk of squid but got nothing. We yelled and beat the hull. But they only cruised alongside for a few hours, then veered east. They foretold weather, a first storm at sea and a night carried to the end of this life. I know that now.

I ran charters a couple years here, until the boat got storm wrecked and fell into foreclosure during drydock and had to be sold. Between the repair work and the sale, we had a couple months free, no payments, and ran every charter up to the last day, gray and choppy, unfit for water fun. But with four hundred bucks on board, we went out, set the anchor, laughed hardy and stayed cheerful for the passengers.

To show them a four-foot breaking wave meant great snorkeling, I dove in. I'd seen many sharks. But diving onto a ten-footer who hovered three feet under, who wiggled once and cruised on, nearly stopped my heart. "Goddamn," I choked and sputtered up. "This is nice!" It foretold salvation.

Phil wore a black shark's tooth around his neck, nitty-gritty, as he liked to be if not fine dining and drinking. The Saturday after Phil died, but I didn't yet know it, I took Marie, the puppy dog, on a beach walk.

Marie might someday get calm enough to curl up by a fire, if she lives that long. Her energy crisis must be reconciled often or it turns destructive. Her record is a grand in landscaping in under thirty minutes. At the beach, we could vent the pressure.

We went the length of *Kiawekapu*. I walked, Marie ran zigzags and circles, plunging through the surf for the distance swimmers. She had plenty of piss and vinegar left by the end of *Makapu* and still as well by the end of *Ulua*. So we crossed the hotel grounds and hit *Wailea* for another mile of it.

At the end, we stood and watched the late afternoon, little waves and blue water. Two fins, dorsal and caudal, broke the surface a few feet out. I turned quickly and yelled, "Marie!"

That was a mistake, game on. She jumped back and side to side. I knew if she spotted the fins she'd be in the water. So I chased her, another distraction, and caught her fifty yards away, where we calmed down, and I put her on the leash to walk back for a look. But it had been fantasy, illusion, until fins broke again, and into a foot of water, a yard away, up rolled a six-foot tiger shark.

It rolled up dead, limp and floppy, awash in shallow foam. But the roll continued, belly up, belly down, belly up again, the little tiger grinning ear to ear. It wasn't dead. It was a casual feed, slow and easy, on small fry in the shallows. High and dry above the pectoral fins, he rested a moment then shimmied through the foam, out a bit, deeper and gone.

"Woof," Marie said.

Aumakua, I told her.

I wondered for two days what the contact meant. I would have thought it a signal from Phil, but Phil hadn't died, I thought.

I asked two people, Hawaiians, and they said yes, aumakua, but it is not from someone else.

Contact is ambient. I tingle. So does the shark. Wait and see.

Phil's passing brought many reflections on adventure, beauty and contact. But the next week was busy, with a trip to Honolulu for business, and with tickets to the symphony, too, for urban stimulation.

A young composer had innovated unique sounds from percussive instruments.

Tchaikovsky came next.

Finally, the oldest and greatest Slavic pianist in the world was introduced. He would play Dvorak.

Like many masters of arts, his old age showed in marginal decrepitude, frail posture. Yet, as masters will, approaching the muse, he seemed young and strong with the softest touch. His fingers drew notes in perfect syncopation, his body guiding the melody in a slow steady shimmy that was easy to follow. My eyes closed on a drift, not toward sleep but in release. I smiled at the onset of the small electric wave and succeeded in doing nothing. I floated freely behind it. I let it lead. I thought of Phil and knew that by now he realized he was beyond, yet for a little while he would remain.

A tremulous refrain near the high end sounded perfect, delicate as spun glass, and as the high notes got higher, I realized the lunker eyed my bait. I felt muscles let go of bones and knew that soon, soon we would bump and run. I smiled again, knowing the lunker was me, way past poundage, and as the movement inside opened up and folded over, Dvorak went to higher notes still for a casual swirl and to the highest notes ever heard, up to where crystals ting.

I laughed then, cracking open to surge — laughed at the instant resolution of all things bearing weight, like want, confusion, loss, love and transitory nature. I laughed hard, as if drug induced, without reason. I felt naked and going quickly mad, and I covered my face with my hands.

That was a strange sight, I suspected; some guy sitting in the concert hall heaving sobs to the greatest Slavic pianist alive.

About the Author

Robert Wintner crossed two continents on motorcycles, sailed four of the seven seas, dove tropical reefs around the world and rose from ashes to success in a place *Forbes Magazine* called the most difficult business arena in America. Profiled in a dozen metro daily papers, interviewed on a hundred radio shows, he declined Leno when asked to arrive in mask, fins and snorkel. He is committed to style, story and entertainment of lasting value. As a front-line activist in reef defense, he lives on Maui with Anita, Cookie the dog, Yoyo, Tootsie, Rocky, Buck, Inez and Coco the cats, and Elizabeth the chicken.

Robert Wintner has authored over twenty books—novels, story collections, memoirs and reef photo books—garnering great reviews. Known in Hawaii tourism for Snorkel Bob's and media against the grain, Wintner is Executive Producer of *The Dark Hobby*, a feature-length documentary on the aquarium trade.

.

www.ingramcontent.com/pod-product-compliance
Lightning Source LLC
Chambersburg PA
CBHW070631260626

47161CB00007B/2656